I0821434

AMERICAN STUDIES – A MONOGRAPH SERIES
Volume 155

Edited on behalf
of the German Association
for American Studies by
REINHARD R. DOERRIES
GERHARD HOFFMANN
ALFRED HORNUNG

KATHRIN KRÄMER

Walking in Deserts, Writing out of Wounds

Jewishness and Deconstruction in Paul Auster's Literary Work

Universitätsverlag
WINTER
Heidelberg

Bibliografische Information der Deutschen Nationalbibliothek
Die Deutsche Nationalbibliothek verzeichnet diese Publikation in der Deutschen Nationalbibliografie; detaillierte bibliografische Daten sind im Internet über *http://dnb.d-nb.de* abrufbar.

UMSCHLAGBILD
Foto: Werner Schandor, textbook at,
unter der Bearbeitung von Uwe Kohlhammer.

ISBN 978-3-8253-5366-7

Imprimé en Allemagne · Printed in Germany
Druck: Memminger MedienCentrum, 87700 Memmingen

Gedruckt auf umweltfreundlichem, chlorfrei gebleichtem und alterungsbeständigem Papier

Den Verlag erreichen Sie im Internet unter:
www.winter-verlag-hd.de

Acknowledgements

I am very grateful to Paul Auster for giving me permission to quote from his unpublished manuscripts which can be found in The Henry W. and Albert A. Berg Collection of English and American Literature, The New York Public Library, Astor, Lenox and Tilden Foundations.

Thanks are also due to the staff of the Berg Collection, curator Stephen Crook and Philip Milito, for helping me to deal with the uncatalogued manuscripts.

I would like to thank the Jewish Studies Association at Champaign, Illinois for their colloquium in 2005. Special thanks are due to Rachel Shulman and Elana Jakel.

I am grateful to Prof. Michael Rothberg, University of Illinois at Urbana Champaign, for his inspirational questions.

Special thanks are also to Lucy and Jonathan Green for their support.

Besides, I would like to thank Werner Schandor and Uwe Kohlhammer for making visible what this book is about with the help of the front cover.

In particular I would like to thank Catherine Lewis very much for her support and patience.

I am deeply indebted to Prof. Alfred Hornung for giving me the opportunity to write this investigation as my doctoral thesis at the University of Mainz, Germany, and for his encouragement throughout my studies.

Finally, I would like to thank Dave J. Karloff very much for encouraging me to write this book, for his constant support, and his patience.

Table of Contents

1. Introduction

In his essay "Book of the Dead" on the French-Jewish writer Edmond Jabès (1976), Paul Auster draws the following conclusion: "If language is to be pushed to the limit, then the writer must condemn himself to an exile of doubt, to a desert of uncertainty. What he must do, in effect, is create a poetics of absence" (114). This quotation refers to one of the most crucial aesthetic demands that Auster, a third-generation American Jew, also fulfills with his own writing: the continuous quest for challenging ways of expression, the urgent appeal to "shake as a whole, to make tremble in entirety," as the French-Jewish philosopher Jacques Derrida puts it in his essay "Différance" published in 1972 (21).

However, this endeavor to explore, and to seriously question, the possibilities of language is the very cause of the writer's insecurity, his grave doubts about the adequacy of words. In spite of his incessant search for the most appropriate words possible, which will hopefully express what he sees and feels, he will never reach his desired aim. Since language is characterized by inconsistency and changeability, the writer will not stop yearning to capture the most precise image of "reality" with his words. In his analysis of Jabès' *Book of Questions* (1963), Paul Auster sums up this situation with the Jewish metaphor of the desert ("Book of the Dead" 114) and thus indirectly refers to the historical fact and biblical motive of the Israelites' flight out of Egypt (Exod. 12.1-18.27). In parallel to the Israelites' arduous, forty-year-long walk towards the promised land (Exod. 33.1-3), the writer "walks" on a stony path, while his destination to render some sort of "truth" remains out of sight. With resignation, the I-narrator of Auster's autobiographical memoir *The Invention of Solitude* (1982) claims: "Just because you wander in the desert, it does not mean there is a promised land" (32).

In Auster's interview with Edmond Jabès, published in *The Art of Hunger* (1992), the latter also parallels the Jewish metaphor of the desert with the writing process. He admits that after finishing the *Book of Questions*, he did not have the feeling that he had arrived where he expected: "It was as if I were reliving the experience of the desert . . . as if I had suddenly come to a blank page" ("Providence" 150). In parallel,

Jacques Derrida, who, like Auster, wrote an article on Jabès' *Book of Questions*, depicts the writing process as a long walk through the desert that will not lead to any kind of truth: "This way, preceded by no truth, and thus lacking the prescription of truth's rigor, is the way through the Desert. Writing is the moment of the desert as the moment of Separation" ("Edmond Jabès and the Question of the Book" 68). Because of the inadequacy of his words, the writer will always feel the distance between himself and language as such. This uncertainty of the accuracy or objectiveness of words, that Auster, Derrida, and Jabès express with the metaphor of the desert, goes along with the renunciation of any definite aim which may be reached through the process of writing.

Jacques Derrida's philosophical theory of deconstruction circles around the impossibility of pinpointing unequivocal meanings and irrefutable truths, and thus breaks with "the basic metaphysical assumptions of Western philosophy since Plato" (Selden 84). A multitude of philosophers and literary critics has devoted itself to the analysis of Derrida's challenging theory. However, what has been analyzed by only a few is the Jewish dimension in his oeuvre which is connected with his theory of deconstruction. At first glance, one would expect that Judaism, interwoven with traditional Western metaphysics, did not influence Derrida to a great extent. However, to provide a theoretical introduction to the analysis of major texts by Auster, the second chapter of this investigation will show that "Derrida cannot be thoroughly understood without elucidating the Jewish current running through his philosophy" (Ofrat 1).

In fact, Paul Auster's literary work, which constantly questions, or even denies, the existence of unambiguous meanings in language and absolute certainties in consciousness, seems to correspond to Derrida's project of deconstruction. His characters keep on looking for definite answers or the right ways of expression. They are continuously forced to face up to "the lack or absence of a center or origin," which results in the supplementation of signifiers "taking the center's place in its absence" (Derrida, "Structure, Sign, and Play" 289). They are caught within a network of allusions, often of contradictory nature, and thus become so disoriented as if they were "lost in the desert" (Auster, *Leviathan* 55). This ramified network of references, which confuses the protagonists on their quest for truth, can be seen as the surface of Auster's texts. Behind this "deconstructive surface" of signifiers that constantly supplement and erase each other, the fragmentary depiction of a Jewish identity – similar to Jacques Derrida's philosophical texts themselves – seems to be hidden. In short, the main objective of this analysis is to show the interconnection of Auster's literary rendition of the theory of deconstruction with Jewish thought. This interconnection can, however, only be recognized if we put Auster's fragmentary references to Jewish history, belief, and culture together as if doing a jigsaw puzzle.

Critics like Dennis Barone, Alison Russell, Tim Woods, or Marc Chénetier have also recognized Auster's affiliation with Derrida's theory. However, the Jewish aspect in his texts has been greatly neglected – with the exception of references to Auster's preoccupation with Franz Kafka and his use of the 'hunger' motif. Derek Rubin, for instance, focuses on the "Jewish trait of longing, of yearning, of 'hunger,'" which he sees at the core of *The Invention of Solitude* (63).[1] An analysis of Auster's poetry and his subsequent novels with regard to this and other Jewish traits has, however, been avoided by secondary literature up till now. In particular, the similarities between Auster and French-Jewish writers and philosophers in their treatment of Jewish experience have not been assessed, despite the fact that Auster spent five years in Paris and has translated and analyzed many texts of French writers.[2]

The answer to the question why the subject of Auster's Jewishness has been avoided for such a long time seems to lie in Auster's writing itself and the way he has dealt with his Jewishness in public. In fact, Auster has never emphasized his Jewishness in any interview, and he has not given any details on the impact his Jewishness may have had on his

[1] Derek Rubin points out that "[h]unger in the sense in which it figures in *The Invention of Solitude*, is probably best defined by looking briefly at an essay by Isaac Rosenfeld entitled 'The Fall of David Levinsky' (1952). Rosenfeld's essay, which is a review of Abraham Cahan's novel, *The Rise of David Levinsky* (1917), is particularly relevant to [his] account. . . . In his discussion of *The Rise of David Levinsky*, Rosenfeld describes the central trait of the protagonist as that of 'hunger, in [a] broader, rather metaphysical sense of the term' (155). He explains how physical, spiritual, emotional, and sexual deprivation in Levinsky's youth made dissatisfaction an integral part of his character. This, he says, expresses itself in his adulthood both as 'a yearning for fulfillment' and as 'an organic habit' as a result of which 'no satisfaction is possible' (155). In short, '[b]ecause hunger is strong in him, he must always strive to relieve it; but precisely because it is strong, it has to be preserved' (155)" (61-62).

[2] Auster's unpublished manuscripts, which can be found at the Berg Collection of the New York Public Library, show that he was not only in contact with Edmond Jabès, whom he interviewed, but with Jacques Derrida as well. Most interestingly, Jabès gave Paul Auster Jacques Derrida's address in Paris in a letter written in 1978.

work. In an interview with Joseph Mallia, Auster even points out that the novels of *The New York Trilogy* (1987) are not "religious" texts. He only admits that "these books are mostly concerned with spiritual questions, the search for spiritual grace" (*The Art of Hunger* 280).

By avoiding any detailed comment on the Jewish dimension of his writing, Auster resembles Derrida, who did not speak openly about his Jewishness before the end of the 1980s, when he had already written his major texts, such as *Of Grammatology* (1967), *Writing and Difference* (1967), *Dissemination* (1972), or *Glas* (1974). Until that time, Derrida's allusions to the time of the "Vichy" government in Algeria (1940-44) with its colonial, anti-Semitic policy and its effects on his Jewish identity appear only "between the margins" of his philosophical texts. They are hidden within a deconstructive analysis of other Jewish philosophers or writers such as Emmanuel Lévinas, Edmund Jabès, Paul Celan, or Franz Kafka. But until the 1990s, Derrida never wrote about his own religious and cultural background in an unmistakable, straightforward manner. The question of course is why neither Auster nor Derrida has openly written about or commented on his Jewishness. It is not the objective of this investigation to give an answer in psychological depth; it rather tries to hint at fragmentary answers veiled within Derrida's philosophical texts and, foremost, the literary ones by Auster.

During the time of the Vichy government, Derrida did not only lose all rights of French citizenship, but also became estranged from his Jewish family background. These early childhood experiences left Derrida wounded and had a great impact on his writing, as the second chapter of this investigation will show in greater detail.[3] Paul Auster as a third-generation American Jew, whose grandparents immigrated to the United States at the beginning of the 20th century, has of course experienced a totally different past. In contrast to the French philosopher, he has not been persecuted by an anti-Semitic policy. "Like most of the members of his generation, he is fully Americanized," as Derek Rubin underlines (61).

[3] Geoffrey Bennington expands on the experience of being wounded in *Jacques Derrida* (1991), a biography he wrote together with the philosopher. He points out that Derrida became sensitive towards every form of racism because of the fact that he himself had been persecuted. He also became sensitive towards mass phenomena in general. Moreover, Bennington points out that the effects of the experiences in Algeria are visible in Derrida's texts written before "Circumfession" (332-33).

However, the assimilation, especially of the second generation of Jewish immigrants, to American culture seems to have had a great impact on the third generation.[4] Indeed, in his autobiographical piece of writing *The Invention of Solitude*, Auster speaks about his estrangement from his Jewish family background only indirectly, i.e., in the voice of his I-narrator: "I was brought up as an American boy, who knew less about my ancestors than I did about Hopalong Cassidy's hat" (28). In short, Auster seems to be separated from traditional Judaism like Derrida, even though for different reasons. In *The Art of Hunger*, he also deals with the separation from traditional Judaism only indirectly, i.e., by analyzing other Jewish writers such as Edmond Jabès, who have also become alienated from traditional Jewish life. In his poetry and prose, the estrangement from Jewish beliefs and customs is a topic that appears between the lines. Its reasons are never illustrated to a great extent, whereas the characters' disorientation often seems to be the effect of their alienation from the past or of the personal losses they had to experience. They are rootless and confused figures, aimlessly wandering in desert-like places, always in search for answers.

In particular, this investigation tries to show that the issue of alienation, loss, and despair is frequently expressed with the image of the wound in Auster's poetry and prose. In "Choral" from his poetry collection *Wall Writing*, for example, Auster depicts the act of speaking, and indirectly the writing process, as taking root in a wound: "Slowly, / you dip your finger into the wound / from which my voice / escapes" (70). Surprisingly, the image of the wound also runs through Derrida's philosophical texts, as the beginning of the second chapter will show. It alludes to the very personal experience of being separated from one's religious and cultural roots. Yet does the image of the wound not also express a timeless experience, since it refers to the history of Judaism? In Auster's and Derrida's texts, it refers to the enslavement of the Israelites

[4] *Jewish American Literature. A Norton Anthology* stresses that with the help of certain statistics "it is easy to conclude that Jews are no longer outsiders – that, in fact, they are deeply embedded in the social structures of this [the American] nation. And perhaps they are. Yet sociological acceptance should not be confused with religious and cultural homogeneity. Even as these statistics suggest a narrative of progress, they also suggest several new challenges; such thorough integration has not been without cost. . . . the success of acculturation has led to rapid assimilation and has posed a serious threat to the welfare of the Jewish American community. Only with great difficulty can American Jews continue to maintain an alternative religious practice and cultural distinction when they so wholly participate in a national culture that is largely based in Christian ritual and tradition" (Chametzky 979).

in Egypt and the times of European pogroms, the Shoah in particular.[5] For instance, in Auster's "The Book of Memory," the second part of Auster's *The Invention of Solitude,* the third-person narrator A. emphasizes that he felt so desperate after he had visited Anne Frank's little room in Amsterdam, which is today a museum, that he immediately needed to put something on paper: "It was at that moment, he later realized, that The Book of Memory began. As in the phrase: 'she wrote her diary in this room'" (83). Here, A.'s sadness as a result of his attempt to face up to the effects of the Shoah leads to his identification with Anne Frank as a writer.

As in this passage from "The Book of Memory," we need to ask in which of Auster's poems and prose texts the experience of an inner wound triggers off the writing process and second, what kind of influence it has on the writing process. In a conversation with Paul Auster, published in *The Art of Hunger,* Edmond Jabès indeed equates the age-old wound of Judaism, the experience of dispersion, persecution, and death, with the experience of the poet who constantly looks for the most precise ways of expression:

> This idea has become very important for me, to such an extent, in fact, that the condition of being a writer has little by little become almost the same for me as the condition of being a Jew. I feel that every writer in some way experiences the Jewish condition, because every writer, every creator, lives in a kind of exile. (Auster, "Providence" 149)

In Auster's writing, the image of the wound also seems to be linked with the writer's efforts to find the "right" words. It is an existential experience of desolation which is at the core of these early poems and connected with the writer's struggle to capture "the real" with words (Finkelstein, "Introduction" 11). Influenced by the Objectivists such as Charles Reznikoff, George Oppen, or William Carlos Williams, Auster

[5] This investigation prefers the Hebrew term 'Shoah' over the term 'Holocaust' which is "most widely employed for the persecution of the Jewish people by Nazi Germany from 1933 to 1945, first in Germany itself and subsequently in Nazi-occupied Europe, culminating in 'extermination' camps and resulting in the murder of nearly six million Jews. However, the Hebrew term *Shoah* (total destruction) would be more fitting, since holocaust also connotes 'burnt sacrifice.' It is true that, like ancient Moloch worshipers, German Nazis and their non-German henchmen at Auschwitz threw children into the flames alive. These were not, however, their own children, thrown in acts of sacrifice, but those of Jews, thrown in acts of murder" (Fackenheim 399).

incessantly tries to depict what he sees in front of him as precisely as possible. "He reaches from the world in his head to the world that he knows his body inhabits, with language, as he realizes, as his only 'means of organizing experience'" (Finkelstein 11). In his early "Notes from a Composition Book" (1967), Auster further explains the function of the written language:

> The word is an attempt to arrest the flow, to stabilize it. And yet we persist in trying to translate experience into language. Hence poetry, hence the utterances of daily life. This is the faith that prevents universal despair – and also causes it. (204)

The despair Auster speaks of here, but also the faith in the word, results from the anxiety of never being able to express what one hopes to say, of feeling alienated or separated from language: "To feel estranged from language is to lose your own body. When words fail you, you dissolve into an image of nothingness. You disappear" (205). This fear of becoming alienated from language and the simultaneous belief in the strength of the word are two major major themes in Auster's poetry as well as his prose. The question is of course in which ways Auster depicts this fear of feeling lost in his poems and novels and the desire to catch "the real" with words, and to what extent the two issues have an effect on the behavior of his characters. Another crucial question is whether he alludes to possibilities of overcoming this fear in his more recent texts.

After a short introduction to the interaction of Derrida's theory of deconstruction with Jewish thought, the third chapter, the main part of this investigation, will demonstrate the similarities in the way of thinking of the American writer and the French philosopher. It will examine major poems of different collections written by Auster in the 1970s, his autobiographical memoir *The Invention of Solitude* (1982), his anti-detective novel *City of Glass* (1985), the apocalyptic novel *In the Country of Last Things* (1987), and the more recent novel *The Book of Illusions* (2002). Above all, the fragments of Jewish teaching and experience which are hidden within Auster's texts will be investigated. They will be analyzed in connection with the development of Auster's writing, i.e., his affiliation with poststructuralist thought and his later gradual withdrawal from it.

Indeed, long before Auster wrote his apocalyptic novel *In the Country of Last Things*, he already tried to capture disseminating thoughts with his words and thus to satisfy his yearning to understand and grasp reality. In the seven poetry collections Auster wrote between 1970 and 1979, the intention is always to prevent thoughts from disappearing, and thus to reach the desired place of homecoming by writing. This yearning will lead the lyrical I to a multiple of imaginary places where it has not been before. It continually wanders into the unknown and incessantly hopes that it will become more sure of itself and the world it is confronted with: "Gaping eye / in the hunger of day. / Where we have not been / we will be. A tree / will take root in us / and rise in the light / of our mouths" ("Pulse" 68). However, the walk to the desired place of homecoming needs to be continued incessantly, since the writing process would otherwise come to a halt or stop altogether. This constant readiness to search for the most suitable ways of expression becomes the prerequisite of creating art: ". . . Do not / emerge, Eden. Stay / in the mouths of the lost / who dream you" ("Hieroglyph" 86).

To this extent, Auster's poetry collections can be understood as his groundwork. The Jewish image of the quest for the promised land is transferred onto the field of aesthetics and depicted as an inevitable necessity which will not, however, lead to full satisfaction on Earth. The analysis of selected poems written by Auster will demonstrate that the writer's intention to express what he thinks, feels, and observes in his familiar surroundings is connected with references to Jewish experience. The following investigation will furthermore ask to what extent the connection of Auster's aesthetic intention with Jewish thought led to his decision to stop writing poetry and to turn exclusively to the medium of prose.

In his transitional piece *White Spaces* written in 1979, Auster deconstructs the attempt to pinpoint any moment of beginning or end. In other words, with the turn to prose Auster seems to resign himself to the fact that neither the starting point or origin of his imaginary journey is definite, nor the destination itself. In order to be able to face up to his surroundings, the writer needs to become conscious of the infinite in which he is embedded:

> And yet nowhere can we find the place or the moment at which we can say, beyond a shadow of a doubt, that this is where it begins, or this is where it ends. For some of us, it has begun before the beginning, and for others of us it will go on happening after the end. Where to find it? Don't look. Either it is here or it is not here. And whoever tries to find refuge in any one place, in any one moment, will never be where he thinks he is. (157)

The impossibility of finding "refuge" during the writing process is also part of Auster's autobiographical novel *The Invention of Solitude*. In an interview, Auster admits that he wrote this memoir "in response to [his] father's death" ("Interview with Joseph Mallia" 276).[6] At the beginning of "Portrait of an Invisible Man," the first part of this memoir, Auster similarly emphasizes the "obligation" the I-narrator feels to create a coherent picture of the father by putting his fragmentary memories on paper. Otherwise, as he knows, the father's "entire life [would] vanish along with him" (6). Thus he tries to gather as many memories as possible and to explore his father's life. During the search for the father in his consciousness, the I-narrator momentarily gains some deeper, but still fragmented knowledge of his Jewish family history. He will indeed understand that the Jewish paternal line of his family did not start to crumble with his father's inaccessibility, but even earlier, i.e., around the time when his grandparents immigrated to America. By putting the I-narrator's memories together, we as readers can assume that the shattered family ties had an influence on the father's development, in particular his later superficiality and absentmindedness.

In other words, the separation from traditional Jewish religion and culture is not only at the core of Derrida's philosophical texts, but at the core of Auster's literary work as well. The analysis of "Portrait of an Invisible Man" and "The Book of Memory" points at the reasons for this separation which are veiled within the deconstructive surface of the two texts, and explains to what extent the separation from Jewish tradition affects the I-narrator and the third person narrator A.

The investigation of Auster's *City of Glass* aims to demonstrate the similarities between the autobiographical memoir, *The Invention of Solitude*, and this anti-detective novel. It tries to show that the biblical image of man's yearning to finally reach the promised land is again

[6] Auster also points out that it is "not so much an attempt at biography but an exploration of how one might speak about another person, and whether or not it is even possible" (276). In other words, *The Invention of Solitude* arises from autobiographical facts, but foremost deals with "certain questions that are common to us all: how we think, how we remember, how we carry our pasts around with us at every moment," i.e., with existential questions ("Interview with McCaffery and Gregory" 307). In order not to answer, but to raise those questions, Auster tried to "enter a state of solitude, . . . the moment when you start to feel your connection with others" ("Interview with Mallia" 277). In particular, Auster tried to "turn [himself] inside out and examine what [he] was made of" by concentrating on the father ("Interview with McCaffery and Gregory" 307). In other terms, *The Invention of Solitude* is an exploration of the self through the search for the other in oneself.

mirrored by an ongoing quest for a father-figure. Furthermore, Auster seems to connect the impossibility of finding the desired father-figure with the protagonist's logocentric project to undo the "fall of language," i.e., to find the pure, perfect language that seems to have existed in Eden. The question will be to what extent Auster's deconstruction of the elements of the detective novel underlines the failure of this project as well as the protagonist's desire which cannot be stilled.

The tone in Auster's apocalyptic novel *In the Country of Last Things* apparently becomes more pessimistic, as the book is "firmly anchored in historical realities" (Auster, "Interview with McCaffery and Gregory" 320). In particular, it refers to the Shoah and anarchic European cities during the Second World War. The Jewish protagonist Anna Blume has to fight for survival in this nightmarish world of decay where everything is "in constant flux" (1) and "[d]eath is no longer an abstraction, but a real possibility that haunts each moment of life" (*In the Country of Last Things* 15).

The analysis of this novel will investigate Auster's hints at historical events of the immediate past and their influence on the present. In particular, it will especially show to what extent these references to the cruelties of the 20th century mirror aspects of Jewish experience in a wider context. Above all, it tries to demonstrate the link between Jewish experience and poststructuralist thought. Indeed, the city through which Anna Blume continuously wanders is depicted as a text that has to be "read" carefully (Woods, "'Looking for Signs in the Air'" 115). Anna Blume's readiness to keep "looking for signs in the air" keeps her from becoming lost from the start (Auster, *In the Country* 25). But since an unmistakable correspondence between signifier and signified is never guaranteed, and the signified might always disappear or change its meaning, Blume needs to fight against her own forgetfulness and the fragmentation of her writing process. The "confusion of semantic and phenomenological horizons" (Woods 116) is at the core of Auster's apocalyptic novel and again interconnected with Derrida's interpretation of the Old Testament motive of the desert or of man's seemingly never-ending walk towards the promised place of homecoming where all suffering can hopefully be left behind.

This strong belief in a positive outcome of the events, in a flight out of the city of decay, makes Anna Blume and the other main characters act in an exemplary manner. With their untiring willingness to help, Auster indirectly transmits the Jewish-Christian message of a necessary responsible form of behavior. The question is of course to what extent this ethical dimension is embedded in poststructuralist thought. The most important philosopher who has influenced Derrida in this context seems to be Emmanuel Lévinas. His vision of "the humanity of human beings" ("The Pact" 226), which he developed against the background of the Jewish religion, will be outlined in the second chapter of this analysis. With the characters' readiness to do their utmost for the other, Auster's 1987 novel seems to reflect Lévinas' and Derrida's vision concerning a peaceful future.

The "possibility of hope" (Auster, *In the Country* 107) is also part of Auster's novel *The Book of Illusions*. Here, the I-narrator David Zimmer, who has lost his wife and his children in a plane crash, comes across the vanished Jewish silent comedian and film-maker Hector Mann. He decides to analyze his films and to find out what has happened to him. By following the traces of Hector Mann's past, Zimmer is eventually confronted with his own experiences. As in *City of Glass*, Auster again depicts the pursuit of a man whose life story reflects the protagonist's inner wounds. Only by trying to get to the bottom of the other person's experiences does it seem possible for the I-narrator to keep on living.

However, the question is whether Zimmer will find the desired answers on his quest for truth, or whether he will need to cope with the dissemination and erasure of words and thoughts. In other terms, the analysis of *The Book of Illusions* investigates whether the novel again conveys poststructuralist thought, or whether Auster has already moved to overcome it with the detailed depiction of Zimmer's and Mann's life stories and of fictional film plots. Moreover, Auster has left his description of nightmarish, apocalyptic settings behind and instead concentrates on extreme, but possible situations in our everyday-life. So he seems to approach his earlier wish to grasp what he sees and feels in his surroundings with a language that develops into "a means of organizing experience" ("Notes from a Composition Book" 204).

The separation from Jewish experience and teaching seems to remain a crucial element in Auster's writing. In *The Book of Illusions*, he circles around it by inventing the figure of a Jewish actor who has become uprooted as a result of the Russian pogroms at the end of the 19th century. Since the actor's life is connected with the I-narrator's present experiences, Auster does not treat anti-Semitism as a past phenomenon, but as a fact that can still be observed in our Western world and that will have its effects on the future.

However, the often unexpected, sometimes even miraculous coming together of people who have never seen each other before, but who begin to open up and to help each other, is contrasted with the depiction of sorrowful experiences. This moment of hope based on a necessary sense of responsibility that Lévinas has continuously spoken about, is not only part of Auster's *The Book of Illusions* and the other novels mentioned above, but also, for example, of *Timbuktu* (1999) or *Oracle Night* (2004). Indeed, Willy, the protagonist of *Timbuktu*, who shuffles around the streets of Baltimore with Mr. Bones, his dog, does not stop believing in a positive outcome of events. For the two of them, "Timbuktu" becomes an imaginary place of hope that can only be reached by wandering through desert-like places:

> At one place, Willy described it as 'an oasis of spirits.' At another point he said: 'Where the map of this world ends, that's where the map of Timbuktu begins.' In order to get there, you apparently had to walk across an immense kingdom of sand and heat, a realm of eternal nothingness.' (60)

In parallel, Auster depicts Sidney Orr, the protagonist of *Oracle Night*, as a disoriented writer, who aimlessly wanders around the streets of New York like Daniel Quinn in *City of Glass*: "I had lived in New York all my life, but I didn't understand the streets and crowds any more, and every time I went out on one of my little excursions, I felt like a man who had lost his way in a foreign city" (2). However, Sidney Orr recovers from a near-fatal illness at least for a while, begins to write again, and has got the feeling that he "[has] come home from a long and difficult journey, an unfortunate traveler who had returned to claim his rightful place in the world" (11).

In other words, some of Auster's (more recent) texts, which are not analyzed in detail in this study, also reflect Jewish thought and experience. However, the interconnection of Jewishness and deconstruction can be most clearly recognized in the texts that were chosen for examination in this analysis, which should justify the selection of Auster's expressive, but neglected poems and his most significant novels. In particular, it will be shown that Auster's poetry can be regarded as the groundwork of his later deconstructive prose writing with regard to the motives of the wound and the desert.

In her recent study of Auster's prose texts, Ilana Shiloh concentrates on the topic of the postmodern quest, which, in her opinion, runs like a thread through all of them (1). In particular, she maintains that although "the end of the creative quest can never be reached, [it is never] completely exhausted" (156). In *City of Glass*, Daniel Quinn knows that he will reach the end of his notebook, and yet he yearns to go on writing forever (Auster, *City of Glass* 156). Anna Blume in *In the Country of Last Things* also hopes to write a letter without an end, although she continuously faces the disappearance and erasure of words and thoughts. However, Shiloh does not recognize the ongoing quest and yearning of Auster's wounded characters as a typical Jewish theme. His figures continuously hope to reach a particular destination on their arduous walks through desert-like forlorn places. The end of this wandering is only imaginary. Moreover, the writing process remains a never-ending search for the most appropriate words. Definite answers will not be given, neither in aesthetic nor in metaphysical respect. Nothing is certain, and yet, hope is not surrendered in spite of all devastation. As Emmanuel Lévinas puts it in "Time and the Other" (1947): "hope . . . is in the very margin that is given, at the moment of death" (42).

2. Jacques Derrida's Theory of Deconstruction and (his) Jewishness: a selection of aspects

"I am the end of Judaism," Jacques Derrida wrote in "Circumfession," originally published in French under the title "Circonfession" in 1991 (122). This statement provokes (at least) two different interpretations, of which the first is extremely irritating and pessimistic. It implies that "Judaism is at an end and [Derrida is] its last remnant." The statement could, however, also mean that Derrida sees himself as being "entirely remote from Judaism," estranged from Jewish beliefs and customs (Ofrat 9). The difficulty is that we cannot interpret Derrida's statement without seeing it in connection with his theory of deconstruction which destabilizes fixed centers of meaning and which breaks free of apparently irrevocable definitions. Indeed, the two contrasting interpretations leave the reader "entangled . . . in what Derrida terms (in English) a 'double bind'" (Ofrat 9). His intention of confusing the reader results from the difficulty of defining what a Jewish identity is, as he points out in an interview with Elizabeth Weber ("A Testimony Given" 42). It is the impossibility of explaining why he calls himself a Jew although he feels separated from Judaism. In Derrida's opinion, this difficulty, however, means a chance for Judaism: "'I am the end of Judaism,' and so the death of Judaism, but also its one chance of survival, ... because in order to say 'I am Jewish' you perhaps have to say how difficult it is to say 'I am Jewish'" (42).

At the beginning of his career, i.e., during the time he developed his project of deconstruction, Derrida did not make any comment on his remoteness from Judaism. However, the texts he wrote from the end of the 1980s onwards illuminate the often hidden, not clearly recognizable references to his Jewishness beneath the surface of his early books. In particular, "Circumfession" (1991), *Archive Fever* (1995), *Monolingualism of the Other* (1996), and certain interviews give us essential answers, especially concerning Derrida's past experiences. They help us to make out the interconnection of deconstruction and Jewishness in general. Indirectly, they demand what the philosopher himself had in mind with his theory of deconstruction: the necessity of reading between the lines, of adding missing connotations, or of making visible what is already there. With the help of selected passages from these more recent texts, the following chapters on Derrida try to hint at and illustrate the often hidden references to (his) Jewishness in his early texts. In particular, they assess the impact of his Jewishness and his preoccupation with Jewish writers on his theory of deconstruction.

The following subchapter concentrates on Derrida's early experiences of anti-Semitism during the time of the "Vichy" government in Algeria and investigates the metaphors of the wound and the desert as "central" concepts of his thought. The subsequent chapters will then deal with Derrida's understanding of the image of the absent or unattainable God in connection with his rejection of 'logocentrism.' Another question will be to what extent the French-Jewish philosopher Emmanuel Lévinas has influenced Derrida with his philosophy of ethics based on the 'face-to-face' relation with the other. Lévinas' "concept" of the "absolutely Other" seems to stand in connection with Derrida's renunciation of logocentrism and his discussion of colonialism, in particular his interpretation of the story of the Tower of Babel in Genesis. Apart from Derrida's theory of deconstruction, Lévinas' idea of the other seems to find its literary rendition in Paul Auster's literary work. In particular, the images of the Tower of Babel and the absent or silent God are used by Paul Auster, too, next to the images of the wound and the desert.

2.1. Being separated from Jewish roots and the ambiguity of circumcision

In *Monolingualism of the Other* (1996), Derrida depicts the French interdict of not having been allowed to speak Hebrew at his school in El-Biar. At the beginning this interdict worked subliminally, as he points out: "I do not recall anyone ever learning Hebrew at the lycée. The interdict worked therefore through other ways. More subtle, peaceful, silent, and liberal ways. It took other forms of revenge" (32). More concretely, French was taught as the "mother tongue," "the very language of the Law" (39) that went along with "the growing uselessness, the organized marginalization of [the other] languages" (38), namely Arabic, Berber, and Hebrew. Derrida thus had to learn French as his "first" language and paradoxically as a language "whose source, norms, rules, and law were situated elsewhere" (41). This new language was forced on him, but excluded him at the same time: "For never was I able to call French, this language I am speaking to you, 'my mother tongue'" (34). It always remained the language of the conqueror, of "the Other," or of French colonial policy itself. Hence Derrida calls it the "monolingualism of the Other":

> [T]he monolingualism of the other would be that sovereignty, that law originating from elsewhere, certainly, but also primarily the very language of the Law. And the Law as Language. Its experience would be ostensibly autonomous, because I have to speak this law and appropriate it in order to understand it as if I was giving it to myself, but it remains necessarily heteronomous, for such is, at bottom, the essence of any law. (39)

To Derrida, this heteronomous experience of language meant to speak the "language of the master" (42), of a country that was far away, ungraspable and therefore also mysterious: "the Metropole was Elsewhere, at once a strong fortress and an entirely other place. . . . The language of the Metropole was the mother tongue; actually, the substitute for a mother tongue (is there ever anything else?) as the language of the other" (42). This transformation of a mother-tongue into a "substitute for a mother-tongue" went along with the transformation of Judaism into a religion of "'external signs'" (54), the religion of the other, which was caused by "Christian contamination" (54):

> Social and religious behavior, even Jewish rituals themselves were tainted by them, in their tangible objectivity. The churches were being mimicked, the rabbi would wear a black cassock, and the verger [chemasch] a Napoleonic cocked hat; the 'bar mitzvah' was called 'communion,' and circumcision was named 'baptism.' (54)

Through the forced adaptation to the French-Christian culture, the Algerian Jews, as Derrida emphasizes, were alienated from their religious and cultural heritage. In *Monolingualism of the Other*, he describes this community as being "cut off, finally, or to begin with, from Jewish memory, and from the history and language that one must presume to be their own, but which, at a certain point, no longer was" (55). In another passage, Derrida draws attention to this separation from religious and cultural heritage when he speaks about a "language of refuge that, like Yiddish, would have ensured an element of intimacy, the protection of a 'home-of-one's-own' [un 'chez-soi'] against the language of official culture . . ." (54). The use of the Conditional II here accentuates the yearning for such a cultural place of retreat, a sanctuary within language itself that Derrida could never enjoy. In 1940, he was expelled from school and deprived of French citizenship. But, as he points out, the alienation from roots and tradition, this cruel form of "amnesia" (59), had become obvious even before.

In the interview with Elizabeth Weber titled "A Testimony Given," he also points out the consequence of the French policy of suppression in Algeria, namely his ignorance of Hebrew and thus of Jewish history and culture in general. Because of this separation from the original language he was later unable to immerse in the Judaic texts, the Old Testament, and the Kabbalah, but had to concentrate on certain metaphorical aspects:

> . . . it happens that I don't know Hebrew, or hardly any; I am very unfamiliar with Jewish history or the texts of the Jewish culture . . . this lack of culture obliges me not to settle down, but to move about in the metaphorical, rhetorical, allegorical dimension of Judaism. That of circumcision, for example. (43)

Jacques Derrida's Jewishness cannot, therefore, be viewed from his attachment to the sources of Judaism and especially not to 'halakhah' (the traditional Judaic law), but from the fissure or rift between himself and Judaism (Ofrat 13). Hence it is not surprising that the Jewish ritual of circumcision, which symbolizes both the covenant between man and God and a lasting wound, has become a metaphorical "center" in Derrida's philosophical writing – or better: the trace or disturbing thread which runs all the way through his texts. It is also present in his early texts, as he explains in "Circumfession" by citing an unpublished passage from one of his early notebooks (the title of this autobiographical text is a Derridean word-formation of "circumcision" and "confession"): "*Circumcision, that's all I've ever talked about, consider the discourse on the limit, margins, marks, marches, etc., the closure, the ring (alliance and gift), the sacrifice, the writing of the body, the* pharmakos *excluded or cut off . . .*" (70). This early passage presented by Derrida quite late in his career shows to what extent his Jewish background, or the separation from it, is directly linked with his theory of deconstruction. Another text from 1977 (mentioned in "Circumfession" for the first time) concretizes this fact: "[c]ircumcision remains the threat of what is making me write here, even if what hangs on it only hangs by a thread and threatens to be lost . . ." (202).

In "Circumfession," Derrida transfers the literal meaning of the Jewish ritual of circumcision onto the field of language itself, i.e., the breaks, fissures, or rifts existing within, or even created by it, and thus emphasizes the more general, universal meaning of being "circumcised" by language: "every man is 'circumcised by language . . . therefore so is every woman'" ("A Testimony Given" 39). Derrida illustrates this observation of the wound existing within language and being caused through it by emphasizing the similarity of the two Hebrew words mijlah (circumcision) and milah (word), which are pronounced in exactly the same way ("Circumfession" 88). 'Circumcision' means, to sum up, both the Jewish ritual of indicating or denoting and of reminding of the covenant between the Jewish people and Yahweh. Furthermore, Derrida turns this ritual into an image for the pre-existing "circumcised language" itself, which has its effects on man in general. It thus expresses, on a metaphorical level, a "universal mark" ("A Testimony Given" 40).

This universality is, as Derrida points out, a characteristic of Judaism itself and thus comprises every thinkable responsibility for humanity:

> 'I am Jewish,' which means: I am testifying to the humanity of human beings, to universality, to responsibility for universality. 'We are the chosen people' means: We are par excellence, and in an exemplary way, witnesses to what a people can be, we are not only God's allies, God's chosen, but God's witnesses, and so on. ("A Testimony Given" 41)

"Universality" also means for Derrida

> that circumcision is there where there isn't any and that what it marks, namely belonging to a community, alliance, the relationship to the father, the symbolic, etc., is something that happens in all cultures, in all languages: the straightforward fact of speaking establishes us from the outset in the alliance of circumcision, in general. It's the paradox of 'All poets are Jews.' ("A Testimony Given" 43)[7]

The poetic experience of language is an "experience of circumcision" and hence, as Derrida puts it, "in quotation marks and with all the necessary rhetorical precautions . . . a 'Jewish experience'" ("A Testimony Given" 43). However, the experience of circumcision cannot be reduced to Judaism alone, but is, in a wider sense, part of other cultures, too.

[7] Here, Derrida quotes the Russian poet Marina Tsvetaeva. Her phrase "All poets are Jews" was also used by Paul Celan as a motto for his poem "Und mit dem Buch aus Tarussa" (Weber 148).

On the basis of these comments, certain previous texts need to be read, such as his article “Edmond Jabès and the Question of the Book” or “Violence and Metaphysics,” an article on Emmanuel Lévinas, both published in *Writing and Difference* (1967). Here, Derrida circles around the “circumcised language” or the “wound within language,” as will be shown more concretely. The following chapter, however, first tries to explain what the act of “circling around a wound” means to Derrida and what it has to do with his “concept” of ‘différance’ which he introduced in an article with the very same title published in 1972.

2.2. The “concept” of ‘différance’ and the impossibility of circling around a wound

In “A Testimony Given,” the interview with Elizabeth Weber, Derrida maintains that the act of “circling around a wound” encloses a paradox: the obsession with the wound, the attempt to get to the bottom of it on the one hand and the simultaneous inability to come closer to it on the other hand. The contradiction lies within these two meanings of the act itself. It is unsolvable, because the wound has already happened, it cannot be negated or erased any more. From the beginning, it is an enterprise doomed to failure:

> And how can you turn around a wound which in one way is your own? From a topological point of view, this already resembles the logical game of an impossible geometry: you can’t turn around your wound. A wound has already taken place that marks an incision in the body; it forbids you this distance or this play which consists in turning around. The game is no longer possible. (“A Testimony Given” 40)

In this passage, Derrida directly connects the act of “circling around a wound,“ this “impossible geometry,” as he calls it (40), with one of the key terms of his theory of deconstruction: the term ‘play.’ It concretizes Derrida’s concept of ‘différance’ with which he takes Ferdinand Saussure’s assumed differential character of the sign a step further:

> Essentially and lawfully, every concept is inscribed in a chain or in a system within which it refers to the other, to other concepts, by means of the systematic play of differences. Such a play, différance, is thus no longer

simply a concept, but rather the possibility of conceptuality, of a conceptual process and system in general. ("Différance" 11)

'Différance' must be understood as a "conceptual process" on the basis of the two meanings of the French verb 'différer': to differ and to defer. This double meaning of 'différer' is not part of the Structuralist concept of 'différence' that Derrida describes as "the condition for signification . . . [which] affects the totality of the sign, that is the sign as both signified and signifier" ("Différance" 10). He maintains, however, that "the signified concept is never present in and of itself, in a sufficient presence that would only refer to itself" ("Différance" 11). In other words, his "concept" of 'différance' summarizes "a configuration of spacial and temporal difference" (Kamuf 59): Differences are floating freely within the system and are able to postpone any notion of 'presence' to a later time.

Above all, Derrida emphasizes the activity of the verb 'différer,' i.e., the production of differences, with the help of the letter 'a,' as it goes back to the French Present Participle. However, the ending '-ance' makes clear that Derrida does not allude to a direct activity, but also to 'mouvance' or 'résonance' (Kimmerle 79). Or, to put it differently, 'différance' stands between a passive as well as an active realization of differing and deferring (Kamuf 59). It describes an "operation which is no operation" (Derrida, "Différance" 11) and is hence, strictly speaking, neither a concept nor a method, but a pre-existing trace showing its effects.

What is consequently dissolved is the metaphysical fixation on any origin. The movement of 'différance,' this playful operation of differing and deferring between the active and the passive, indeed works against any seeming irrefutable fixed principle, any centeredness. It must be understood as the concrete opposite of origin:

> What is written as différance, then, will be the playing movement that 'produces' – by means of something that is not simply an activity – these differences, these effects of difference. This does not mean that the différance that produces differences is somehow before them, in a simple and unmodified – in-different – present. Différance is the nonfull, nonsimple, structured and differentiating origin of differences. Thus, the name origin no longer suits it. ("Différance" 11)

Moreover, Derrida concretizes the playfulness of 'différance,' which depends on the non-existence of a center or origin, with the term 'supplementarity': The function of the sign is to "[replace] the center, which supplements it, [to take] the center's place in its absence" ("Structure, Sign, and Play" 289). In short, by acting as a supplement or surplus, by adding something, the sign takes the center's place. Signification as a whole must hence be understood on the basis of a network of supplemented signifiers that is becoming more and more ramified.

As an effect, the present is differed and deferred against itself and also "everything that is thought on the basis of the present, that is, in our metaphysical language, every being, and singularly substance or the subject" ("Différance" 13). In other words, the decentering of the present, the basis of metaphysical thinking, leads to the fissuring or dispersing of the subject and object that Derrida further explains with the term 'dissemination': "Dissemination affirms . . . endless substitution, it neither arrests nor controls play . . ." (Derrida, "Positions" 86). If the present is however differed and deferred against itself, if it disseminates, it becomes the past and the future at the same time. Time in general is thus spaced up, or, as Derrida puts it, it is the "becoming-space of time or the becoming-time of space" ("Différance" 13) which the movement of 'différance' aims at.

Furthermore, he depicts this phenomenon with the term 'trace' which can be understood as a certain interval being necessary to let things come to the surface and disintegrate again ("Différance" 13). It constantly refers to everything lying in a certain exteriority and is in itself part of a network of references. The trace points to "the enigmatic relationship of the living to its other and of an inside to an outside" ("On Grammatology" 42).

In the interview with Elizabeth Weber, Derrida also connects the meaning of 'différance' enclosing 'supplementation' and 'the trace' with the impossibility of "circling around a wound." Indirectly, he refers to his personal inner wound, the separation from Jewish roots mirrored in a "circumcised language," and points out that the act of circling around it contains a paradox: On the one hand, it is marked by the desire, the wish to approach a certain origin by moving "toward the future or the past, toward the eschaton, which means the extreme" ("A Testimony Given" 55). On the other hand, 'différance' blocks this origin or source, it "bars the origin" (55). The latter becomes differed and deferred. It is divided from itself, it is dissolved. In short, the movement of 'différance' illustrates the impossibility of "circling around" an initial wound; its paradox parallels the contradiction of the personal undertaking. Or, to put it the other way round, the impossibility of reaching an original inner wound hides within itself the movement of 'différance':

> In a word, the compulsion of 'turning around' is also the experience of an impossible circle or circulation: the impossibility of closing the circle. You turn around because you can't bring the circle to a halt. It can't come back to itself. The impossibility of a coming-back-to-oneself, in the sense of a reappropriation, but just as much in the sense of consciousness – in French we say revenir à soi, 'to come back to oneself. . . .' ("A Testimony Given" 44)

In another part of the interview, Derrida concretizes the impossibility of circling around a wound with the act of remembering. The latter encloses, as he further explains, the insight that past experiences often elude the attempt to get hold of them. Trying to approach an inner wound means to confront oneself with the risk of forgetting, i.e., with a certain boundary also describing one's own inability (50).

However, Derrida emphasizes that this boundary must not be neglected, since it can be transcended. In other words, he points out the confrontation with the future, with everything lying behind this boundary, as well as the welcoming of 'the Other.'[8] Consequently, the boundary needs to be understood as a certain "gift": "You cannot and should not avoid the risk of forgetting if you want to remember. Memory without risk of forgetting is no longer a memory. It's dreadful, but that is finitude itself, the limit and the chance of what comes, of the other and the event: the gift" ("A Testimony Given" 51). The boundary of not-coming-to-oneself is thus not a standstill, but in fact the prerequisite for the ethical chance of noticing the other and then of giving:

> [T]he impossibility of recovering, of recovering oneself, of coming back to oneself, that's what it is, the openness of the gift, if there is such a thing. If it were possible to recover, recover oneself, come back to oneself, the gift would be calculation, programming, reappropriation, thanks. (44)

Moreover, Derrida makes clear that the double meaning of "circumcision" and the motive of "gift" refer to each other and that the ambiguity of these terms is essential. He consciously keeps them in

[8] From the mid-seventies onwards, Derrida was influenced by Emmanuel Lévinas and his concept of 'the Other,' as will be more concretely discussed in chapter 2.5., with particular reference to Derrida's early article "Violence and Metaphysics" (*Writing and Difference* 79ff.).

suspense, which is, in his view, necessary for the existence of Judaism in general:

> These paradoxical motifs of being Jewish, the gift, and circumcision, are indissociable for me. In order for them to be indissociable, for them to form a chain in some way, the main thing is that it mustn't come to a halt and that you can't assign an identity, a stable self-identity, to one of those notions. If you think you know what it is to be Jewish, what giving is, what circumcision is, you can be sure that there won't be any more of them: that there never has been any of them! (44)

These late Derridean explanations and illustrations can, as the following chapter will demonstrate, already be detected in one of his early texts: "Edmond Jabès and the Question of the Book," published in *Writing and Difference*. Here, Derrida circles the ambiguity of circumcision by interpreting Jabès' *Book of Questions* and connects it with the character of writing in general. Indirectly, he seems to circle his own language, which is marked by breaks and gaps, and his inner wound of being divided from Jewish roots, too. The contradiction of this undertaking, i.e., the necessity to get to the bottom of one's wounds and the irrefutable prediction that it will meet with its boundaries, is, to say it once more, the paradox of the Derridean concept of différance itself.

2.3. Writing in the desert, "between the fragments of the broken Tables," and the deconstruction of the subject

Right at the beginning of his article "Edmond Jabès and the Question of the Book," Derrida maintains that Jabès' "poetic discourse *takes root* in a wound" (64). This wound is a personal one, which Derrida opens up while playing with the word "root"; he refers it to the past and at the same moment depicts it as being timeless: "A powerful and ancient root is exhumed, and on it is laid bare an ageless wound (for what Jabès teaches us is that roots speak, that words want to grow . . .)" (ibid.). The writing process, as he additionally argues with regard to Jabès, but also more generally, emerges from this inner, age-old wound and is simultaneously connected with Judaism itself: "[I]n question is a certain Judaism as the birth and passion of writing" (ibid.). A bit further, he specifies this interconnection or alliance by quoting a very generally formulated statement by Jabès: *"[The] difficulty of being a Jew, which coincides with the difficulty of writing; for Judaism and writing are but the same waiting, the same hope, the same depletion"* (65).

In other words, Derrida, in his interpretative study of the French poet, parallels the situation of the writer with the situation of "the Jew" by referring to the history of Judaism which is marked by the experience of dispersion, persecution, torture, and death. Depletion, waiting, and hope have not only been the consequence of the pogroms of the 19th century and the Shoah in the 20th century, but can be dated back to the moment when Adam and Eve were expelled from the Garden of Eden and became "outcasts from God's presence . . ., destined to seek (and hide from) their creator" (Eisen 220). This experience of depletion, but also of hope, is especially present in the Five Books of Moses when Abraham leaves for Canaan (Gen. 12.1-9) and Moses frees the Israelites out of slavery in Egypt (Exod. 1-18).

In short, Derrida speaks, by using Jabès's words, about the longing for the promised land, the place of fulfillment that Jahwe once assured His people. This yearning is, in Derrida's view, not only present in Judaism, but is equally expressed by the poet, who, over and over again, feels himself separated from his roots or from language itself. Consequently, the poetic undertaking is described as a walk through the desert, while the desired destination remains out of sight (Derrida, *Writing and Difference* 68).

In Jabès' case, writing does not emerge out of the strict adherence to Judaism, but out of the separation from it, enforced from the outside, but possibly also as the consequence of a personal decision. "Poetic autonomy . . . presupposes broken Tables" (67), writes Derrida and alludes to Moses, who broke the Tables of the law out of anger that the Israelites did not respect the law, but worshipped other gods (Exod. 32.1-20). The fact of being separated is in Derrida's understanding the prerequisite for the creation of literature. Out of or within it, the poem comes into being: "Between the fragments of the broken Tables the poem grows and the right to speech takes root" (67).

The language used by the poet mirrors the inner conflict, the wound. It is described as being "far from 'the fatherland of the Jews'" (67) and hence can be called a "form of exiled speech" (67). Moreover, this "exiled speech" does not only characterize poetry, but is also "[t]he necessity of commentary" (67) and thus of Derrida's interpretative study of Jabès' *Book of Questions* itself. To this extent, it goes along with one of the key statements of deconstruction: the renunciation of the metaphysical idea of the subject as an authoritative, "unified principle from which all things flow. . ." (Lawlor 183).

In "Semiology and Grammatology: Interview with Julia Kristeva," Derrida explains "that the subject . . . depends upon the system of differences and the movement of différance, that the subject is not present, nor above all present to itself before différance, that the subject is constituted only in being divided from itself, in becoming space, in temporizing, in deferral . . ." (29). The subject which is part of the movement of différance, as Derrida also illustrates in "Différance" (20/21), consists of an innumerable amount of differences, is differing from and deferring itself, or is, in short, spaced up.

In his early essay on Edmond Jabès as well as in "Freud and the Scene of Writing" (196 ff.), Derrida anticipated the deconstruction of the subject, which cannot be extricated from the network of supplementations within time and space. Here, he rejects the 'subject' of writing understood or defined exclusively as the "sovereign solitude of the author" ("Freud and the Scene of Writing" 226) and extends it to the book, actually the object, which "becomes a subject in itself and for itself" ("Edmond Jabès" 65). Furthermore, the 'subject' comprises all sorts of relations ("Freud and the Scene of Writing" 227) and is therefore "shattered and opened" ("Edmond Jabès" 65).

Writing is, to sum it up, "ruined, made into an abyss" ("Edmond Jabès" 65). It is situated "on the vague estate, in the non-place" (69), which is also depicted as "the desert" or "the city," "for in either the root is equally rejected or sterilized. Nothing flourishes in sand or between cobblestones, if not words. City and desert . . . besiege the poetry of Jabès . . ." (69). Here, the Jewish image of old age, the desert, is replaced by the image of modernity, with which the poet is daily confronted. Both stand for separation, alienation, and yearning and are in themselves characterized by supplementation and dissemination. Derrida describes them, by quoting Jabès, as a "labyrinth," where "'*we will go over the same way ten times, a hundred times . . . And all these pathways have their own pathways. – Other wise they would not be pathways*'" (69).

The images of the desert and the city connect the situation of the modern writer and the history of Judaism with each other. Or, to put it differently, the situation of the writer mirrors the history of Judaism and vice versa. Jabès' "home" is depicted as "a fragile tent of words erected in the desert where the nomadic Jew is struck with infinity and the letter. Broken by the broken Law. Divided within himself" (69). Being confronted with infinity means the infinity of the writing itself. The past steps of the poetic undertaking often dissolve themselves, and the future of writing, which will never end, cannot be made out. Hence the writer sees nothing but a "white page" in front of him that is marked by the moment of death: "'*At noon, he found himself once more facing infinity, the white page. Every trace of footsteps had disappeared. Buried*'" (70). Or, in another passage, Derrida maintains that "[d]eath strolls between letters. To write, what is called writing, assumes an access to the mind through having the courage to lose one's life, to die away from nature" (71).

But although the writer is confronted with the moment of death, hope is never surrendered. It remains visible in the "fragile tent of words" in the sand – or, as a fragment of life which, in Jabès' case, "differs from itself, defers itself, and writes itself as différance" (78). Derrida describes this fragment as "the solitary arising of an unseen root, beyond the reach of the sun. Toward a hidden sky" (72).

2.4. God as the unattainable source and the renunciation of logocentrism

In his essay on Edmond Jabès, Derrida emphasizes that "[t]he breaking of the Tables articulates, first of all, a rupture within God as the origin of history" (67). God has, in Derrida's view, "separated himself from himself . . . by keeping still, by letting silence interrupt his voice and his signs, by letting the Tables be broken" (67). With this statement, Derrida refers to the passage in Exodus, when God repents His intention of punishing the people of Israel, who are worshipping a golden calf, and silently observes Moses' anger and his impulsive reaction, the shattering of the first Tables (Exod. 32.7-20). In Derrida's understanding, God does not interfere or judge Moses for not having presented the law, His writing, to the Israelites. Only later, He speaks to Moses, but buries His face in front of him and everyone else, too (Exod. 33.20-23).

Derrida calls the moment of God's seeming absence or silence "the moment of the desert as the moment of Separation" (68), which, however, also means that man becomes responsible for his own actions, his own words: "God no longer speaks to us; he has interrupted himself: we must take words upon ourselves" (68). This responsibility expressing itself in writing is directly connected with the original sin. Because of our innate inability to listen to God's words, we are condemned to writing and the search based on it: we "must entrust ourselves to traces, must become men of vision because we have ceased hearing the voice from within the immediate proximity of the garden . . . '*The garden is speech, the desert writing*'" (68).

Moreover, Derrida points to the fact that the image of the absent God, the One who does not show His face, and its connection with "man's writing as the desire and question *of* God" (74) is part of the Kabbalah: "Negativity in God, exile as writing, the life of the letter are all already in the Kabbalah. Which means 'Tradition' itself" (74). Derrida probably thinks of the Kabbalistic depiction of God as "'*Reisha delo yada*'" (the unattainable head)" (Ofrat 55), which can be linked with one of the cornerstones of Derrida's theory of deconstruction, his rejection of 'logocentrism.' With this term he means the metaphysical dependence on an authoritative voice, the act of holding onto a source or origin, as he explained in his lecture "Structure, Sign, and Play in the Discourse of Human Sciences" at Johns Hopkins University in 1966: "Structure – or rather the structurality of structure . . . has always been neutralized or reduced . . . by giving it a center or of referring it to a point of presence, a fixed origin" (278). Through this longing for an origin, "[t]he permutation or the transformation of elements" (278), especially the "substitution of contents, elements, or terms" (278), have been repressed, as Derrida maintains. In short, with the term 'logocentrism' he speaks against the metaphysical "determination of Being as presence" (280).

Moreover, the Greek term 'Logos' for 'word' appears in the well-known declaration of the Gospel of St. John "In the beginning was the Word" (John 1.1), i.e., the spoken word, and also refers to the first chapter of Genesis which depicts the creation of the world through the voice of God. Speech, as it is formulated here, cannot be separated from God as the absolute origin who existed before everything else came into being. God's voice or 'Logos' in general is the seemingly unassailable source, the center of life and death. If in the beginning there was nothing but the spoken word, writing must be regarded as an inferior phenomenon, as in Aristotle's thesis: "written words are the symbols of spoken words" (Kamuf 31). Here, writing can only define its identity through speech by serving as "phonetic transcription" (Kamuf 31) and is thus unable to grasp "'the thing itself'" (Kamuf 31), the signified.

In contrast, Derrida wants to deconstruct this hierarchy depending on speech as the center. He subverts it by treating writing as a signifying process having its own modes of expression and connects it with his idea of the self-concealment of God, with His separation from Himself and the absence of His original, primary voice. He regards God as "utter secret shrouded in the veils of 'writing'" (Ofrat 37), keeping silent behind the Tables and at the same time in between them, but always unattainable. In short, Derrida seems to link his key statement, the rejection of 'logocentrism,' with the vocabulary of negative theology.

However, we must not equalize deconstruction with negative theology, as Derrida himself points out in *Psyché* written in 1987 (546).[9] Here, he responds to false interpretations of his texts and emphasizes that 'différance' should not be understood as a concept, and in particular not as a theological concept (Kimmerle 119). This however does not mean that deconstruction is not connected with Jewishness. In "Circumfession" or in the interview with Elisabeth Weber, he clearly refers the themes of the wound, memory, circumcision, and the question of the interference of God to the movement of différance, and hence links his theory with (his) Jewishness. In his early essay "Violence and Metaphysics," he moreover points to the possible impossibility of the existence of God, this 'double bind,' which can be regarded as being part of 'différance': "Did not the Kabbala also speak of the unnameable possibility of the Name?" (137).

In other words, God is depicted as being ungraspable, absent, and silent. He is characterized by separation and division, and between man and God there opens an abyss, a chasm, or a desert. However, Derrida has not followed Freud's or Nietzsche's undertaking of putting God to death. On the contrary, in "Faith and Knowledge," an essay published in

[9] In *Psyché*, Derrida investigates the theme of negative theology and "[refers] to his own presence in Jerusalem" (Ofrat 129): "Comment parler convenablement de la théologie negative? Y en a-t-il une? Une seule? Un modèle régulateur pour les autres ? Peut-on y ajuster un discours ? . . . Oui, en toute vérité, ce qui est à plus de mille lieux plus loin que Jérusalem est aussi proche de mon âme que mon propre corps; j'en suis aussi sûr que d'être un homme" (Derrida, *Psyché* 546).

Religion (1998), he emphasizes the distinctness of Judaism (and Islam) in rejecting this modern, seemingly irrevocable "truth" (25 ff.). Furthermore, he affirms the essence of Judaism which rabbi Louis Jacob, for example, sums up with the following words: "When all is said and done, it is impossible to know God. But it is possible to know that there is a god" ("God" 298).

This statement on the possible impossibility of God hints at Derrida's interpretation of Franz Kafka's parable "Before the Law" ["Vor dem Gesetz"] in "Préjugés: Devant la loi" (1985), as Gideon Ofrat points out (54). In this story, a villager is kept at a distance from the law, as the title already reveals. Although he urgently asks for entry, right up to the end of his life, the law does not stop being arcane, obscure, hidden – in short, an unattainable secret marked by a 'double bind': The gate to the law is always open, but the guard prevents the man from walking through it. Until his death, the latter will neither get to know anything about the content of the law, nor about its source, origin, or father-figure since it is entangled within the movement of différance – the way to it will always be blocked (Derrida, "Préjugés" 126). In "Préjugés," Derrida however points out that the parable ends "at the most religious moment," i.e., when the villager, now an old, almost blind man behaving like a child, recognizes light within the darkness of the law, this absolute secret (126). The religious experience or moment of hope is contrasted to, and at the same time forms an alliance with, the absence of the source, the hidden origin, or, in other words, God.

2.5. In dialogue with Lévinas or facing the Other

In *Altérités* (1986), Jacques Derrida claims that he would raise no profound objection to the philosophy of Emmanuel Lévinas, that he would indeed "be ready to sign everything what he [said]" (qtd. in Taureck 100). This quotation is surprising since Derrida also criticized Lévinas quite sharply over the years. However, his early essay "Violence and Metaphysics. An Essay on the Thought of Emmanuel Lévinas" – an interpretation of *Totality and Infinity. An Essay on Exteriority* (1961) – shows, in spite of its criticism, Derrida's deep-rooted affinity with

Lévinas and the challenge his philosophy meant for him. Here, Derrida especially comments on Lévinas' restriction of the exclusiveness of the Greek similarity principle with the help of the Otherness principle. This principle influenced Derrida to a great extent, i.e., it pointed the way to his renunciation of logocentrism, and is therefore depicted in this chapter.

In *Totality and Infinity* (1961), Lévinas stresses that the violence of Socratism lies within the concentration on the same and the autonomous, within self-centeredness and the fixation on origins. Hence he, as Derrida puts it, "summons us to depart from the Greek site and perhaps from every site in general, and to move toward what is no longer a source or a site . . ." ("Violence and Metaphysics" 82). More concretely, Lévinas speaks in favor of a desire that "tends toward *something else entirely*, toward the *absolutely other*" (Lévinas, *Totality and Infinity* 33). It does not, according to him, focus on "the essence of being," but is directed towards the unknown, the ungraspable, or mysterious. It transcends any self-centeredness, is insatiable, and hence belongs to the sphere of infinity. In fact, as will be later shown more concretely, Judaic thought shines through this longing for the other:

> The metaphysical desire does not long to return, for it is a land not of our birth, for a land foreign to every nature, which has not been our fatherland and to which we shall never betake ourselves. The metaphysical desire does not rest upon any prior kinship. It is a desire that cannot be satisfied. (33/34)

Based on this understanding of desire is an ethics defined as a "proceeding from the I to the other, as a *face to face*. . . ." In short, "[t]he absolutely other is the Other" (39).[10] That means "the Other" is characterized by absolute difference. He/She is the one forever remaining foreign to the I and who thus can never be possessed:

> He and I do not form a number. The collectivity in which I say 'you' or 'we' is not a plural of the 'I.' I, you – these are not individuals of a common concept. Neither possession nor the unity of number nor the unity of concepts link me to the Stranger [l'Étranger], the Stranger who disturbs the being at home with oneself [le chez soi]. But Stranger also means the free one. Over him I have no power. (39)

[10] The original French sentence is "L'absolument Autre, c'est Autrui" (*Totality and Infinity* 39).

This relation between the I and the other as autonomous subjects being separated from each other forms the basis of Lévinas's ethics. To this extent, it differs from the 'I-Thou'-relationship in Martin Buber from which Lévinas already distanced himself in his early essay "Time and the Other" (1948). In Buber, as Lévinas points out, "reciprocity remains the tie between two separated freedoms, and the ineluctable character of isolated subjectivity is underestimated" ("Time and the Other" 54). Since Buber believes in a duality, he does not fully recognize the division between two subjects presented as autonomous persons. At the same time, he does not develop the idea of a relation to the absolutely other as an ethical necessity (Taureck 37).

Lévinas dissociates himself from Buber and turns to the Jewish-German thinker Franz Rosenzweig, the author of *The Star of Redemption* [*Der Stern der Erlösung*] (1921). With this book, Rosenzweig opposed the idea of totality of the philosophical tradition, especially in Hegel, and is consequently, as Lévinas points out, "a work too often present" in *Totality and Infinity* (28). The danger of the idea of totality, according to the two philosophers, lies in excluding or extinguishing everything that deviates from the understanding of sameness, i.e., in the renunciation of Otherness (Putnam 35 and Ofrat 137). The use of violence, in addition, most often goes along with the striving for power, order, and control. In contrast, the idea of infinity stands for the recognition and welcoming of Otherness, for "the unknown and untried," and, as a consequence, for "freedom and creative advance" (Wild, "Introduction" 17).

In a later work, *Otherwise than Being or Beyond Essence* (1974), Lévinas introduces the phrase "me voici" (i.e., "here I am") as the necessary "speech-act of presenting myself, the speech-act of making myself available to another" (qtd. in Putnam 38). This speech-act cannot be understood in depth if one is not aware of its biblical connotation. In fact, the Hebrew word for "me voici" is "hineni," which, for example, Abraham says to God in the story of the sacrifice of Isaac (Gen 22.1). Here, Abraham trusts God, the absolutely other, without hesitation and places himself in God's service. In parallel, the prophet Isaiah places himself at God's disposal by saying "hineni," too (Isaiah 6.8).

The necessity of saying "hineni" to the Other thus constitutes one of the cornerstones of Lévinas' ethics. The 'I' is obliged to present itself to the face of the other in the same way Abraham or Isaiah do – candidly, without thinking twice. Here, Lévinas universalizes a Jewish theme: The unrestricted openness to God's command is paralleled to the ethical demand of offering oneself to the face of the Other. At the same time, the 'I' needs to become aware of the Other's distance from itself that can never fully be dissolved. The closer the relationship indeed becomes, the more the 'I' understands that the Other can never be totally grasped. Its face remains "an exteriority that does not call for power or possession, an exteriority that is not reducible, as with Plato, to the interiority of memory" (*Totality and Infinity* 51). In other words, Lévinas transfers an attribute of God, His inaccessibility, to the concept of the other. Just as God's face can never be seen by anyone (Exod. 33.20), so it remains impossible to take hold of the other. Indeed, Derrida extends the encounter between the I and the other to the field of religion itself:

> Face to face with the other within a glance and a speech which both maintain distance and interrupt all totalities, this being-together as separation precedes or exceeds society, collectivity, community. Lévinas calls it religion. It opens ethics. The ethical relation is a religious relation (Difficile liberté). ("Violence and Metaphysics" 95/96).

With his metaphysics as ethics, Lévinas works against metaphysics as ontology in the tradition of Plato, against a theory of being a totality of identical entities. He develops a theory of a relation between the 'I' and the other who are separated entities, but who place themselves at each other's disposal. In the encounter with the face of the other, speech becomes possible enclosing respect and responsibility for the other. This responsibility for the need of the other is grounded, as Lévinas stresses, within Judaism itself, i.e., he regards it as a pre-philosophical or "originary" one. The age-old wound of persecution and imprisonment in Egypt stands at the outset for humane behavior, as he declares in his essay "Revelation in the Jewish Tradition" (1977):

> The traumatism of my enslavement in Egypt constitutes my very humanity, that which draws me closer to the problems of the wretched of the earth, to all persecuted people. It is as if I were praying in my suffering as a slave, but with a pre-oratorial prayer; as if the love of the stranger were a response already given to me in my actual heart. My very uniqueness lies in my responsibility for the other; nobody can relieve me of this, just as nobody can replace me at the moment of my death. (202)

In his essay "The Pact" (1982), Lévinas additionally illustrates the Judaic principle of reciprocal responsibility:

> His concern is my concern. But is not my concern also his? Isn't he responsible for me? And if he is, can I also answer for his responsibility for me? Kol Yisrael 'arevim zeh lazeh, 'All Israel is responsible one for the

> other', which means: all those who cleave to the divine law, all men worthy of the name, are all responsible for each other. (225/226)

In the following sentences, Lévinas points to "the theme of asymmetry" (Putnam 44) and links it with the topic of infinity in Judaism:

> I always have, myself, one responsibility more than anyone else, since I am responsible, in addition, for his responsibility. And if he is responsible for my responsibility, I remain responsible for the responsibility he has for my responsibility. Ein ladavar sof, 'it will never end'. In the society of the Torah, this process is repeated to infinity. (Lévinas, "The Pact" 226)

The concern for the other as a Judaic necessity will never be completely fulfilled. It remains, according to Lévinas, "an ideal" that includes "the humanity of human beings" as a whole. He, in other words, universalizes a Judaic value and opens up a general theory of ethics.

Jacques Derrida's affinity with Lévinas of course lies within the latter's concept of the "Other." However, in his essay "Violence and Metaphysics," Derrida criticizes that Lévinas's philosophy still moves within the boundaries of the Greek notion of being: "There is no speech without the thought and statement *of* Being" (143). Lévinas has not, as Derrida points out, reached his aim, i.e., of completely turning away from Hellenism to an ethics based on Judaic thought. Derrida is hence ready to ask openly: "Are we Jews? Are we Greek?" (153). With the following remark, he seems to give an answer himself: "We live in the difference between the Jew and the Greek, which is perhaps the unity of what is called history. We live in and of difference . . . " (153). These sentences again point to Derrida's distance from Judaism, to the rift he talks about in *Monolingualism of the Other.* By interpreting Lévinas, he clearly comes close to himself – or better: the Other within himself that here cannot be fixed to either "the Greek" or "the Jew."

2.6. The collapse of the Tower of Babel and the impossibility of translation

Derrida's rejection of logocentrism influenced by Lévinas' principle of "the Other" and his depiction of God as an indefinable, ungraspable essence, the opposite of a center or origin, can be linked to his discussion of colonialism and its effects on religious, cultural, and linguistic identity. In *Monolingualism of the Other*, Derrida sums up his childhood experiences in Algeria, where he was forced to speak French as his first language, from which he was later excluded: "I only have one language; it is not mine" (1). On the basis of this paradoxical past experience, he makes a general remark on language: ". . . [T]here is no such thing as *the* language, . . . there is no such thing as absolute monolingualism" (7). In a following passage, Derrida adds that colonial policy works through this monolingualism, "through the power of naming, of imposing and legitimating appellations" (3), and hence aims "to reduce language to the One, that is, to the hegemony of the homogeneous" (40).

This is, however, an attempt that cannot be fully achieved "since the One of a language . . . is never determined" (30). Language is in itself, according to Derrida, characterized by supplementation, fragmentation, and spacing, and thus will not infinitely become the unshakable center or instrument of a sovereignty. Moreover, language is, in dialogue, always directed to the other or it "originates" from the other; it will never stay with oneself alone, and thus cannot be possessed (40).

About ten years before Derrida discussed the effects of colonialism in general on the basis of his personal experiences in *Monolingualism of the Other,* he had written his essay "Des Tours de Babel" (1985). Here, he also speaks clearly against the creation and the imposition of a single, universal language – but more distanced from himself, by citing the story of the Tower of Babel in Genesis (Gen 11.1-9). This story tells of Yahweh punishing the tribe of Shem ("Shem" means "name" in Hebrew) for having built the Tower of Babel, an image for the haughtiness of a yet undivided mankind (Mertens, *Handbuch der Bibelkunde* 145 and Bennington, "Derridabase" 174). Because of the tribe's desire to make a name for itself, "'to accede to the highest, up to the Most High'" ("Des Tours de Babel" 248), Yahweh gives the erected town His own name "Bavel" or "Babel" which resembles the word "balál," i.e., "to confuse" (Mertens 145). Then He scatters the people all over the Earth and impels them to speak other languages.

Hence the story constitutes a paradoxical pair – or 'double bind': God who has created language and given it to man divides man from it and through it. Out of His anger that the people have misused His gift for god-like purposes, He erases their name, replaces it with His own, and splinters the one existing language into a multitude of different ones. Consequently, He prevents the erection of a state aiming at universality and uniformity.

By scattering the people all over the Earth and by splitting up their language, Yahweh imposes on them the necessity to translate each other – but without accomplishing a perfect translation, since this would again mean speaking one language only (Bennington, "Derridabase" 175). With this focus on a translation infinitely taking place within confusion, Derrida reacts on Walter Benjamin's essay "The Task of the Translator" ["Die Aufgabe des Übersetzers"] (1923). According to Benjamin, the translator needs to complement the meaning of the original by having the idea of a pure or "true" language in mind and yearning to reach it (56ff.). This undertaking will, however, not be accomplished, since the act of translating cannot be understood as the restoration of the original text, but as a stony or dusty path on which the translator is constantly confronted with his inability (Ofrat 70). According to Derrida, the translator needs to work with a fragmentary language differing and deferring itself and thus will never come close to any pure or true meaning of words. In *Monolingualism of the Other,* Derrida uses biblical vocabulary to describe the act of translating and calls it "a desert without a desert crossing" (72). In "Des Tours de Babel," he maintains that "[f]rom the origin of the original to be translated, there is fall and exile . . ." (250). The translator circles around the original meaning without ever reaching it; he is confronted with the movement of différance and hence will come to the conclusion that "the pure language remains concealed, hidden (*verborgen*), walled up in the nocturnal intimacy of the 'core'" (253). In other words, "translation contains something of the divine, messianic, religious promise" (Ofrat 71), which, however, eludes its fulfillment. Any "pure" translation will not be accomplished.

In "On Language as Such and the Language of Man" ["Über Sprache überhaupt und über die Sprache des Menschen"], an essay published in 1916, Benjamin declares that man's "originary" divine nature shows itself in giving objects their name, in a more or less godlike act of creation (33ff.). With the movement of 'différance,' the play of differences preventing the signified concept of being present in itself, Derrida clearly opposes this conception and declares it as hubris that might develop into concrete acts of (political) violence ("Différance" 11). God, as he emphasizes, "interrupts . . . the colonial violence or the linguistic imperialism" ("Des Tours de Babel" 253) signified by the tribe's dedication to a universal tongue; He creates confusion showing itself indirectly in every translation: "In a sense, nothing is untranslatable; but *in another sense*, everything is untranslatable; translation is another name for the impossible" (*Monolingualism* 57). Derrida has logically chosen a title for his essay which "is itself untranslatable," as Peggy Kamuf notes (243). Joseph F. Graham, the American translator, emphasizes that

> 'Des Tours de Babel' . . . 'can be read in various ways. *Des* means 'some'; but it also means 'of the,' 'from the,' or 'about the.' *Tours* could be towers, twists, tricks, turns, or tropes, as in a 'turn' of phrase. Taken together, *des* and *tours* have the same sound as *détour*, the word for detour.' (qtd. in Kamuf 243)

The title of the essay eludes any definite meaning. It must in itself be regarded as an "original" demanding translation which, however, will not be fully accomplished. In other words, Derrida's conception of translation can be opened up to a more general view of reading, as Geoffrey Bennington explains in "Derridabase": "We can say, too, generalizing a little the meaning of the word 'translation,' that all of Derrida's own texts are (only) readings or translations of 'originals,' but we shall assert the originality of these readings by recognizing that in turn they demand translation" (168). This demanded translation or interpretation of Derrida's texts will certainly come across the same multiplicity and diversity that he himself tracks down, such as in Jabès' and Celan's poems or Joyce's novels. More generally expressed, every reading is an impossible translation of a language that will never be owned, or completely grasped. The translation does not reproduce the original meaning, but always creates something new:

> At the same time, this untranslatable translation, this new idiom makes things happen [fait arriver], this signature brought forth [fait arrivée], produces events in the given language, the given language to which things must still be given, sometimes unverifiable events: illegible events. Events that are always promised rather than given. Messianic events. But the promise is not nothing; it is a non-event. (*Monolingualism* 66)

2.7. The borderline nature of death and "archive fever"

The translator or interpreter follows, as explained above, a dusty, stony, desert-like path by being confronted with the movement of différance. The purity of language remains an unrealizable desire. An absolute truth cannot be achieved. The translator constantly meets with a border, with stoppage, or erasure – in other words, with the moment of death itself. In his early essay "Freud and the Scene of Writing," Derrida puts this more generally with his emphasis on "the trace [which] is the erasure of selfhood, of one's own presence, and is constituted by the threat or anguish of its irremediable disappearance" (230). Or, in short: "This erasure is death itself" (230), with which the subject is always confronted.

However, death should not just be understood as an ending or absolute border-post behind which there is no transit, as Derrida explains in *As if I were Dead*, an interview on the occasion of a conference in 1995 entitled "Applied Derrida." This title gave Derrida the ghostly feeling of looking at or listening to himself as if he were a different person, an other, as if he himself did not exist anymore: "You can imagine that when one comes to a conference entitled 'Applied You,' you experience the situation in which it is as if you were dead. Finally" (16). As a consequence, Derrida asks the question what it really means to be dead. He decides for an experiment in which he takes on the role of the corpse. Thus he seemingly observes himself and the others from a sphere exterior to ours, and, by doing so, tries to answer the question why we are afraid of death:

> On the one hand, we are scared because we think we won't be there anymore. So that would be the end of the world, not simply the end of our world but the end of the world. But, on the other hand, what is scarier is the fantasy . . . that we are going to be present at and in attendance at this non-world, at our own death. We will continue to be dead, that is, absent, while attending the actual world. . . . What is absolutely scary is the idea of being dead while being quasi-dead. . . . (19-20)

Derrida explains man's deepest anxiety by defining death as being characterized by a "double bind." Death appears as an absolute mark, break, or stoppage, as the finite itself which is inherent in life. With this definition, Derrida partly covers the Judaic notion of death, namely "the profound acceptance of the fact of mortality: death as part of a natural process marks the inevitable end to life in this world and is a fate common to all God's creatures" (Abramovitch, "Death" 131). In Judaism, "[t]his awareness of the imminence and inevitability of death" has the consequence that man "ought to treat each day as if it were to be his last" (135). Looking at ourselves as mortal beings brings us closer to life. Rabbinical authorities in fact differentiate between

> a biological reality and a theological conception of death. . . . The body, after death, returns to the dust, fulfilling the observation of Genesis 3:19, 'for dust you are, and to dust you shall return'; whereas the soul, often identified as the divine spark, finds its way back to the divine creator, as in the saying, which forms part of the funeral service, 'The Lord has given and the Lord has taken away, blessed be the name of the Lord' (Job 1:21). (Abramovitch 131/132)

The traditional Jewish funeral ritual reveals this dialectic understanding of death and "completes a cycle of an eternal return to the Garden of Eden, which began personally with the birth of the individual and mythically with the expulsion from paradise" (134).

In *Archive Fever,* Derrida does not elaborate on the Jewish conception of death; but he concentrates, on the one hand, on the awareness of our mortality and, on the other hand, on death as a crossing from here to there, on the in-between, and our anxiety that is connected with it. Eight years before, in *Psyché,* he defined this crossing in the following way: "At the moment of death, we can no longer be concerned with anything but the Other in ourselves" (qtd. in Kamuf 203). Again, Derrida is here close to Lévinas who points out that at the moment of death "we are in relation with something that is absolutely other, something bearing alterity not as a provisional determination we can assimilate through enjoyment, but as something whose very existence is made of alterity" ("Time and the Other" 43).

Lévinas regards death as something absolutely unknowable and ungraspable, as the mysterious which is separated by an abyss from the present ("Time and the Other" 39ff.). Besides, at the moment of death, the subject experiences "the limit of [its] virility" (42), i.e., it is reduced to absolute passivity. Death comes, as Lévinas puts it, "at a certain moment we are no longer *able to be able (nous ne 'pouvons plus pouvoir')*. It is exactly thus that the subject loses its very mastery as a subject" (42). Since the French verb 'pouvoir' can be translated by 'to be able' or 'can' and the noun by 'power' or 'force,' this sentence may be interpreted in the following way: At the moment of death, the subject is no longer in possession of its powers – or, to be more precise: "[I]t loses its very ability to have powers, its 'I can' – that is to say, its very self-constitution as an existent" (Hand 55).

Furthermore, the knowledge of death as the essential possibility of being goes along with the necessity or responsibility of opening up oneself to the other – in particular to the death of the other, which is already marked by his name. The name will still be there after its bearer's death, it will function at his place and will remind of his past existence. In "Derridabase," Geoffrey Bennington sums this up in the following way:

> [A]ny experience of the other must be engaged, however minimally, in this reciprocal indebtedness produced by the relation to death inscribed by a signature: we shall say that this indebtedness (let's call it friendship) is grounded in a certainty underlying any encounter, namely that one of us will die before the other, will in some sense see the other die, will survive the other, and will therefore live in memory of the other, wearing the other's mourning, like it or not. (165-166)

Remembrance is one major theme of Derrida's *Archive Fever. A Freudian Impression* (1995) that he here connects with the phenomenon of the "archive" coming into being at the moment of death. The meaning of "archive" can be referred to the Greek word "arkheion" which, as Derrida explains, originally meant "a house, a domicile, an address, the residence of the superior magistrates, the *archons*, those who commanded" (*Archive Fever* 2). Derrida adds that at the archons' homes, i.e., within the private sphere, the official, legislative documents were written. The word "archive" thus refers to the public sphere and at the same time includes the private and personal: "It is thus, in this *domiciliation*, in this house arrest, that archives take place. The dwelling, this place where they dwell permanently, marks this institutional passage from the private to the public . . ." (2).

On the basis of this "double bind" of the archive, Derrida turns to the "Freudian signature" which has left its traces, i.e., to Sigmund Freud, the name, on the one hand, and to "the invention of psychoanalysis on the other hand: "project of knowledge, of practice and institution, community, family, domiciliation, consignation, 'house' or 'museum,' in the present state of its archivization" (5). In particular, he concentrates on "memory as *internal* archivization" (13) and its connection with the Freudian theory of the death drive. To Freud, the death drive, that he sometimes also calls destruction drive or aggression drive, influences human consciousness in so far that it "incites forgetfulness, amnesia, the annihilation of memory, as *mnēmē* or *anamnēsis*" (11).

However, the death drive does not only affect man's memory, but especially has an impact on everything external, i.e., it "also commands the radical effacement, in truth the eradication, of that which can never be reduced to *mnēmē* or to *anamnēsis*, that is, the archive, consignation, the documentary or monumental apparatus as *hypomnēma*" (11). For Derrida, the archive seems to mean a conscious process or an instrument of gathering material, of trying to compile everything that will possibly disappear or that is already partly forgotten: "[T]he archive takes place at the place of originary and structural breakdown of the said memory" (11). In other words, the death drive is regarded as the prerequisite for every archive understood as a term that includes both the private and the public in itself. The lost memories, facts, or material awake the yearning for an archive:

> There would indeed be no archive desire without the radical finitude, without the possibility of a forgetfulness which does not limit itself to repression. Above all, . . . there is no archive fever without the threat of this death drive, this aggression and destruction drive. (19)

Furthermore, the archive, which becomes necessary because of the loss or the disappearance of memories, cannot only be called the home or stockroom for past contents, but is also directed towards the future (16/17). Its aim is to reveal what has been covered or hidden, to bring to light the traces of what has seemingly been buried. It is, in short, not only bound by death, but by life as well and thus makes obvious what deconstruction is about.

Derrida's autobiographical work "Circumfession" can be called the attempt of an archive, a writing that is bound to life and death at the same time. With it, Derrida turns to "the conventionally conservative genre of autobiography" (Hornung, "Autobiography" 221). He seems to be as fascinated by the self, by "the private sphere" as Thoreau or Walt Whitman once were. Yet he turns "the traditional autobiographical form, for which Saint Augustine's *Confessiones* . . . stand[s] paradigmatically" upside down, i.e., "Circumfession" is the opposite of a "construction of narrative continuity and unfragmented subjecthood" (221).

At the moment of his mother's death, Derrida tries to capture pictures of his past, his childhood and youth in Algeria. Yet his thoughts accelerate in the face of death, and his words on paper disseminate into all sorts of directions. One sentence runs into the other without a pause, as Derrida longs "to overtake each second, like one car overtaking another, doubling it rather, overprinting it with the negative of a photograph already taken with a 'delay' mechanism . . ." ("Circumfession" 39). This restless zapping from one fragmentary memory to the next leaves the reader irritated and confused. But this is exactly what Derrida tries to achieve: "I write to alienate, drive mad all those that I will have alienated by not saying anything" (274). The reader indeed needs to put the different moments of Derrida's life and the elements of his theoretical work together like a jigsaw puzzle, but realizes that "[a] nonfinite number of . . . narrative links are plausible" (Bennington, "Acts" 321). According to Geoffrey Bennington, Derrida depicts "*one life* among others, real ones, possible ones, fictive or secret ones" ("Acts" 321) and hence creates "*the contrary of a construction*" (322).

In spite of, but also because of this resulting confusion, "Circumfession" comes to be a very personal work. While looking death in the face, Derrida opens up himself to the other within himself, to his own mortality, and also to the future: "I see myself dead cut from you in your memories that I love and I weep like my own children at the edge of my grave, I weep not only for my children but for all my children, why only you, my children" (39/40). The mourning for the mother's foreseeable death goes along with a search for the inner self. In particular, Derrida connects himself with certain traces of death before he was born, most of all with his elder brother Paul, who died before him. He felt like a substitute, like "the twin brother of a dead one" (277), like "his double" (138). Because of the presence of death in his life, he was always "interested in his own identification" (138). He has constantly been looking for an answer to the question "'who am I?'" (138), but has not found one. This inner search for an identity goes along with Derrida's choice of the autobiographical form, which is "a vehicle for self-representation" (Hornung, "Autobiography" 222). As it serves as a means to ask "existential questions" (222), the autobiographical piece of writing can be regarded as a quest for "orientation and stability in a disoriented and unstable world" (222). In comparison to Derrida's linguistic and philosophical theory, the use of the autobiographical form can therefore be interpreted as an inconsistency.

However, we must not forget that such as quest is depicted as an extremely demanding, arduous undertaking. The author of an autobiographical piece continues circling around his inner wounds, the "*scars*, escarres" (97), as Derrida also calls them. The moment of death becomes a signifier which directs attention to all sorts of conceivable moments and places in time and space. Hence the writer might get lost during his quest or become utterly confused. He also runs the risk of losing his identity altogether (Derrida, "Circumfession" 22). In other words, Derrida's "Circumfession" can be called a dispersed piece of "writing without interruption which has been looking for itself forever. . ." (201). It is writing marked by fragmentation, by cuts and incisions – in short, by the moment of circumcision, the Jewish ritual which here in particular is turned into a philosophical and literary means and image.

3. Jewishness and Deconstruction in Paul Auster's literary work

In his essay collection *The Art of Hunger* (1992), Paul Auster describes modern Jewish writers as "solitary wanderer[s]," driven by the inner urge to arrive at a place of homecoming through the act of writing (42). Very much like Jacques Derrida's interpretation of Edmond Jabès, he depicts Franz Kafka's prose writing as a perpetual search for the right words that must never end, since the desired destination will never be in sight:

> He wanders toward the promised land. That is to say: he moves from one place to another, and dreams continually of stopping. And because this desire to stop is what haunts him, is what counts most for him, he does not stop. He wanders. That is to say: without the slightest hope of ever going anywhere. ("Pages for Kafka" 22)

In another passage from "Pages for Kafka," a little essay Auster wrote on the fiftieth anniversay of Kafka's death, Auster specifies his interpretation of Kafka's paradoxical aesthetic undertaking. It is the act of walking itself that seems to be at the core of Kafka's texts. According to Auster, the writer is forced to follow his path through desert-like places continuously:

> . . . so that at each moment, even as he continues on his way, he feels he must turn his eyes from the distance that lies before him, like a lure, to the movement of his feet, appearing and disappearing below him, to the road itself, its dust, the stones that clutter its way. . . . (24)

On this stony, apparently never-ending path, the writer always feels like an outsider, a stranger in the world he struggles with: "He wanders. On a road that is not a road, on an earth that is not his earth, an exile in his own body" (24/25). In his essay "The Decisive Moment" on the Jewish-American writer Charles Reznikoff, Auster also emphasizes the poet's missing sense of belonging or the feeling of having become excluded from a larger community. Desperately, the poet tries to cope with it: "It is more than just loneliness, however. It is exile, and a way of coming to terms with exile that somehow, for better or worse, manages to leave the condition of exile intact" (42). By quoting Reznikoff, Auster explains that this feeling of living in exile results from the poet's alienation from Jewish tradition: "'How difficult for me is Hebrew: / even the word for *mother*, for *bread*, for *sun* / is foreign. How far have I been exiled, Zion" (43).

Yet, it is not only the alienation from Jewish beliefs that is apparently at the core of Reznikoff's writing. As a second-generation American Jew, he always had to cope with his "state of *otherness*" (42) he was born into, the fact that he was treated as someone not really belonging to modern America. In short, "he has been exiled twice – as a Jew, and from Judaism as well," as Auster emphasizes (43).

This condition of being exiled seems to lie at the "center" of Derrida's theory of deconstruction, too, as the first part of this investigation showed. Similar to Reznikoff, Derrida was "exiled twice," not in America though, but in Algeria through its colonial, anti-Semitic policy in the 1940s. Here, he was separated from traditional Jewish life and became alienated from the French-Algerian culture (cf. ch. 2.1.). Primarily, it is the impossibility of circling around this wound, of ever coming nearer it through the act of writing, that Derrida emphasizes, for example in the interview with Elizabeth Weber, "A Testimony Given" (55). This impossibility he connects with his "concept" of différance, the playful operation of differing and deferring. In other words, the writer will consequently fail with his attempt to get to the bottom of his wounds, since the movement of différance will block the way towards them. Any origin becomes differed and deferred and thus eludes the writer's intention to get hold of it (ch. 2.2.).

The desire to come to terms with the wound of alienation also runs through Auster's poetry and prose. This attempt is often described as an unbearable undertaking, or, as in Auster's essays on Jabès, Kafka, or Reznikoff, an apparently never-ending walk through the desert. At the beginning of Auster's career, it seems to be connected with the aesthetic necessity to find the right words, to regard language as a tool to come closer to given facts or even truths, as the following chapter on Auster's poetry will show. Influenced by the Objectivists such as Charles Reznikoff, George Oppen, or William Carlos Williams, Auster is interested in concentrating on the things he is surrounded by and to depict them as precisely as possible. In his essay "Private I, Public Eye" on Oppen, Auster emphasizes the poet's "refusal of any pre-arranged or inherited system of values" and his genuine, unadulterated observation resulting in a "language [that] is almost naked" (115). Oppen's fascination with the physicality of the object, his "wonder in the sheer this-ness of things, against the confusion and brutality of the social world" (116) will lead "to larger questions of society and the possibility of community" (117). However, his attempt to face up to the reality of the modern world seems to result from "a feeling of isolation and loss [rather] than from a naïve hope in the future: '. . . because we find the others / Deserted like ourselves and therefore brothers'" (118). In parallel, Auster's early writing also springs from a profound "feeling of isolation and loss" – similar to Derrida's project of deconstruction which seems to be directly connected with his personal experience of separation from Jewish religion and culture. It is the "origin" of alienation from traditional Jewish knowledge which turns out to be the starting point of the writing process.

Besides, "the necessity of seeing the world – that is to say, of entering it" ("Private I, Public Eye" 118), which Auster sees at the core of George Oppen's texts, is an aesthetic demand in Auster's poems that will develop to an ethical question in his prose. In other words, Paul Auster's writing stands in contrast to the aesthetic postmodernists of the 1960s and 70s, such as John Hawkes, who exclusively tried to negate the differences between facts and fiction (Hornung, "Hungerkünstler" 124). In an interview of 1965, Hawkes declared "plot, character, setting, and theme" as the "true enemies of the novel" and substituted them through his "totality of vision or structure" (Enck 149). However, these constituents of narrative structure remain crucial for Auster, although he makes use of postmodern writing techniques (Hornung, "Hungerkünstler" 125). When he leaves poetry writing altogether and turns toward prose, he more and more tries to depict what he sees and feels at present and what he remembers from the past. However, this shift will go along with the insight that it will never be possible to find the right words for depicting the separation from Jewish roots and the moment of death. Or, as Derrida puts it in "A Testimony Given," the desire to get to the bottom of an originary wound will never be satisfied; it remains "an origin that is constantly delayed, toward the future or the past" (54-55).

Moreover, the experience of loss and alienation is not only a personal theme in Auster's writing, but also seems to be a more general cultural Jewish one. According to Derrida, man's separation from God, his experience of alienation, and the image of the absent God, who might hide Himself from man, "are already in the Kabbalah. Which means 'Tradition' itself" ("Edmond Jabès" 74). This "moment of Separation" as a traditional-cultural Jewish experience also runs through Auster's texts.

For instance, the I-narrator of *The Invention of Solitude* or Anna Blume, the protagonist of *In the Country of Last Things*, seem to have lost any connection to their Jewish past. Auster generalizes this personal kind of loss, when he refers to moments of extreme suffering in Jewish history, especially at the time of the Shoah. The Rabbi in *In the Country of Last Things* describes the experience of alienation and persecution as a specific Jewish experience: "Every Jew, he said, believes that he belongs to the last general of Jews. We are always at the end, always standing on the brink of the last moment, and why should we expect things to be any different now?" (112)

The personal experience of being exiled from traditional Jewish life through the anti-Semitic policy in Algeria in the 1940s seems to lie at the "center" of Derrida's theory of deconstruction. In parallel, the Jewish experience of persecution, especially during the Shoah, and the separation from religious and cultural roots are two of Auster's major themes. Yet he writes about them only in fragmentary form, since one of his "central question[s]" seems to be the same as Jabès'. In his essay "Book of the Dead" on Jabès' *Book of Questions* he sums it up in the following way: It is the question "how to speak what cannot be spoken. The question is the Jewish Holocaust, but it is also the question of literature itself" (107).

This statement on the impossibility of writing must not be understood in Theodor Adorno's sense of the term who claimed that writing poetry after Auschwitz is barbaric. In Auster and in Jabès, it is rather the question how the incomprehensible could be put into words, i.e., if it will ever be possible to write about a time in history for which there is no comparison. In order to write about the Jewish experience of alienation and persecution, the Shoah in particular, "writing itself is first put into question," as Auster claims at the end of his essay on Jabès (114). In other words, the incomprehensibility of this experience goes hand in hand with the realization of the insecurity or indeterminancy of language and the refusal to give any definite answers.

Indeed, when Auster's writing turns to prose, the rejection of logocentrism, the awareness of absence in presence, and the use of a fragmentary language will become a necessity. With Auster's understanding of the inadequacy of language, which can never express totally what the writer sees, feels, and wants to remind us of, his writing will more and more correspond to Derrida's theory of deconstruction. The Objectivists' guiding principle, "the purity of perception," Auster describes as an "effort [which] takes on the value of a religious act"

("The Decisive Moment" 15). In the course of time, Auster distances himself from it and instead turns toward the playful possibilities of language and emphasizes the impossibility of getting closer to one's wounds through the act of writing.

3.1. The early fragmented poems – the foiled desire for purity in writing

In the interview with Larry McCaffery and Sinda Gregory, Auster explains that he "remain[s] very attached to the poetry [he] wrote, [he] would still stand by it. In the final analysis, it could even be the best work [he had] ever done" (303). Indeed, between 1974 and 1980, Auster published six collections of poetry, "a substantial and highly original body of work," as Norman Finkelstein rightly points out ("Introduction" 9-10). Most poems of *Unearth* (1970-1972) and *Wall Writing* (1971-1975) were written in Paris and in the south of France. During this time, Auster did not only read and translate French-Jewish writers, for example Edmond Jabès, but also non-Jewish ones. Among them were Stéphane Mallarmé, who is considered to be one of the most significant symbolist poets, Jacques Dupin, and André du Bouchet. Foremost, Auster seems to have been fascinated with Mallarmé's aesthetic quest for purity and his belief in an absolute (Niebylski 39). In his "oevre pure," Mallarmé concentrates on the color of white, which also runs as a metaphor through Auster's poetry (Hauck 317). One poem from *Wall Writing* is even called "White," and in his transitional piece of writing "White Spaces," Auster deals with the question of approaching some absolute truth through the process of writing.

Like Hegel, Mallarmé assumed that the "absolute" can be reached through the principle of negation that he regarded as the liberating principle par excellence. Thus, his poetic personae, for example in "Hérodiade," which Mallarmé began writing in 1864, are in quest for freedom and hope to get rid of their psychic limitations (Mallarmé, "Hérodiade" 40 ff.). However, in contrast to Hegel, for whom truth is inherent in the totality of being, totality for Mallarmé is always evasive, i.e., it may only be perceived by allusion to its absence (Niebylski 40). Mallarmé indeed holds onto this principle of absence or nothingness throughout his writing career. Already in 1866, he connects it with the principle of beauty: "After having found nothingness, I found beauty" (qtd. in Niebylski 41). One year later, in another letter to his friend Henri Cazalis, Mallarmé develops the connection of nothingness and beauty in poetry: "I have made a long descent into Nothingness in order to speak with exactitude. There is only Beauty – and it has but one perfect expression: Poetry" (qtd. in Niebylski 41).[11] Mallarmé's fascination with nothingness, emptiness, or silence in connection with his principle of exactitude or purity in writing influenced Paul Auster at the early stages of his career. At that time, the latter's preoccupation with the inner self went hand in hand with his attempt to find the most precise words, as the following chapter will show.

In "Search for a Definition," a poem of *Facing the Music*, Auster speaks of the desperate undertaking "of looking for a place / to enter the world, a way of being / present / among the things / that do not want us" (145-46). This feeling of alienation and exclusion, that is also expressed by Jacques Derrida, and the desperate undertaking to find a place of homecoming are directly connected with the writer's struggle to find the right words. Embedded in Auster's early search for precision in writing is the question of the existence of God in spite of His invisibility, as the following chapters try to demonstrate, too. In "Edmond Jabès and the Question of the Book," Jacques Derrida links the image of the absent God, who does not show His face, and that is part of the Kabbalah, with one of his main theses, the renunciation of 'logocentrism.' He regards God as "utter secret shrouded in the veils of 'writing'" (Ofrat 37), keeping silent behind the Tables and at the same time in between them, but always unattainable (cf. ch. 2.4.). Already in Auster's poetry, the uttainability of God during man's search for Him is a major theme that will develop in his prose writing. Here, it goes hand in hand with his rejection of any dependence on an original source or origin, with his continuous questioning of seemingly definite answers in writing.

Most interestingly, the theme of the wound which runs through Derrida's philosophical theory of deconstruction as a personal and more general Jewish experience will also appear in Auster's poems and later on in his prose texts. In "A Testimony Given," the philosopher emphasizes the contradiction between the obsession with a wound, the attempt to get to the bottom of it and the inability to approach it. Auster, for example, writes about this contradiction in *White Spaces* (1978). His early poems show that the act of writing emerges from wounds,

[11] Mallarmé's remarks on the principles of nothingness and beauty are conveniently available in Niebylski. See Mallarmé, *Correspondances* 220 and 243.

primarily from the experience of alienation or uprooting, as will be shown in the next chapter. The attempt to get closer to this original wound is often connected with the search for the most suitable words. What the lyrical I will however be confronted with is the dissemination of signifiers. Confused and disoriented, it will not stop walking on dusty paths in desert-like places, always in search for coherence.

According to Jacques Derrida, language is in itself characterized by fragmentation and dissemination and thus cannot infinitely become the unshakeable center or instrument of a sovereignty. In his essay "Des Tours de Babel," he speaks clearly against the creation and the imposition of a single, universal language by interpreting the story of the Tower of Babel in Genesis (Gen. 11.1-9). The necessary confusion of language is at the core of the story which Auster also refers to in his poetry. Because of this confusion, the attempt to create a most precise text can never be fully achieved. Like Derrida, Auster depicts the purity of language as an unrealizable desire and hence distances himself from the Mallarméan ideal. The writer will constantly try to come closer to his wounds, but will meet with a border, with stoppage, or erasure – in other words, with the moment of death itself.

3.1.1. Writing out of wounds and the turn to a narrative style

In his essay "Book of the Dead" (1976) on Edmond Jabès, especially on his *Book of Questions* (1963), Paul Auster declares that "Jabès found himself as a writer in the act of discovering himself as a Jew" (*The Art of Hunger* 114). With this statement, he is close to Jacques Derrida's conviction that Jabès' writing emerges from an age-old wound of Judaism, i.e., the experience of dispersion, persecution, and death, but also of a never-ending hope (cf. ch. 2.3). Auster, in parallel to Derrida, also quotes a remark made by the Russian poet Marina Tsvetaeva, namely that "[i]n this most Christian of worlds / all poets are Jews" (114), and explains that this equation is the essence of Jabès' writing, the central conviction from which his *Book of Questions* developed.

In particular, Auster refers to the deep longing and the ongoing search for the "promised land" as a biblical image and poetic experience. The writer becomes estranged from his own ideas and from language itself over and over again. Nevertheless, he continues looking for the most appropriate words possible. In the conversation between Paul Auster and Edmond Jabès, which is mentioned in the introduction of this investigation, the latter equalizes "the condition of being a writer" with “the condition of being a Jew” (Auster, “Providence” 149). Then he generalizes this personal experience, which he describes as a central experience of his development as a writer, by arguing that every writing process mirrors the condition of being a Jew, which is the condition of living in exile (ibid.). This age-old Jewish experience of being exiled, the wound of being separated from Jewish roots, is indeed at the heart of Auster’s poems, too, as this chapter tries to show. More concretely, the wound is a personal poetic experience which at the same moment refers to the history of Judaism in general. Or, to put it the other way round with the help of Derrida’s words: “In question is a certain Judaism as the birth and passion of writing” (“Edmond Jabès” 64).

In his gloomy, sinister poem No. 24 of his early collection *Unearth* (1970-1972), Auster indeed describes the act of writing as a process of coming into being within a wound of an impersonal “you.” Uncanny, spine-chilling images of death emerge from this wound. The writing process thus becomes a ghost-like experience, a mysterious, unfathomable nightmare:

> . . . Your sinew
> does not mend, it is
> another rope, braided
> by ink, and aching through
> this raw hand – that hauls the images
> back to us: the clairvoyant
> corpse, singing
> from his gallows-mirror; a glance,
> heavier than stone, hurled
> down to April
> ice, ringing the bottom
> on your breath-well. . . . (60)

In his poem “Choral” of his later poetry collection *Wall Writing* (1971-1975), Auster takes up the image of writing taking root in a wound. But the shift is now to the wound of the lyrical I that the impersonal “you” touches, with the consequence that the lyrical I begins to speak: “Slowly, / you dip your finger into the wound / from which my voice / escapes” (70). In parallel to poem No. 24 of *Unearth*, this wound is connected with the moment of death. A former battle-field is mentioned, now overgrown by clover. Here, the impersonal “you” rides in its dream: “Whinnied by flint, / in the dream-gait that cantered you across / the clover-swarmed / militant field" (70). In the second stanza, this battle-field becomes a lively memory. The noise of fighting is audible and makes the impersonal "you" rebellious. It falls into an insurgent, combative way of speaking: "this bit / of earth that inches up / to us again, shattered / by the shrill, fife-sharp tone / that jousts you open, million-fold, / in your utmost / heretic word" (70).

In the first poem of *Unearth*, Auster also circles around the moment of fighting and of death. Again, an impersonal "you" is addressed and now depicted as being exiled, imprisoned, and completely left alone in the middle of a city, Jabès' and Auster's modern equivalent for the traditional Jewish image of the desert (37). The barren landscape mirrors the inner state of the impersonal "you," its experience of being alienated. It is confronted with nothing but its writing process becoming an act of rebellion and echoing the insurgent atmosphere of the late 1960s in Europe and the States. Influenced by this political uproar, Auster has produced a "radical anarchist subtext" (Finkelstein, "Introduction" 12). The impersonal "you" seems to have taken on the violent gesture of its surroundings, namely of "the wall," here an image of unjustified imprisonment or of hopelessness. Its only chance to survive is in adapting to the mercilessness of the modern wilderness, symbolized by the image of "the wolves" at the end of the poem:

> Along with your ashes, the barely
> written ones, obliterating
> the ode, the incited roots, the alien
> eye – with imbecilic hands, they dragged you
> into the city, bound you in
> this knot of slang, and gave you
> nothing. Your ink has learned
> the violence of the wall. Banished,
> but always to the heart
> of brothering quiet, you cant the stones
> of unseen earth, and smooth your place
> among the wolves. Each syllable
> is the work of sabotage. (37)

These lines exemplify the symbolically condensed and at the same time mysterious, concealed nature of Auster's early work that asks for the reader's unrestricted concentration (Troester 532). In an interview with Larry McCaffery and Sinda Gregory, Auster describes his poetry of the early 1970s in the following way: "I had started out by writing poems that resembled clenched fists; they were short and dense and obscure, as compact and hermetic as Delphic oracles" (301). The obsessive treatment of the self lies at the core of these early poems. They are an attempt to get to the bottom of inner wounds, a search for certain roots, or for the inmost nature of things, as Auster explained in another passage of the interview with McCaffery and Gregory:

> My poems were a quest for what I would call a uni-vocal expression. They expressed what I felt at any given moment, as if I'd never felt anything before and would never feel anything again. They were concerned with essences, with bedrock beliefs, and their aim was always to achieve a purity and consistency of language. (304)

This attempt to find "purity and consistency of language" can be detected in Auster's poem "Pastoral" of *Wall Writing* (1971-75). It goes along with the hope of getting as close as possible to certain depths. Surprisingly, the rebellious tone of *Unearth* now gives way to a more optimistic, momentarily idyllic atmosphere. A past scenery where everything is different from the present is at the core of the poem. This scenery is still waiting for the impersonal "you" to get explored. During its undertaking, the (written) word becomes an aid to throw light upon the hidden depths, to bring the roots to the surface. It is a seemingly endless journey which is depicted here. Through it, the impersonal "you" understands that even at a violent moment, symbolized by the axe striking off the roots, it goes on living:

> In the hinterland of moss and waiting,
> so little like the word
> that was a waiting as well,
> all has been other
> than it is, the moss
> still waits for you, the word
> is a lantern
> you carry to the depths
> of green, for even the roots
> have carried light, and even now
> your voice
> still travels through the roots, so that
> wherever an axe may fall
> you, too, shall know that you live. (92)

Here, the impersonal "you" tries to illuminate the mysteriousness of the past with the help of the word. The emphasis is put on the writer's search for the most suitable word that might sum up a situation or atmosphere most exactly. This quest "is present throughout Auster's work, most often in the guise of the stone as the irreducible element which refers to nothing but itself" (Troester 529), such as in "Interior," also a poem of *Wall Writing* (67). It expresses Auster's early striving toward the real, the ordinary scenes which surround him, and thus also shows the influence the Objectivists have had on him with their precise manner of description (70). In his essay "The Decisive Moment" on Charles Reznikoff, Auster connects the Objectivist's striving to stay on the surface of life, to present concrete details of ordinary scenes with the Jewish experience of being exiled:

> Even as he becomes a part of the landscape he has entered, he continues to be an outsider. Therefore, objectivist. That is to say – to create a world around oneself by seeing as a stranger would. What counts is the thing itself, and the thing that is seen can come to life only when the one who sees it has disappeared. . . . And yet, it is as if each act of seeing were an attempt to establish a link between the one who sees and the thing that is seen. As if the eye were the means by which the stranger could find his place in the world he has been exiled to. (39)

This attempt to get in contact with the surrounding world, in which each "sound of a word [is] married to death" (67), lies at the center of Auster's poem "Interior." Here, the lyrical I points out its ability to vanish (". . . and the life / that is this force in me / to disappear" (67)) while it is opening up itself to the ordinary things it notices around itself. It leaves itself behind in order to write about the real:

> Night repeats. A voice that speaks to me
> only of smallest things.
> Not even things – but their names.
> And where no names are –
> of stones. The clatter of goats
> climbing through the villages
> of noon. A scarab
> devoured in the sphere
> of its own dung. And the violet swarm
> of butterflies beyond. (67)

The wish to find a moment of purity and precision in language is also the theme of an unpublished poem titled "Land's End" and of a piece in prose format with approximately the same content, titled "City of Words" (Troester 527-529). Let me first quote "Land's End" before elaborating on the shift to the prose version and its meaning in the context of Auster's later deconstructive writing:

> Like a message in a bottle.
> A last word scrawled in the blood
> of shipwreck –
> rescued from life at the end of life
> and therefore lost. A word
> addressed to no one, coming at the end
> of all other words – addressed to no one,
> to everyone, to you.
> Like a single word, thrown out to sea.
> As if I could begin
> from nothing.
> . . . .

Here, the lyrical I yearns to begin anew with its act of writing by trying to rescue the "last word." It hopes to trace back the moment at which language once came into being in order to create a "pure," most precise language. With this quest, "Land's End" foreshadows one of the main themes of Auster's following texts, especially of *City of Glass*. In this anti-detective novel, Stillman, Sr., the culprit, searches for a "prelapsarian language" (57) based on the total correspondence of signifier and signified (see 3.3.3). However, the more he yearns to become a new Adam by naming things most suitably (Kierkegaard 168), the more he will deviate from his logocentric undertaking. His wanderings through the city of New York will not lead him anywhere. Similarly, the longing of the lyrical I for creating a new, innocent sort of language in "Land's End" will come to nothing. The image of the last word sums up this project which is doomed to failure before it has even started. It will repeat itself at the beginning of Auster's deconstructed epistolary novel *In the Country of Last Things*: "These are the last things, she wrote. One by one they disappear and never come back" (1).

Moreover, the image of the "message in a bottle" in "Land's End" expresses the improbability of ever getting in touch with an other by taking down words. It is especially unlikely that the message thrown out into the sea will ever reach the addressed person. Consequently, it is not only meant for a specific "you," but also for a general audience ("A word addressed . . . to everyone") and simultaneously for "no one." This theme of the word lifted up from a fixed communication between an "I" and a "you" will develop in Auster's work (Troester 529). In particular, it will again be present in *In the Country of Last Things*. Here, a letter is written by Anna Blume, the protagonist, to an undisclosed recipient who will probably never receive the young woman's lines. At the same time, the novel is addressed to a general readership as is "Land's End," and of course, because of the autonomy of words, to no one as well.

In the prose version of "Land's End," "City of Words," an interesting shift occurs: The stress is not on a single word any more, but on many words that substitute the former depicted silence (Troester 529). The fixation on the single word "thrown out to sea" to reach a specific person is abandoned, since it immediately "drowns in the sea of words":

> Like a message in a bottle.
>
> Like a single word written in blood and thrown out to sea in a bottle.
>
> A word that is the last word. A word, rescued from life at the end of life, and therefore lost. A word addressed to no one. A word, after all the other words are lost – addressed to no one, to every one, to you.
>
> There is no word. Only the many words that stand in the place of silence. For the city is all that cannot be said, and it is each word that drowns in the sea of words.

With the last two quoted lines, Auster leaves behind the "shipwreck of the singular"[12] and turns towards the modern urban scenery of the many. This shift hints at Anna Blume's description of an apocalyptic place in *In the Country of Last Things* where nothing new comes into being any more, but where things and words just vanish. "City of Words" was, as the unpublished holographs and notebooks in the Berg Collection at the New York Public Library indicate, a title Auster had in

[12] This phrase is borrowed from George Oppen and occurs again in *The Invention of Solitude*, especially with regard to the story of Jonah (see 79 and 126).

mind for his later novel (Troester 529). This prose piece, written about fifteen years before the novel, surprisingly ends in a very similar way to the beginning of the novel:

> The words come, therefore, at the moment there are no more words. And they belong to no one. She writes the words from the city and then vanishes back into the city. There is no city except for the evidence of words. And her words have been lost from the very beginning – from the moment she began to write.

In the deconstructed epistolary novel, Anna Blume will write prose and tries to depict her surroundings as exactly as possible – an undertaking that is doomed to failure since her own words are always at risk of disappearing. In other terms, the turn to prose goes hand in hand with the striving to describe the external world. Finally, Auster will leave behind poetry altogether and, with it, his almost exclusive concentration on the internal world of the singular. The first poem of his poetry collection *Disappearances* (1975) indicates this process:

> Out of solitude, he begins again –
>
> as if it were the last time
> that he would breathe,
>
> and therefore it is now
>
> that he breathes for the first time
> beyond the grasp
> of the singular.
> . . . . (107)

This attempt to leave behind the "grasp of the singular" goes along with the insight that a specific origin or center cannot be pinpointed. In particular, the search for the word that might depict a specific situation most exactly will come to nothing. A passage in *White Spaces*, the transitional piece between Auster's poetry and prose, illustrates this:

> I dedicate these words to the things in life I do not understand, to each thing passing away before my eyes. I dedicate these words to the impossibility of finding a word equal to the silence inside me. (160)

The renunciation of perfection, i.e., the aim at finding purity and precision in language, runs parallel to the impossibility of circling around the reason of one's longing, one's inner wounds. This understanding is already formulated in poem No. 21 of the early collection *Unearth*. Here, Auster is close to Derrida's conviction that the more one tries to get to the bottom of one's wounds, the more unlikely it becomes to reach them. It is a paradoxical, very disturbing undertaking Auster writes about:

> Rats wake in your sleep
> and mime the progress
> of want. My voice turns back
> to the hunger it gives birth to,
> coupling with stones
> that jut from red walls: the heart
> gnaws, but cannot know
> its plunder; . . . .   (57)

According to Jacques Derrida, the way to the original wound will always be blocked; it remains hidden or seems to be too confusing to be followed. In parallel, the theme of the writer's quest for his inner self, that will always be inaccessible, runs through Auster's poetry and later through his prose fiction as well. For example, in his poem "Quarry" of his collection *Fragments from Cold* (1976-77), the lyrical I comes to the conclusion that "[t]he world / that walks inside [it] / is a world beyond reach" (138). In the later autobiographical writing "Portrait of an Invisible Man," the I-narrator will also understand that his act of writing about a father who has always been absent will not heal him, but will only keep his inner wounds open (32). In parallel, the longer the protagonist of *City of Glass*, Daniel Quinn, looks for paternal authority, for orientation, and truth, the more confused he becomes until he finally loses himself completely in the street network of the postmodern metropolis.

With the turn to prose and the insight that a center or origin will always elude itself, words begin to disappear into the unknown as soon as they emerge. They disseminate into all sorts of directions and supplement each other in the Derridean sense of the term. The female writer in "City of Words" for instance takes down some lines that seem to be lost from the very beginning. Nevertheless, she continues her (paradoxical) undertaking. In short, on the threshold between poetry and prose, Auster creates a deconstructive text that opens the writing process up and at the same time deprives it of every security. In *White Spaces*,

Auster becomes concrete in deconstructing the beginning and the end of writing. Neither the one nor the other can be pinpointed to a specific moment in time:

> In the realm of the naked eye nothing happens that does not have its beginning and its end. And yet nowhere can we find the place or the moment at which we can say, beyond a shadow of a doubt, that this is where it begins, or this is where it ends. For some of us, it has begun before the beginning, and for others of us it will go on happening after the end. Where to find it? Don't look. Either it is here or it is not here. (157)

However, although the writer knows that he will never find the purity or precision he has been yearning for, he keeps on searching. Although he will not come close to the aim he has tried to reach, he will start all over again – such as in poem No. 7 of *Disappearances*. Here, time is slipping by while the third-person-figure feels the urgency to continue its way, since the end of all efforts can also be their beginning:

> and he who would begin to breathe
> will learn there is nowhere to go
> but here.
>
> Therefore, he begins again,
>
> as if it were the last time
> he would breathe.
> For there is no more time. And it is the end of time
>
> that begins. (113-114)

In *Archive Fever*, Derrida refuses the meaning of death as a definite ending. Instead, he elaborates on the uncertainty of death and human anxiety connected with it and on the chance to get in touch with "the absolutely other" in Lévinas' sense of the term (c.f. ch. 2.7). As in poem No. 7 of Auster's *Disappearances*, any seemingly fixed ending contains the possibility of beginning anew or of facing the unknown.

To sum up, Auster's poetry contains the traces of a later deconstructive prose writing that develops with "City of Words" or *White Spaces* to his subsequent novels, *City of Glass* or *In the Country of Last Things*. In his philosophical texts, Jacques Derrida metaphorically transfers the Jewish ritual of circumcision onto his situation in Algeria and his alienation from Jewish religion and culture, in particular through "the organized marginalization" of Hebrew (*Monolingualism of the Other* 38). This personal inner wound, which Derrida connects with experiences of alienation, persecution, and death in Jewish religion and history, seems to be the starting point for the development of his theory of différance and his critique of logocentrism. In parallel, the image of the wound referring to the Jewish experience of dispersion, separation, and waiting is at the heart of Paul Auster's early poems and is directly connected with the experience of the poet himself who endlessly looks for the perfect, most precise words. However, the way to perfection in writing can never be reached, just as any original wound will always remain inaccessible (Derrida, "A Testimony Given" 55).

The development of a deconstructive prose writing, from Auster's transitional pieces onwards, goes hand in hand with the insight that the act of circling around a wound as well as the search for the purity of language are doomed to failure from the very beginning. Instead of being concentrated on finding the most suitable word possibly existing, the I-narrator of *White Spaces* eventually tries to let go: "I . . . began, slowly and painfully, to empty my mind. Now emptiness is all that remains: a space, no matter how small, in which whatever is happening can be allowed to happen" (160).[13] In this (white) space, an active reading-process might set in. It is the place for a multiple of associations from the exterior (Troester 537). However, this does not mean that the I-narrator will ever be satisfied, that he will ever feel at home. In the last poem "Facing the Music" of Auster's collection with the same title, written after *Disappearances*, the lyrical I also continues its journey while looking for suitable, new ways of expression. In this context, the poem can also be interpreted as Auster's "valediction to poetry" (Finkelstein, "Introduction" 14):

> . . . The tongue
> is forever taking us away
> from where we are, and nowhere
> can we be at rest
> in the things we are given
> to see, for each word

[13] Paul Auster wrote *White Spaces* after a rehearsal of a dance piece he visited in December of 1978. In an interview, he describes the writing process as "a liberation," "a tremendous letting go" that initiated a "whole new period" ("Interview with McCaffery and Gregory" 302).

is an elsewhere, a thing that moves
more quickly than the eye, even
as this sparrow moves, veering
into the air
in which it has no home. . . . (151)

3.1.2. The everlasting walk in the desert: "There is no promised land."

In his article "Edmond Jabès and the Question of the Book," Jacques Derrida equals the lyrical undertaking of the French-Jewish poet with an arduous walk through the desert (68), while the destination can only be dimly perceived on the horizon (66). Similarly, the image of the wanderer who continuously walks on his stony path to a particular destination which disappears from sight lies at the core of Auster's poetry. For example, in poem No. 25 of the early collection *Unearth*, an impersonal "you" is again addressed and described as walking endlessly in a desert-like landscape to an unspecified destination. This journey is, especially in the first three lines, connected with an impossible act of speaking or the difficulty in letting words go:

Nomad –
till nowhere, blooming
in the prison of your mouth, becomes
wherever you are:
....
As if to say,
wherever you are
the desert is with you. As if,
wherever you move, the desert
is new,
is moving with you. (61)

In the gloomy, extremely dense poem No. 17, Auster becomes more detailed in listing a number of biblical images. They seem to come to the mind of the lyrical I on its search for words (53). In particular, the image of the desert is splintered into different associations: a "tent-speech" (l. 1), "our forty-dark . . . next year" (l. 2), "dunes that whirled free" (l. 7-8), and "the grate of sand" (l. 10). The use of the number forty in the second line alludes to the forty years the Israelites spent walking through the desert to the promised land (Num. 20.1 – 21.9), and it hints at the forty days and nights Moses spent in the desert of Mount Sinai for taking down the words of the Covenant, the words of the Tables (Exod. 34.28-29).

Moreover, the image of the desert is connected with the image of "scree-words," a torrent of words disseminating in the writer's memory. However, the poetic experience of walking in a desert by taking down words is not only a past experience. The lyrical I sees a long ordeal in front of it, a path marked by suffering and violence that the impersonal "you" will not be able to cope with, either. This negative outlook on the future is mirrored by the unequal length of the lines and their abrupt breaking-off:

> Mirrored by the tent-speech
> of our forty-dark, alodial-hued
> next year –
> the images,
> ground in the afterlight
> of eyed, the wandered
> images absolve you: (dunes
> that whirled free, – scree-words
> shuttled
> by the grate of sand, – the other
> glass-round hours, redoubling
> in remembrance). And in
> my hand – (as, after the night, – the night) –
> I hold what you have taken
> to give: this path
> of tallied cries, and grain
> after grain, the never-done-with
> desert, burning on your lips
> that jell in violence. (53)

In his poem "White," dedicated to the German-Jewish poet Paul Celan (Finkelstein, "Introduction" 15), Auster also makes use of the symbolic number forty at the end. Here, it alludes, beside its other meanings, to the forty days Noah spent in the ark after the Earth had been flooded (Gen. 8.1-6) and to the Jewish-Christian symbol of the dove *(Wall Writing* 102). In Genesis, Noah sends out a dove three times. The third time it returns with an olive branch, in its beak the symbol for peace in the Jewish-Christian cultural context (Gen. 8.8-12). The last four lines of Auster's poem "White" (". . . that forty days / and forty nights / have brought no dove / back to us") can consequently mean that either a long time of waiting (symbolically, for the dove) or the words of the Tables have not brought along peace between men. Both interpretations would include the assumption of a certain distance from Judaism, out of which the writing process might emerge, similar to Derrida's interpretation of Jabès' writing: "[p]oetic autonomy . . . presupposes broken Tables" (Derrida, "Edmond Jabès" 67).

With its beginning, Auster's poem "White" furthermore hints at the unpublished piece "Land's End." Again, the written lines are "thrown out to sea in a bottle" (87). It is a symbolic action with which the writer tries to do the impossible, to get in touch with the sphere of death. Indeed, the poem is addressed to Paul Celan who committed suicide on 20 April 1970 by jumping off a bridge into the Seine in Paris ("For one who drowned . . ." (87)).

In parallel, Auster's poem No. 7 of his collection *Disappearances* sets in at the moment of death which is simultaneously the moment of birth – a theme which Auster expands on at the end of *The Invention of Solitude*. It reminds us of Derrida's elaboration on the double nature of death in "Circumfession" or *Archive Fever* (cf. ch. 2.7.). The philosopher regards the moment of death as the prerequisite for the attempt to reveal what has been covered or hidden, to bring to light the traces of what has seemingly been buried (*Archive Fever* 16-17). In so far, the moment of death does not appear as a final ending, but as a turning point or crossing to a different form of being.

In Auster's poem No. 7, the depicted isolated third person-figure is thrown into nothingness ("He is alone. And from the moment he begins to breathe, / he is nowhere. Plural death, born / in the jaws of the singular, . . ." (113)) where it understands that there is no other place to go to, that it is unable to reach any destination (". . . and he who would begin to breathe / will learn there is nowhere to go / but here" (113)). In the colossal city, the modern equivalent of the biblical image of the desert, the search for the individual word will come to nothing ("For the city is monstrous, / and its mouth suffers no issue / that does not devour the word / of oneself" (113)). However, by reaching rock bottom the third person-figure already makes a new step. It starts its journey through life all over again and keeps on moving, the end of its path always in sight ("Therefore, he begins again, / as if it were the last time / he would breathe" (113)).

In "Quarry" from *Fragments from Cold*, Auster puts the experience of being surrounded by a desert-like landscape on an existential level, too. An unspecified "we" has been walking in circles to a particular origin and has hence lost its way (138). The natural image of the light, which no longer gives any orientation, illustrates this. By continuing to walk on the stony, crumbling path in a lonely area, the unspecified "we" is forced to hear nothing but its own voice. It is set back to experience solitude – as much as the I-narrator in "The Book of Memory" of *The Invention of Solitude* or Quinn in *City of Glass* is forced to. At the end of "Quarry," Auster introduces a lyrical I which fails in its attempt to reach any of its past moments and, by doing so, the essence of its inner self. Any possible center or origin will elude forever:

> We have been here, and we have never been here.
> We have been on the way to where we began,
> and we have been lost.
> There are no boundaries
> in the light. And the earth
> leaves no word for us
> to sing. For the crumbling of the earth
> underfoot
> is a music in itself, and to walk among these stones
> is to hear nothing
> but ourselves.
> I sing, therefore, of nothing,
> as if it were the place
> I do not return to –
>
> and if I should return, then count out my life
> in these stones: forget
> I was ever here. The world
> that walks inside me
>
> is a world beyond reach. (138)

The theme of losing one's orientation by trying to understand particular past moments again appears in *White Spaces*, now in prose format. It is the confusion of time by which the wanderer is confronted. The past and the present are differed and deferred against themselves; the meanings of beginning and end are turned upside down:

> Something begins, and already it is no longer the beginning, but something else, propelling us into the heart of the thing that is happening. If we were suddenly to stop and ask ourselves, "Where are we going?", or "Where are we now?", we would be lost, for at each moment we are no longer where we were, but have left ourselves behind, irrevocably, in a past that has no memory, a past endlessly obliterated by a motion that carries us into the present. (155)

The image of the journey through a desert-like landscape is now further developed and depicted in detail. It is a writer's journey Auster concentrates on. The I-narrator is walking through his room and investigating the little space around him. He is patiently looking for possible words that might express what he feels or sees at a specific moment. Consequently, the room becomes an image of the mind and the dissemination of the writer's thoughts. It is an "archive" in the Derridean sense of the term, a conscious process or prerequisite for gathering material, for compiling everything that might otherwise disappear (Derrida, *Archive Fever* 11). The writer's thoughts, which are always in danger of getting lost, awake the yearning for this sort of "archive." However, the room is not only depicted as the home for present thoughts and past memories, but it is also directed towards the future – similar to Derrida's elaborations on the nature of the "archive" in *Archive Fever* (16-17). It is a journey "into space," i.e., into the infinite, that the writer has set out on and that he will continue, although he might just circle around his starting point.

Besides, Auster again makes use of the modern image of the city to illustrate the writer's multiple paths ramifying into the unknown. He equates it with the biblical image of the desert. He also uses the image of the ocean as in his poem "White" (87) or the unpublished piece "Land's End." In all three texts, thoughts might metaphorically sink down to the seafloor where they will remain out of reach:

> I remain in the room in which I am writing this. I put one foot in front of the other. I put one word in front of the other, and for each step I take I add another word, as if for each word to be spoken there were another space to be crossed, a distance to be filled by my body as it moves through this space. It is a journey through space, even if I get nowhere, even if I end up in the same place I started. It is a journey through space, as if into many cities and out of them, as if across deserts, as if to the edge of some imaginary ocean, where each thought drowns in the relentless waves of the real. (*White Spaces* 158-59)

Within the room, it becomes extremely difficult to find the right words since the meanings of words supplement each other and disappear to some space in one's mind: ". . . I find these words falling from my mouth and vanishing into the silence they came from" (180). In short, the writer will never end his journey, he might never arrive at any home-like place: "And whoever tries to find refuge in any one place, in any one moment, will never be where he thinks he is" (178). In his poem "Late Summer," Auster expresses this conviction in even more definite terms. Here, the Jewish hope of reaching the expected destination is abandoned like in *The Invention of Solitude*: "There is no promised land" (98).

The impossibility of finding shelter or the difficulty in reaching home is also the theme of the poem "Between the Lines" from the collection *Facing the Music*, written shortly after *White Spaces*. This poem is an interpretation of, or, in Jewish terms, "a midrash on the biblical figure of Jacob" (Finkelstein, "Introduction" 15).[14] In Genesis, Jacob, Isaac's son and Esau's brother, flees from Canaan to Haran, since his brother has decided to kill him for having obtained the right of primogeniture and the father's blessing by devious means (27.1 – 28.22). After a long time away from home, Jacob returns to Canaan and finally reconciles himself with Esau (31.1 – 33.20). On his journey, he fights with an angel during the night until the early morning (32.23-32).

In the first stanza of "Between the Lines," Auster puts the emphasis on Jacob's absence, his life in foreign parts of the country, or the troublesomeness of his return, the long, tiring journey back home that seems to be predestined: "Stone-pillowed, the ways / of remoteness. And written in your palm, / the road" (147). He then declares that "home" does not mean one's birthplace, abiding-place, or native land, but "the distance between blessed and unblessed," i.e., the hatred between the twins Jacob and Esau that they needed to overcome. Auster is close to Lévinas when he stresses the necessity to put oneself in the position of

[14] Midrash ("from the Hebrew word meaning 'study'") "as a body of literature essentially is the interpretation of sacred texts, usually the Bible but also Mishnah" (a comprehensive book of *halakhah*, the body of the Jewish Oral Law). In the Tannaitic period (130-160 AC), two sorts of midrashim (the plural form) came up: "*halakhic midrash* developing out of academies and the *aggadic midrash* rising from the pulpit, from the sermons of rabbis." Today, there are three types of midrashim: "exegetical, that is, explanatory (this group includes the *halakhic midrash* as well as the *aggadic*); homiletical, containing parables and moral lessons . . .; and narrative, expanding on the storytelling of the Torah" (Robinson 355-357). Auster's poem "Between the Lines" can thus be called a narrative midrash.

the other who is absolutely different and remote from oneself.[15] It's an ethical message that Auster gives here with the help of the biblical figures: the one who makes himself available to the other as Jacob once did will understand the need of the other, his grief, and pain: ". . . And whoever puts himself / into the skin of his brother, will know / what sorrow is / to the seventh year / beyond the seventh year / of the seventh year. . . ." (147). The use of the symbolic number seven refers to the Pharaoh's dream of seven well-fed and seven emaciated cows as well as seven firm and seven withered ears of corn. Joseph, Jacob's and Rahel's eldest son, interprets this dream in the way that seven years of abundance will be followed by seven years of hunger (Gen. 41.1-36).

Moreover, Auster's poem "Song of Degrees" from *Wall Writing* also hints at the biblical figure of Jacob and circles around the theme of walking through the desert. In this fallow land the wanderer's steps wipe out themselves: "A footstep / gives ground: what is more / is not more: nothing / has ever been / enough. . . ." (94). The arduous act of walking does not bring the wanderer any further, which simultaneously means that the writer's yearning to take down most precise words or even to discover a new sort of language will not be stilled: ". . . So much / the better – so many / words, / raked and murmured along / by your bedouin knees, will not / conjure you home . . ." (94). However, the wanderer does not stop walking through the desert, and he will not stop yearning to arrive at a particular destination. In parallel, the writer does not give up his hope of finding suitable words, as Derrida equally emphasizes in his essay on Edmond Jabès ("Edmond Jabès" 69-70). Being confronted with infinity means the infinity of the writing itself. The past steps of the poetic undertaking often dissolve themselves, and the future of writing cannot be made out. Hence the writer sees, as in Derrida's interpretation of Jabès' *Book of Questions*, nothing but a "white page" in front of him which is marked by the moment of death: "'*At noon, he found himself once more facing infinity, the white page. Every trace of footsteps had disappeared. Buried*'" (70). In the last passage of *White Spaces*, Auster also points out the never-ending walk to an unspecified destination, which is marked by the moment of death, symbolized by the falling snow. However, the colour white, here transported by the image of the snow, connects the hopelessness of this walk with the innovative imaginative potential of the writer's undertaking: "Never to be anywhere

[15] Jacob and Esau are different in various ways: Esau's body is, from birth on, covered all over with hair. Besides, Esau becomes a hunter, whereas Jacob remains at home, looking after the tents (Gen. 25.27).

but here. And the immense journey through space that continues. Everywhere, as if each place were here. And the snow falling endlessly in the winter night" (162).

3.1.3. The invisible God and his unpronounceable name

In his interpretation of Edmond Jabès' *Book of Questions*, Jacques Derrida points out the Jewish image of the silent, hiding God who does not show His face ("Edmond Jabès" 67 ff.). In particular, he quotes the Old Testament scene when Moses breaks the Tables and God does not appear (Ex. 32.19-20). In fact, in one of Paul Auster's interviews with Edmond Jabès, the latter elaborates on this image of the ungraspable, unattainable God. In the following passage of the interview, Jabès emphasizes the moment of separation and division between man and God, the conviction that a chasm or a desert opens which cannot be walked through. Jabès then points out God's remoteness by alluding to his inexpressible name:

> What I mean by God in my work is something we come up against, a void, something against which we are powerless. It is a distance . . . the distance that is always between things . . . We get to know where we are going, and then there is still this distance to cover. And a moment comes when you can no longer cover the distance; you get there and you say to yourself, it's finished, there are no more words. God is perhaps a word without words. A word without meaning. And the extraordinary thing is that in the Jewish tradition God is invisible, and as a way of underscoring this invisibility, he has an unpronounceable name. (Auster, "Providence" 160)

In his poem "Song of Degrees," Auster also points out the distance, the moment of separation between man and God in contrast to the "Song of Degrees" of the Old Testament, the pilgrim songs in the fifth book of the Psalms (Ps. 120-134). These pilgrim songs praise God for having freed Israel, whereas Auster stresses the troublesomeness of the way through the desert. The images of "vacant lots" (l. 1), "rubble" (l. 3), and "sand heaps" (l. 4) hint at this arduous journey, on which man cannot reach God, although he is praying: "In the vacant lots / of solstice. In the light / you wagered for the rubble / of awe, sand heaps: / retched into prayer – the distance / bought / in your name" (94). The parallel syntactical construction of the following sentences and the use of the anaphor "You," with which God seems to be addressed, underline man's powerlessness. The lyrical I continuously walks through the desert and looks for a home-like place. Yet its yearning will not be stilled on Earth: "You. And then / you again. A footstep / gives ground: what is more / is not more: nothing / has ever been / enough. . . . You, / and then we. The earth / does not ask / for anyone" (108).

Moreover, the image of the invisibility of God, which Derrida elaborates on in his interpretation of Jabès' *Book of Questions* ("Edmond Jabès" 67ff.), is also the theme of Auster's poem "Covenant." God is here present and absent at the same moment. He can be sensed, but remains invisible: "Throng of eyes, / myriad, at sunken retina depth: the image / of the great, imageless one, / moored within" (96). The title and, in particular, the second and third stanza hint at the promised land given to Abraham's and Isaac's descendants by Yahweh (Exod. 33.1ff.), and the Israelites' walk through the desert. As the lyrical I sees it, they tried to reach an invisible destination, an indefinable land somewhere on the horizon. In other words, they went into nothingness by following God's voice. This, however, remained silent:

> Mantis-lunged, we,
> the hirelings, alive in juniper and rubble,
> broke the flat bread
> that went with us, we
> were steps, wandered
> into blindness, we knew by then
> how to breathe ourselves along
> to nothing.
>
> Something lost
> became
> something to be found.
> a name,
> followed through the dust
> of all that veering, did not ever
> divulge its sound. . . . (83)

The walk from and into nothingness is also part of the poem "Wall Writing" in Auster's collection with the very same title, as well as the Derridean image of the absent God who does not show His face: "Come from nowhere / in the night / of the one who does not come" (81). However, the invisible God is made visible through the writing process.

He is connected with the "white spaces" of words, i.e., their invisible connotations. The writer brings them to the surface by scribbling them onto a wall which can be one of the four walls of the writer's room; or it may allude to the Wailing Wall in Jerusalem. This interpretation of the poem allows one to regard it as a kind of prayer ("Or the whiteness of a word, / scratched / into the wall" (81)).

In his transitional piece *White Spaces*, Auster speaks of the "silence" of words, i.e., the origin where their connotations vanish to during a writing process or a talk. This image also appears in Auster's poem "Ecliptic. Les Halles," published in *Wall Writing*. Here, the lyrical I yearns to fathom silence. It is a hunger which needs to be stilled. Besides, the addressed impersonal "you" can be interpreted as the absent God watching the lyrical I. However, He will never appear, but instead speaks indirectly, with the voice of the prophet Ezekiel, who, according to the Old Testament, transmits the vision of a new Israel after it has been destroyed (Ezek. 37.1 ff.). The lyrical I identifies with the Israelites of the past. Consequently, this powerful message of the recovery of the people of Israel means a moment of hope. The prophet's words are an indirect yet visible token of the possibility of God's existence that Auster circles around in the last stanza of the poem. Here, his poetic language is again rich in imagery:

> You were my absence.
> Wherever I breathed, you found me
> lying in the word
> that spoke its way back
> to this place.
>
> Silence
> was
> in the prowled shambles
> and marrow
> of a cunning, harlot haste – a hunger
> that became a bed for me,
> as though the random
> Ezekiel-wrath
> I discovered, the "Live," and the
> "yes, he said to us,
> when we were in our blood,

Live," had merely been your way
of coming near –

As though somewhere,
visible, an arctic stone, as pale
as semen, had been
dripping, fire-phrase by fire-phrase,
from your lips. (74)

In *White Spaces*, Auster becomes concrete in explaining the invisibility of God by referring to God's multiple names in Hebrew. Their sense, according to him, lies in "acknowledging that-which-cannot be spoken, that-which-cannot-be-seen, and that-which-cannot-be-understood" (157). The dissemination of words is necessary to point out God's omnipotence and man's inability of ever grasping it. In short, God is not neglected, but confirmed in spite of, or better, because of His invisibility. In *Religion*, Derrida also speaks against Nietzsche's undertaking of putting God to death and instead affirms the possible impossibility of God's existence (27). In a very poetic style, but in prose format, Auster makes this clear by elaborating on man's emotional knowledge and the unnecessary attempt to find words for what he is already sure of:

> We know, even if we cannot put it into words. And the feeling that remains within us, the discretion of a knowledge so fully in tune with the world, has no need of whatever it is that might fall from our mouths. Our hearts know what is in them, even if our mouths remain silent. (158)

3.1.4. The "Babel-roar" within the writer's mind

The theme of a seemingly never-ending journey to a certain origin or place of hope in Paul Auster's poetry is not only linked to the hiding, ungraspable God, but also to the subject of writing itself. In particular, Auster focuses on the biblical image of Babel similarly to Jacques Derrida and connects it with his renunciation of a possibly existing pure language. In many of Auster's early poems, the lyrical I is depicted as a wanderer, constantly following its dusty path in search of the most suitable words. What it will be confronted with, however, is the dissemination and supplementation of different images which cannot be grasped or put into any specific order.

In Auster's poem No. 9 from *Unearth*, the addressed "you" is confronted by a "thunder," a "Babel-roar" drowning out every other sound on the traveler's journey: "It will not be what you wandered to that is heard" (45). While Derrida uses the image of the Babelonian confusion of language as an ethical-political argument against the dangers of colonialism through the possible imposition of a single, universal language (cf. ch. 2.6.), Auster, in his poetry, focuses on the aesthetic necessity of depicting writing as a process characterized by utter confusion. Complementing a text in Walter Benjamin's understanding, i.e., creating a most precise one, will never be possible.

In the first stanza of his poem "Scribe" (*Wall Writing* 69), Auster in fact depicts a third-person figure which suddenly "[finds its] room again in Babel" (74). Here, it is confronted with confusing images disseminating in its mind and simultaneously connecting each other. Their agglomeration, nullification, and renewed emergence create an absurd, almost surrealist effect:

> It was written.
> A flower
> falls from his eye
> and blooms in a stranger's mouth.
> A swallow
> rhymes with hunger
> and cannot leave its egg. (69)

According to Derrida, the translator, i.e., the interpreter of any kind of text, works with a fragmentary language differing and deferring itself and will thus never come in contact with any "true" meaning of words. In parallel, Auster depicts the act of writing as a stony path on which the author continuously needs to come to terms with his own inability. In "White Nights," another poem of *Wall Writing*, the lyrical I even seems to have lost control over his writing process. He seems to be separated from it: ". . . The pen / moves across the earth: it no longer knows / what will happen, and the hand that holds it / has disappeared" (65).

In Auster's poem "In Memory of Myself," the lyrical I is equally unable to speak. Being surrounded by silence, it only hears the pulsating, pounding sound of words within its mind which are, however, inaccessible. Unable to get to the bottom of its inner self, it turns toward the surrounding world:

I cannot speak.

So much silence
to be brought to life
in this pensive flesh, the beating
drum of words
within, so many words

lost in the wide world
within me, and thereby to have known
that in spite of myself

I am here.

As if this were the world. (148)

In *The Invention of Solitude*, Auster will repeat the theme of the writer's inability to reach his inner self and his attempt to raise the hidden words from under the surface. Here, the fragmentary memories and words replace themselves constantly so that any conclusion is deferred to a later time. In parallel, Anna Blume in *In the Country of Last Things* will become utterly confused since she cannot take hold of the words disseminating in her mind. Nevertheless, she tries to keep in touch with her surroundings by taking down what she sees, as she knows that she would otherwise lose herself completely.

The writer's existential dependence on the external world on grounds of the confusion within himself is also the theme of Auster's poem "Credo" from his collection *Facing the Music* (141). Here, Auster focuses on the necessary mergence with the uncountable, little real objects surrounding ourselves, on the wish to become one with the external world: "The infinite / tiny things. Or once merely to breath / in the light of the infinite / tiny things / that surround us. . . . / To say: / our very lives depend on it" (141).

In short, with his last poems written at the end of the 1970s, Auster leaves behind the exclusive fixation on the inner self dominating his early poems. The theme of the writing process coming into being within a wound will however lie beneath the surface of his prose texts, too. Besides, Auster will intensively go on dealing with the writer's yearning to express what he sees and feels, with his "walk through the desert" to find the right word in spite of the "Babel-roar" within the writer's mind.

3.2. *The Invention of Solitude* – the desire to reach the promised land in a deconstructed autobiographical piece of writing

> I can never be sure of where I am. A feeling of moving around in circles, of perpetual back-tracking, of going off in many directions at once. And even if I do manage to make some progress, I am not at all convinced that it will take me to where I think I am going. (32)

These lines taken from "Portrait of an Invisible Man," the first part of *The Invention of Solitude* (1982), comprise Paul Auster's situation while he was writing his autobiographical mosaic shortly after his father had died ("Interview with Joseph Mallia" 276). He set out on a mental journey through which he hoped to find the other, the father within himself, by condensing his memories. This inmost "hunger" or ardent desire to come to terms with his father's identity, his Jewish roots, and thus with himself needed to be maintained with the help of the writing process, because he knew that if he stopped writing, the father would disappear forever ("Portrait" 6).

However, the I-narrator's great expectations, which constantly shine between the "margins" of the text, as Jacques Derrida would depict it, are not fulfilled. He becomes more and more entangled within the network of his own memories, within the movement of 'différance.' At the same time, he does not get to the bottom of his inner wound, i.e., the fact that his father has always been absent. The attempt of circling around the past shows itself as an impossible undertaking. It does not give him any answer except the one that through his father's absence he has been separated from his Jewish roots.

In short, the paradox undertaking to get as close as possible to the wound of separation from traditional Judaism, which is mirrored by Derrida's theory of différance, also shines through Auster's autobiographical novel, even though its reasons are different from the philosopher's texts. The more the I-narrator of *The Invention of Solitude* tries to remember his Jewish family, the more his inner yearning or hunger grows. Very similar to Derrida's essay on Edmond Jabès, the writing process is hence described as a walk through the desert, and the belief in reaching the desired place of homecoming at some point in time is itself questioned ("Portrait" 32).

The following analysis of both "The Portrait of an Invisible Man" as well as "The Book of Memory," the second part of *The Invention of Solitude*, tries to illustrate that Auster bases his prose writing on Derrida's theory of deconstruction and that he uses it as a kind of literary aid. His aim is to depict an innermost yearning to reach a once promised place of homecoming and the impossibility of arrival in the present. So he transfers the Old Testament motive and consequence of Jewish history onto his personal situation, i.e., his desire of coming closer to an always inaccessible father and indirectly to himself. Besides, it is entangled within the network of impressions and memories supplementing and erasing each other constantly, within the movement of différance, which blocks any answer or origin. This interpretation, in other words, focuses on the fragmentary depiction of a Jewish identity that seems to be locked within the *deconstructive surface* of an autobiographical mosaic.

3.2.1. The moment of death as a wound triggering off the dissemination of memories

In an interview with Joseph Mallia, Auster explained that the experience of his father's death left him with a deep, inner wound which triggered off the writing process of *The Invention of Solitude* (and indirectly the following novels, too, since they grew out of this autobiographical mosaic (Kierkegaard 174)):

> He [the father] simply dropped dead one day, unexpectedly, after being in perfect health, and the shock of it left me with so many unanswered questions about him that I felt I had no choice but to sit down and try to put something on paper ("Interview with Joseph Mallia" 276).

The beginning of "Portrait of an Invisible Man" similarly shows how deeply the I-narrator is shaken by the suddenness of his father's death, how disoriented he seems to be. He now feels "the invisible boundary between life and death . . . and no longer know[s] which side [he is] on" (5). In short, the experience of death is characterized by a double bind. On the one hand, it clearly marks an end, but on the other hand, it is depicted as a crossing, and the I-narrator is conscious of the in-between of life and death. The words of the I-narrator are similar to those of Derrida in *As if I were Dead* or in "Of Grammatology," where the latter places "the relationship to death as the concrete structure of the living presence" (43). In parallel, the I-narrator is now convinced that "life becomes death, and it is as if this death has owned this life all along" (5).

Like Derrida, Auster does not make use of a theological concept of death. However, he also underlines that death hints at the creation of something new, here the writing process, and that it thus cannot be reduced to the finite. The foreseeable death of the philosopher's mother triggered off his 59 autobiographical comments or periphrases which he later called "Circumfession," whereas Auster felt the inner urgency to put his feelings and memories into words after his father had died: "I knew that I would have to write about my father" (6). In experiencing death, the "trace of erasure" or deep, inner wound ("Portrait" 32), they both choose the conventional genre of autobiography. Yet "Circumfession" as well as *The Invention of Solitude* are characterized by fragmentation, by breaks, gaps, and fissures.

This of course does not mean that "The Portrait of an Invisible Man" is an altogether pessimistic piece of writing. In spite of the experience of death, the words on paper have a positive function for Auster. They stand between life and death, "between [the narrator] and a silence that continues to terrify [him]" ("Portrait" 65). The writing process defers the absolute darkness of death for a moment. It provides a chance to think about the father, about the other within himself and to understand that death lies within life and life within death. Death "shake[s] the self from its apathy, from the pseudo-intimacy it maintains with itself" (Bruckner 28) and thus touches off a lively process of thinking, a "dissemination" of memories and images. In short, Emmanuel Lévinas' concept of the other and Derrida's elaboration on death as the moment in time when "we can no longer be concerned with anything but the Other in ourselves" (qtd. in Kamuf 203) shines through Auster's first part of *The Invention of Solitude* (c.f. ch. 2.7.).

Besides, the more the I-narrator of "Portrait of an Invisible Man" writes, the more he becomes entangled within the network of supplemented signifiers. He soon begins to feel lost, and, as a consequence, even questions his role as son. At the funeral, he recognizes that "his cousin [is] more shaken by [his] father's death than any of [his] other relatives" (62). The emotional bonding that must have existed between the two is obvious to him, and he admits that "he [the cousin] was the real son, he was the son [he] could never bring [himself] to be" (63). The I-narrator feels insecure and is, because of the dissemination of his ideas, unable to express what he wants to say:

> Again and again I have watched my thoughts trail off from the thing in front of me. No sooner have I thought one thing than it evokes another thing, and then another thing, until there is an accumulation of detail so dense that I feel I am going to suffocate. Never before have I been so aware of the rift between thinking and writing. For the past few days, in fact, I have begun to feel that the story I am trying to tell is somehow incompatible with language. . . . ("Portrait" 32)

By comparing "Circumfession" with "Portrait of an Invisible Man," we can see that the event of death had a similar effect on Derrida and his writing process that is also characterized by the supplementation and dissemination of signifiers. Derrida's thoughts, as already mentioned, accelerate in the face of death. From the beginning, he "[knows] how to 'zap'" (176), i.e., he quickly moves from one memory to the next one and lets his words run into each other without a pause. In Auster's autobiographical mosaic, the past impressions also supplement each other and disseminate into all sorts of directions; after one idea has appeared on the surface, others follow step by step until everything is flowing. Besides, the memories also erase each other similar to "Circumfession." To use Derrida's terminology, each trace lets a thought appear, whereas a second one reduces it to a fragment or dissolves it one second later:

> The rampant, totally mystifying force of contradiction. I understand now that each fact is nullified by the next fact, that each thought engenders an equal and opposite thought. Impossible to say anything without reservation: he was good, or he was bad; he was this, or he was that. All of them are true. At times I have the feeling that I am writing about three or four different men, each one distinct, each one a contradiction of all the others. Fragments. (61)

The dissemination of all sorts of memories and the erasure by each other are reflected by the form of *The Invention of Solitude*. Every one of the little paragraphs is a piece of writing in itself, i.e., concerning its content, a specific memory, image, or conclusion, it is mostly independent from the one preceding or following it. It often does not directly repeat or develop the thoughts mentioned beforehand, but presents a new idea, or it begins at a totally different point in time. The fissures, rifts, and ruptures running through the text mirror the narrator's inner wounds which the experience of death has opened. Moreover, because of the writing process coming into being and expanding at the moment of death, these already forgotten memories, especially those of an always absent father, suddenly resurface and appear livelier than ever:

> There has been a wound, and I realize now that it is very deep. Instead of healing me as I thought it would, the act of writing has kept this wound open. . . . Instead of burying my father for me, these words have kept him alive, perhaps more so than ever. (32)

On the basis of the included fissures and rifts within the text, Auster's autobiographical mosaic has undergone a formal as well as stylistic development from, for example, James Joyce's *A Portrait of an Artist as a Young Man* (1916), a modern, largely autobiographical novel which is marked by the stream of consciousness. In both works, we are locked within the figures' heads (i.e., the I-narrator and A., the third person narrator of "The Book of Memory," on the one hand and Stephen Dedalus on the other hand) whose experiences and way of thinking are closely linked to the authors' lives themselves. Auster makes use of Joyce's technique of presenting thoughts and sense impressions without any logical sequence, of letting memories and immediate experiences flow into each other. Yet he puts the stress on the fragmentary nature of thoughts which displace each other constantly. As a consequence, any specific meaning or conclusion is deferred to a later time. Any development of the kind that Stephen Dedalus experiences at the end will never be reached, but can only be perceived dimly in the far distance.

In "The Book of Memory," the second part of *The Invention of Solitude*, the dissemination of fragmentary thoughts is also clearly visible. Here, Auster "examines himself by exploring the inner life of a person called 'A.'," reminiscent of Kafka's protagonist K. in his novel *The Trial* [*Der Prozess*] (1925). In "Portrait of an Invisible Man," however, "Auster seeks to reach himself through writing about his father in the first person" (Shibata 186). "He tries, in other words, to probe himself first through the other, then as the other" (Shibata 186). Thus he comes very close to Derrida's idea that sometimes "we *can* no longer be concerned with anyone except the other *in ourselves*" (qtd. in Kamuf 203). In fact, Auster equates himself with Collodi "dipping his pen into the darkness of his inkwell . . . [and] using him [Pinocchio] as the instrument (literally, the pen) to write the story of himself" ("The Book of Memory" 163). In an interview with Larry McCaffery and Sinda

Gregory, Auster explained what he had in mind with his decision for a third person narrator:

> What it came down to was creating a distance between myself and myself. If you are too close to the thing you're trying to write about, the perspective vanishes, and you begin to smother. I had to objectify myself in order to explore my own subjectivity. . . . The moment I think about the fact I'm saying 'I,' I'm actually saying 'he.' It's the mirror of self-consciousness, a way of watching yourself think. (319)

Through A., the narrator, Auster presents a deconstructed, i.e., a distanced, alienated, and also objectified picture of himself. He opens himself up to the reader by creating this figure, and at the same time hides behind it.

Like the I-narrator in "Portrait of an Invisible Man," A. in "The Book of Memory" tries to get to the bottom of himself by withdrawing into extreme solitude, the precondition for taking words on paper. He shuts himself up in his room, also described as "a black hole" (77) or "another dimension" (77), where he seems to be preoccupied with nothing but his own experiences, especially with his fear of losing his son. With the help of his writing, he "wanders" into his inner self which he explores as if it were a yet unknown country and soon jumps from one memory to the next: "He feels himself sliding through events, hovering like a ghost around his own presence, as if he were living somewhere to the side of himself – not really here, but not anywhere else either" (78).

With A.'s decision to isolate himself, to distance himself from others, Auster indirectly parallels "The Book of Memory" with *The Book of Jonah* of the Old Testament. He depicts the latter as "a story of solitude" (124), a story that "is told as if from outside that solitude, as if, by plunging into the darkness of that solitude, the 'I' has vanished from itself. It cannot speak about itself, therefore, except as another" (124). In fact, *The Book of Jonah* is, in contrast to the other prophetic books of the bible, written in the third person, as the narrator A. emphasizes – just like "The Book of Memory" is. On the one hand, Jonah and A. resemble each other in their refusal to speak, in their retreat from the world (124/125); A.'s room can indeed be paralleled to "the belly of the ship," where Jonah hides from God and His directions to go to Nineveh (Jon. 1.1-3), as well as to "the belly of the whale," in which Jonah survives the raging storm (Jon. 2.1-11). On the other hand, A. and Jonah open themselves up to the other in themselves and, indirectly, to their surroundings as well.

Moreover, Auster does not only write about the solitude of one single person, but, since Jonah must be understood as a parabolic figure, of man in general. A.'s room can hence be understood as a place of isolation and of community at the same time (Auster, "Interview with McCaffery and Gregory" 316). A. indeed "feels that he is moving inward (through himself) and at the same time moving outward (towards the world)" (139). On his journey into unknown space he "become[s] more than just himself" (139), because he allows himself to be captivated by extreme narrowness in order to discover the seemingly unthinkable possibilities within his mind, i.e., to break through the isolation he has brought himself into: "A feeling of having been locked up, and at the same time of being able to walk through walls" ("The Book of Memory" 78). The death-like solitude that A. and Jonah encounter is consequently "a preparation for new life, a life that has passed through death" (25) and thus mirrors Derrida's focus on death characterized by a "double bind.". As in Derrida's *As if I were Dead*, death appears as an absolute mark, break, or stoppage, as the finite itself which is inherent in life (19-20). But with A.'s and Jonah's solitude into unknown space, Auster, similar to Derrida, also concentrates on death as a crossing, on the in-between of life and death, and human anxiety about the unforeseeable. Compared to "the belly of the whale," A.'s room becomes a "womb" (89), "a kind of mental uterus, site of second birth. In this enclosure the subject gives birth, in essence, to himself" (Bruckner 28). More concretely, "the tongue is finally loosened" (125) at the moment of looking death in the face. By being enclosed in the solitude of his writing process, A. will, similarly to the I-narrator in "Portrait of an Invisible Man," understand that in his mind,

> a network of paths begins to be drawn, as in the image of the human blood stream (heart, arteries, veins, capillaries), or as in the image of a map (of city streets, for example, preferably a large city, or even of roads, as in the gas station maps of roads that stretch, bisect, and meander across a continent). . . .
> (Auster, "The Book of Memory" 122)

The writer's "thoughts compose a journey" (122) on which they take turns, mirror themselves, but at the same moment emanate their own essence. A.'s memories quickly replace each other – or, to use Auster's words, all thoughts "'come at random, and go at random . . . '" (139). This is illustrated with the following passage. As in Derrida's "Circumfession," a certain beginning or end is not clearly indicated:

> He remembers writing his first book, a detective story he composed with green ink. He remembers thinking that if Adam and Eve were the first people in the world, then everyone was related to everyone else. He remembers wanting to throw a penny out the window of his grandparents' apartment on Columbus Circle and his mother telling him that it would go straight through someone's head. He remembers looking down from the top of the Empire State building and being surprised that the taxi-cabs were still yellow. (168-169)

As this passage shows, memory emits its power within the four walls of A.'s room. It itself becomes "a room, . . . a body, . . . a skull that encloses the room in which a body sits" (88). Memory, in other words, transcends the enclosed space the narrator has brought himself into. Saint Augustine, mentioned by the narrator as well as by Derrida in "Circumfession," observed this, too. He thought about that which is contained by and that which lies outside of memory:

> '. . . I cannot understand all that I am. This means, then, that the mind is too narrow to contain itself entirely. But where is that part of it which it does not itself contain? Is it somewhere outside itself and not within it? How, then, can it be part of it, if it is not contained within it?' ("The Book of Memory" 88-89)

Auster also preoccupies himself with "the nature of the subtle and intricate nexus between the outer world of observable phenomena and the inner world of the endlessly observing . . . human mind" (Bawer 68), when he mentions Emily Dickinson, who similarly withdrew into extreme solitude. Indeed, her solitude made an extraordinary poetry collection possible. By thinking about her, A. understands that "consciousness [is] captivity as well as liberty" (Auster, "The Book of Memory" 123), that "he is both in and outside of himself" (Shibata 186). As for Dickinson, the words he takes down on paper "are a way of being in the world" (Auster, "The Book of Memory" 123) and reflect the movement of his thoughts. They are connected with the space of the exterior, i.e., with all kinds of signifiers hinting at the past, the present, and the future. A. understands that "every body experiences everything that goes on in the universe" (160), that "[e]ach man, therefore, is the entire world, bearing with his genes a memory of all mankind" (114).

Moreover, moments of life and death run into each other. The transitoriness of all things is already present at the beginning of "The Book of Memory," when A. writes: "It was. It will never be again" (75). The experience of the father's death has, to be more concrete, an impact on A.'s relationship to his son Daniel. A. now seems to take on his father's former role or becomes his double – i.e., he feels more plainly what it is like to be a father and thus regards Daniel in a different manner. At the same moment, he identifies with his son to the extent that the remembrance of his own childhood becomes more vivid:

> When the father dies, he writes, the son becomes his own father and his own son. He looks at his son and sees himself in the face of the boy. He imagines what the boy sees when he looks at him and finds himself becoming his own father. Inexplicably, he is moved by this. It is not just the sight of the boy that moves him, nor even the thought of standing inside his father, but what he sees in the boy of his own vanished past. It is a nostalgia for his own life that he feels, perhaps, a memory of his own boyhood as a son to his father. (81)

To sum up, the moment of death triggering off a search for orientation does not only lie at the "center" of "The Portrait of an Invisibile Man," but also of "The Book of Memory." In both texts, Auster points out to what extent the experience of death has affected his way of thinking and writing. Similar to Jacques Derrida's "Circumfession," the search does not give any concrete answer concerning the past, but brings the writer closer to his son or to life in general. But before he feels this, he is, just like Derrida, repeatedly thrown back onto his wounds or "scars" (Derrida, "Circumfession" 15). In the philosopher's case, the physical wound caused by his circumcision, that he refers to in many of his texts, is depicted as a crucial moment of death standing at the beginning of his life, running through his childhood, adolescence, and adulthood. Concerning Derrida's theory of deconstruction, it becomes a symbol for the meaning of incisions, breaks, and shifts in writing. Neither in "Portrait of an Invisible Man," nor in "The Book of Memory" does Auster mention the Jewish custom of circumcising. However, while concentrating on and writing about his relationship to his father, memories of division and separation stand at the "center" – a fact that reflects itself not only in the form of this autobiographical piece as stated above, but in Auster's vocabulary as well. This becomes obvious when he describes the relationship to the father in a metaphorical way. They, as he points out, have always been "cut off from each other on opposite sides of a wall" ("Portrait" 24). It is a "circumcised" relationship Auster writes about and which partly explains the I-narrator's separation from his Jewishness.

3.2.2. The deconstruction of the paternal figures – or: being divided from Jewish roots

Although the I-narrator of "Portrait of an Invisible Man" becomes more and more conscious of the "circumcised" relationship to his father, he paradoxically tries to stop him from disappearing altogether by sticking to his pen, by desperately clinging to his memories.[16] He tries to link these memories with each other in order not to forget what happened to his father, to himself, and to his Jewish ancestors. A. in "The Book of Memory" depicts memory as "a catalyst for remembering his own life and as an artificial structure for ordering the historical past" (116). Similar to Derrida's "Circumfession," the autobiographical mosaic can thus be understood as the attempt of an archive coming into being at the moment of death (c.f. ch. 2.7.). By trying to write it, the I-narrator hopes to create a vessel or stockroom for the past events, to bring to light what has seemingly been buried. He especially wants the father to be present, and thus he has to "act quickly" ("Portrait" 86). However, the undertaking of "looking for him" (7) turns out to be a paradox and a failure from the beginning, as the father "has always been absent, invisible to others, and most likely to him as well" (7). The narrator sees it clearly: "Death hasn't changed anything" (7).

In fact, different aspects of the father's past circle around and disseminate themselves in the narrator's head. It therefore becomes impossible to determine one single idea as the core of his identity. Instead, the father has always struck the narrator as being "a block of impenetrable space in the form of a man" (Auster, "Portrait" 7). The narrator "never had the feeling that he [the father] could be located" (9), because of "this lack of [any] center" (9) within him. As a consequence, the son produces a fragmentary piece of writing which must do without any kind of authority guaranteeing linearity or coherence. It is, like Derrida's "Circumfession," a dispersed piece of "writing without interruption" (Derrida, "Circumfession" 201), a text marked by cuts and incisions, or, to use the Derridean terminology, by the moment of circumcision, understood as a literary means.

[16] In the "Interview with Mark Irwin," Auster argues that "when everything about ourselves is called into question, when the ground drops out from under us . . . memory becomes a powerful force in our lives" (329).

Indeed, the narrator of Auster's autobriographical mosaic circles around his father consisting of a great number of selves. It is a deconstructed subject he tries to depict as exactly as possible without ever coming nearer it in his mind (Ickstadt 44). One idea of his father's identity doubles itself endlessly. In the following scene, the father's self is reduced to nothing but a trick photography, a collage of many copies of the same picture repeatedly put over one another. This shows that the father's identities, which are unconnected and do not refer to one another, vanish to an unfixed point in time and space:

> And then, you study the picture, you begin to realize that all these men are the same man. The seance becomes a real seance, and it is as if he has come there only to invoke himself, to bring himself back from the dead, as if, by multiplying himself, he had inadvertently made himself disappear. There are five of him there, and yet the nature of the trick photography denies the possibility of eye contact among the various selves. Each one is condemned to go on staring into space, as if under the gaze of the others, but seeing nothing, never able to see anything. It is a picture of death, a portrait of an invisible man. (Auster, "Portrait" 31)

The photography demonstrates to what extent one truth about the father doubles, multiplies, and consequently nullifies itself (Barone, "Introduction" 13). It does not really matter what you say about him. Everything is right and wrong at the same time. Hence the idea of an accessible truth fades away in the narrator's mind (Auster, "Portrait" 61).

Besides, by trying to put the fragmentary memories of his father together like a jigsaw puzzle, the I-narrator indeed questions the human nature of his father. He describes him as a man who takes on different roles and always wears a mask, "a person he [the father] had invented, an artificial creature he could manipulate in order to manipulate others . . . , a puppeteer working the strings of his alter-ego from a dark, solitary place behind the curtain" (16). He is a man with "no response" (17) to any conversation, "[a] man without appetites" (17). "He was never a married man, never a divorced man, but a life-long bachelor who happened to have had an interlude of marriage" (17). He is "a defective character" (Barone, "Introduction" 13), a ghost who has always been rattling around "somewhere else, between here and there. But never really here. And never really there" (Auster, "Portrait" 19).

Shortly after the father's death, a girl in fact comes to the narrator telling him that his father is on the phone: "It was gruesome. I thought:

there's a ghost at the other end of the line, and he really does want to talk to me. It was a few moments before I could speak" (13). This passage could also imply that the father looks for his son (if we take the words literally), that he turns the narrator's role of a wanderer searching for him upside down. With his seeming attempt to reach him, the father becomes his son's double. However, this attempt turns out to be nothing but a creepy illusion, a wish the narrator yearns to come true. Of course, this will not happen: without answering the phone, the narrator hangs up.

Obviously, "The Portrait of an Invisible Man," which deals with the possibility of mysterious doubles and admits that its I-narrator has lost his modes of expression, must be called ghost-writing. Its specific vocabulary is also present in the following passage. Here, the father's belongings underline his ghost-like appearance. They are marked by the trace of 'différance': "the objects of a dead man. . . . They are there and yet not there: tangible ghosts, condemned to survive in a world they no longer belong to" (10). The father's house mirrors the disintegration of his identity by "falling apart from within" (31). His clothes are put on a level with "an expression of solitude, a concrete way of affirming his absence" (55).

Indeed, the earliest memory the narrator has of his father is that he never really recognized him, that "he saw [him] only through the mists of his solitude" (24). At this point, Auster builds up a second idea of solitude. It is the opposite of the necessary solitude an author has to find in order to write: the incapability of bringing oneself into contact with others, in this case with the son. Auster clearly favors the first paradoxical nature of solitude, making the connection of thoughts and people possible.[17] But because of his father's mental absence, the narrator is unable to come close to his multiplied self. His project of

[17] Sinda Gregory is also of the opinion that solitude "is a concept that seems to contain a lot of different resonances for [Auster] both personal and aesthetic" (Auster, "Interview with McCaffery and Gregory" 313). Auster agrees with that: "solitude is a rather complex term for me; it's not just a synonym for loneliness or isolation" (313). For him, it is "one of the conditions of being human" and means that "real life takes place inside us" (313). "[T]he life-long conversation we have with ourselves . . . takes place in absolute solitude" (314). Auster only seems to mention the first idea of solitude presented above: "you don't begin to understand your connection with others until you are alone. And the more intensely you are alone, the more deeply you plunge into a state of solitude, the more deeply you feel that connection. It isn't possible for a person to isolate himself from other people" (315).

capturing the "man hidden inside the man who was not there" (Auster, "Portrait" 20), i.e., of bringing the other within the father to light is foreseen as a definite impossibility (20). In other words, "Portrait of an Invisible Man" as an "archive writing" in the Derridean sense of the term, i.e., as an attempt to gather material that is at risk of being forgotten, only seemingly works against the eradication of the narrator's memories. The Freudian death drive, which Derrida elaborates on in *Archive Fever*, "[has incited] forgetfulness, amnesia, the annihilation of memory" probably already years ago (Derrida, *Archive Fever* 11). The narrator generalizes his insight into the effect of the annihilation of memory with the following words: "Impossible, I realize, to enter another's solitude" (19).

Without having come into contact with any paternal guidance or support, the son does not have a clue which course to take and becomes a confused and disoriented figure. He is unable to express what he wants to say and skeptical whether his yearning will ever be satisfied. However, the father's absent-mindedness has paradoxically preserved his hunger for getting hold of and experiencing a more intimate relationship with him (32). As a consequence, the I-narrator is not really capable of facing the moment when he will have reached the last page, although the writing process is extremely painful (Rubin 65). He seems to be imprisoned in his own piece of writing through which he tries to reach his father. At the same time, he fears to finish it because of his certainty that he will then disappear forever. In short, A. needs to maintain his hunger:

> The closer I come to the end of what I am able to say, the more reluctant I am to say anything. I want to postpone the moment of ending, and in this way delude myself into thinking that I have only just begun, that the better part of my story still lies ahead. ("Portrait" 65)

However, by continuing his writing, the I-narrator gains some deeper knowledge concerning his Jewish family-history which is hidden within the deconstructive layer of the text. He soon understands that not only he himself is a wounded, a "crippled" man (32), but that also his father suffered greatly from the disintegration of family relations (50). In particular, he finds out that he didn't have a true father, either, and thus possibly "found life only tolerable by staying on the surface of things" (15).

Indeed, the Jewish paternal line did not start to crumble with the narrator's father, but even earlier, i.e., with the grandmother who killed her husband in 1919. The grandfather has, similar to his son, always appeared as if he had never lived at all or disappeared from the face of the earth without leaving behind any traces. He has also entered some kind of no-man's-land, an indefinable region where he can no longer be located, as a photograph shows that the I-narrator finds:

> And then I realized what was strange about the picture: my grandfather had been cut out of it. The image was distorted because part of it had been eliminated. My grandfather had been sitting in a chair next to his wife with one of his sons standing between his knees – and he was not there. Only his fingertips remained: as if he were trying to crawl back into the picture from some hole deep in time, as if he had been exiled to another dimension. The whole thing made me shake. ("Portrait" 34)

Because of the grandfather's seeming infidelity, his wife decided to erase his existence, to push him out of life. No one of his offspring should remember his face. In this way, the biblical pattern of the father walking hand in hand with his children is given up (Fisch 39-40). The story of Isaac who was first going to be sacrificed by his father, but was then rescued by God Himself (Gen. 22, 1-19), signifies the demanded reconciliation of father and son, the healing of aggression and cruelty between the generations. However, the grandmother abandoned this traditional law of the Old Testament and consequently broke with the Jewish family pattern, "the infrastructure of Jewish existence" (Fisch 42). What has remained is "an emptiness . . . , a state of disintegration in which all familiar landmarks are gone" (Fisch 42).

Both the narrator and his father are left with a void that cannot be filled any more, with the knowledge of a trace which has forever been wiped out. They are haunted by their own detective undertaking of pinpointing the true facts of the past which eventually leads to nothing. The narrator indeed does not know whether he should believe the newspaper articles about the murder that "loom up at [him] with all the force of the unconscious, distorting reality in the same way dreams do" ("Portrait" 36). He reads them "as a cave drawing discovered on the inner walls of [his] own skull" (37). As a consequence, other stories about his grandfather spread themselves within his mind. He does not manage to come to terms with reality. Truth distorts itself and the grandfather remains to be a ghost-like figure – the opposite of the traditional Jewish principle of the father being a benevolent teacher and the symbol for Jewish law and order (Herweg 179).

By concentrating on his memories, the I-narrator becomes conscious of the fact that the paternal role became totally substituted by the grandmother who "acted as a matriarch, [as] the absolute dictator, the prime mover who stood at the center of the universe" (Auster, "Portrait" 33). She is also described as "a tyrant, given to screaming and hysterical fits" (50), as a "fierce, refractory" (49) woman who tied her children to herself and "demanded allegiance" (50). By behaving like this, she appears as the opposite of the traditionally idealized, honoured "Jewish mother" based on the concept of the *Schechina*, the female personification of the divine spirit, of love and care (Num 35.34 and Herweg 37). The narrator's grandmother equals Sophie Portnoy in Philip Roth's novel *Portnoy's Complaint* (1967), who, in an authoritarian manner, prevents the children from becoming independent. Auster's narrator furthermore mentions that "the good of the family was always more important than the good of any of its members" ("Portrait" 50) – with the consequence that the grandmother did not take her son's personal concerns and wishes seriously. Thus he lost faith in the people around him and soon also in himself:

> [T]he sky could fall on top of him at any moment, . . . he could never be sure of anything. Therefore, he learned never to trust anyone. Not even himself. Someone would always come along to prove that what he thought was wrong, that it did not count for anything. He learned never to want anything too much. (50)

On grounds of his fundamental uncertainty, the narrator's father withdrew into some kind of inner exile, into his solitude which was reinforced and reflected by the family's "nomadism." After the grandmother had been acquitted, "they moved constantly" ("Portrait" 48) because of their fear of slander and persecution, and thus cut off every connection to the past. They were continually wandering in foreign parts of the country without building up any sort of center. In short, the family's inevitable flight mirrors the biblical motive as well as the historical fact of the Israelites' flight out of Egypt (Num. 20.1 ff). However, in contrast to millions of Jewish families who were forced to leave their home in times of persecution, the Shoah in particular, the narrator's grandmother chose a life of total isolation. She did not get in touch with other people and thus completely distanced herself from one of the most important pillars of Judaism, the idea of the Jewish community:

> In a family that had already closed in on itself, this nomadism walled them off entirely. There were no enduring points of reference: no home, no town, no friends that could be counted on. Only the family itself. It was almost like living in quarantine. (49)

The family's "restless, unmoored existence" ("Portrait" 9) seemed to have an enormous effect on the I-narrator's father: he later led a life of negligence, superficiality, or, as outlined above, of total absent-mindedness. Similar to his father, he disappeared into a dimension where other people could not get in close contact with him. Thus he became "a perpetual outsider, a tourist of his own life" (9), whom the access to his family history was denied and who then distanced himself completely from the Jewish community (65), which must of course also be regarded as an effect of his assimilation to modern America. Especially for the rabbi of his community, who later conducts the funeral service for him, he became a complete stranger: "He had not known my father, in fact knew nothing about him, and half an hour before the service was to begin I sat down with him and told him what to say in the eulogy" (67).

The I-narrator, influenced by his father's ignorance, loses any connection to the Jewish family history (28). Consequently, he does not identify with any Jewish community institution either. His memories of, for example, his Bar Mitzvah (66) or a dinner in a Jewish restaurant (28) are nothing but fragments disseminated in his writing. They are totally intertwined with the story-line and are sometimes barely recognizable. Or, if we use Derrida's words, they are traces of a far distance that suddenly appear on the surface and then disappear again into the network of the text.

This is also true for "The Book of Memory," when A. remembers his Bar Mitzvah in 1960, but at the same moment points out that Bill Mazeroski's win in the World Series is "the first image that springs to his mind when 1960 is mentioned" (116). Baseball seems to compensate for religion in the traditional sense and is an example to what extent modern America has influenced a young Jewish man. A. even equates "the power of baseball" (116) with "the power of memory" (116), i.e., he enters his inner world with the help of remembering this game and thus regards it as a "religious experience" (117). The vocabulary of religion only serves as a means to bring A.'s enthusiasm about baseball to the point, as the following humorous statement also indicates: "to win the pennant was to enter the promised land" (117).

In short, the I-narrator and A. are, similar to the father, not "bound to a regular participation in organized Jewish life" (Azria 28). They do not identify with Jewishness on the grounds of tradition as a normative, authoritative guideline and thus mirror Jacques Derrida's statements on his separation from Jewish beliefs and customs, the fact that he is "entirely remote from Judaism" (Ofrat 9).

However, the fact that Auster's narrators, whether consciously or unconsciously we cannot say, include the fragments of their Jewish past in their writing proves that they still feel a sense of belonging. They perceive themselves as being connected to the Jewish paternal line of the family. Yet they also realize that they are separated from it and so resemble the father in his feeling of unsatisfied yearning. In short, they identify themselves as Jews "on the grounds of affinity" (Azria 28), but their Jewishness can only be dimly recognized in forms of fragmentary memories in an autobiographical, deconstructed writing.

3.2.3. The absence of God in the present

In "Portrait of an Invisible Man," the I-narrator refers to his Jewish identity "between the margins" and so circles around it without ever coming to its center, its essence, that is to say – God. His name is only mentioned when he retells the parable of Jonah. But in all other passages, God remains invisible, just as in Derrida's interpretation of the biblical scene after Moses has broken the Tables in "Edmond Jabès and the Question of the Book" (67). He appears as the absent, unattainable source, shrouded within the writing process. Since the narrator's father and grandfather also remain ungraspable, we can ask ourselves whether the search for thc biological father indeed means the search for *Jahveh*. However, it seems impossible to analyze Auster's autobiographical mosaic in such psychological depths. What can instead be claimed is "that rupture, the absence of God, the rift . . . are among the basic experiences of Judaism, whether ancient or modern," as Judah David Eisenstein and Otzar Midrashim have clearly outlined:

> 'Rabbi Shimeon Bar Yochai teaches that the Holy Name and all His appellations are contained in a cabinet, Rabbi Hona said and taught that the tablets and fragments of tablets are contained within the Holy Ark of the Torah.' (Bamidbar Raba, Parasha 4, sec. 20,5) The segment is not separate

> from the whole, nor the Torah from its fragments; the divine message is dumb and incomprehensible: 'Who is like unto Thee among the gods, oh Lord, who is like unto Thee among the dumb, oh Lord.' (qtd. in Ofrat 6)

By considering this, we can call the first part of *The Invention of Solitude* a writing of absence created by a writer who, like Derrida, "is in dialogue with death, speaking the language of death, the language of trace" (Ofrat 124). With its renunciation of 'logocentrism,' the theory of deconstruction does not accept any source, center, or origin being present or undivided in itself. The image of God as the One who does not show His face is entangled within the theory of deconstruction and mirrors itself in Auster's "Portrait of an Invisible Man" and in "The Book of Memory." Or, in other words, the absence of God as an experience of Judaism emphasized by Derrida is intertwined with (and also hidden in) the deconstructive layer of these texts and stands in connection with the narrator's father having lost contact to his traditional Jewish family background.

Besides, A. in "The Book of Memory" translates forty fragments by Mallarmé after his son Daniel has almost died of pneumonia. The latter once wrote them while his son Anatole was wrestling with death. By translating the fragments, A. tries to express his thankfulness for Daniel's life and understands these fragments as "the equivalent of offering a prayer" (110). Poetry here substitutes the probably most essential traditional Jewish act by taking on its religious meaning. A., who is divided from his Jewish background, does not address the lines to *Jahveh*, but "to the *modern nothingness*" (110) and at the same moment to "the sense of [Daniel's] life" (110).

The translation is, in other words, marked by a "double bind." It thus expresses that life is ruled by the moment of chance, as Auster repeatedly points out, for example in an interview: "If my work is about anything, I think it's about the unexpected, the idea that anything can happen. You never know what's looming up ahead" ("Interview with Mark Irwin" 333). However, this does not mean that *The Invention of Solitude* is a nihilistic piece of writing. It contains fragmentary memories of Jewish history which, as the following chapter will show more clearly, transport an ethical message: the necessity of remembering the crimes of the past, the Shoah in particular. In so far, *The Invention of Solitude* contains hope and is directed towards the future, as the last sentence clearly demonstrates: "It was. It will never be again. Remember" (172).

3.2.4. The narrators' confrontation with the Shoah and its effects

In several episodes, it becomes obvious that "things take on meaning only in relation to each other" ("The Book of Memory" 161). Auster connects a multitude of facts of Jewish history, especially of the Shoah, fragmentary quotations from other (Jewish) writers, and stories with each other and, as a consequence, transports a deeper meaning. This deeper meaning as an effect of the poststructuralist means of intertextuality becomes obvious when he does not only quote Mallarmé, Israel Liechtenstein, or Anne Frank, but also passages from *The Thousand and One Nights*. Each of its stories contains other stories of storytelling, mirrors them, and runs into them like the streets on a map. Together, they shake the walls of the king's consciousness as they make "the existence of others" clear to him.

This is exactly what Auster tries to do with *The Invention of Solitude*. All the quoted passages from Jewish writers are signifiers pointing to other quotations, thoughts, and experiences. The narrator's impressions are linked to these quotations and are reflected by them. To this extent, the past, the present, and the future cannot be separated from each other. The writing process is not only a search for identity, but is directed to the other as well. The responsibility for the need of the other is grounded, as Lévinas has repeatedly pointed out, within Judaism, i.e., he regards it as a pre-philosophical or "originary" one (c.f. ch. 2.5.). The age-old wound of persecution and imprisonment in Egypt stands for the outset for humane behavior, as he declares in his essay "Revelation in the Jewish Tradition": "The traumatism of my enslavement in Egypt constitutes my very humanity, that which draws me closer to the problems of the wretched of the earth, to all persecuted people" (202). In parallel, Auster conveys the ethical message of responsibility by linking the personal experience of the moment of death with extreme suffering in Jewish history, above all at the time of the Shoah. According to Lévinas, the concern for the other as a Judaic necessity will never be completely fulfilled. It remains, as he stresses, an "ideal" which includes "the humanity of human beings" as a whole" ("The Pact" 226). With the means of intertextuality in his autobiographical mosaic, Auster similarly emphasizes the never-ending importance to feel responsible for the other and to remind us of the past so that it will not repeat itself in the future.

While A., for example, is standing in Anne Frank's little room in Amsterdam, which today is a museum, he is overwhelmed by his own sadness. Here he feels the urge to write "The Book of Memory" (83). Anne Frank's experience of being imprisoned with nothing but her own writing in fact mirrors A.'s retreat into himself: "To imagine a solitude so crushing, so unconsolable, that one stops breathing for hundreds of years" (83). Furthermore, Anne Frank reminds A. of his son Daniel, because her birthday is the same as his: "June twelfth. Under the sign of Gemini" (83). Anne Frank can hence be understood as Daniel's twin sister, and A. indeed comes to the conclusion that in this "world . . . everything is double, . . . the same thing always happens twice" (83). These words must not be interpreted in the way that Daniel will also be forced to go through persecution and torture soon. Instead, they hint at A.'s anxiety of having lost his son forever when he split up from his wife. He feels this anxiety even stronger after a Jewish child called Etan Patz has disappeared from his neighborhood: ". . . every time he saw the photograph of this face he was made to think of his own son – and in precisely these terms: lost child" (101). Etan and Anne Frank reflect A.'s worries about his son's life, or, more concretely, reflect his feeling that the separation from Daniel is a death-like experience.

During his writing process, A. becomes more and more convinced that life is cruel and senseless. This feeling intensifies when he thinks hard about the victims of the Shoah. Similarly to his visit of Anne Frank's House in Amsterdam, he is incapable of saying a word when Marina Tsvetaeva comes to his mind – the well-known Jewish-Russian poet, whose statement "All poets are Jews" is also mentioned by Derrida in "A Testimony Given." In "The Book of Memory," Auster explains that, as a result of the Nazi persecution, "she hanged herself in 1941" (94) and that her son Mur was killed in 1944 (97). With Mur, A. is reminded of all children who were killed, especially all Jewish ones at the time of the Shoah. By looking at some pictures of these dead children, A. becomes aware of the inadequacy of language:

> The dead children. The children who will vanish, the children who are dead. Himmler: 'I have made the decision to annihilate every Jewish child from the face of the earth.' Nothing but pictures. Because, at a certain point, the words lead one to conclude that it is no longer possible to speak. Because these pictures are the unspeakable. (98)

A. is similarly "reduced to saying nothing" (81) when a friend tells him the story about M. who rented a room in Paris, the same room in which his Jewish father had taken shelter from the Nazis for a couple of months (80). This story, which proves that the past is directly linked to the present, that past events may repeat themselves strangely, leads A. to the conclusion that "nothing can be explained anymore" (81). Within his room, he seems to be pursued by his memories and feels that reason does not help him to get to the bottom of them.

Close to the end of the book, Auster emphasizes this emotion by alluding to Freud, who described moments when we are haunted by something as "'uncanny,' or *unheimlich* – the opposite of *heimlich*, which means 'familiar,' 'native,' 'belonging to the home'" (Auster, "The Book of Memory" 148). By referring to Freud, Auster generalizes A.'s inner experiences. Every human being is affected; there is no exception:

> The implication, therefore, is that we are thrust out from the protective shell of our habitual perceptions, as though we were suddenly outside ourselves, adrift in a world we do not understand. By definition, we are lost in that world. We cannot even hope to find our way in it. (148)

In parallel, A. soon becomes entangled by the circular movements of his thoughts. There does not seem to be any way out of the helical, intertwined system of his mind. It is indeed a "chaotic odyssey" he has set out on (Bruckner 32), a "journey" to an uncertain destination within the four walls of his room, which alludes to the room in Auster's *White Spaces*, an image of the mind, i.e., of the dissemination of the narrator's thoughts. It is a journey into the infinite that the I-narrator of *White Spaces* has set out. He is eagerly awaiting to find suitable words that might express what he feels or sees at a specific moment. From the beginning it is clear that he will continue his journey, although he might just circle around his starting point. With the modern image of the city, Auster illustrates the narrator's multiple possibilities ramifying into the unknown and equates it with the biblical image of the desert where words keep out of sight or can only be dimly perceived in the far distance.

In parallel, the third person narrator A. in "The Book of Memory" loses all sense of time (145) and is haunted by "[s]patial disorientation" (Kiely 32) as the metaphor of Amsterdam brings to the point: Shortly before or after A. visits Anne Frank's House, he is eventually imprisoned by the circular, helical structure of the city. Indeed, it is, very much as in *White Spaces*, depicted as a desert-like place where he loses his orientation: "He wandered. He walked around in circles. He allowed himself to be lost" (86). A. equates the circles of Amsterdam with "circles of hell" (Auster, "The Book of Memory" 86), as 16th century writers once did, and with images of memory as well. His conviction that "Amsterdam [is] hell, and . . . hell is memory" (86) shows to what extent he is overpowered by the cruelty of the past.

More concretely, the hellish character of memory is not only marked by being reminiscent of Anne Frank's or Tsvetaeva's suffering, but also by an allusion to Israel Liechtenstein, a custodian of important material which proved the crimes of the Nazis. His last testament written in 1942 is an expression of extreme hopelessness, concerning the future of the Jewish people: "I know that we will not endure. To survive and remain alive after such horrible murders and massacres is impossible" (84).

On the very last page of "The Book of Memory," Liechtenstein's pessimistic prediction is repeated in a letter written by Nadezhda Mandelstam rebelling against the fact that families are separated, that she will perhaps never see her husband Osip again: "How hard and long for each of us to die alone. Can this fate be for us who are inseparable? Puppies and children, did we deserve this? Did you deserve this, my angel?" (171). Nadezhda Mandelstam seems to become A.'s mouthpiece, when she writes of the inadequacy of language at the moment of extreme suffering: "I have no words, my darling, to write this letter . . . I am writing it into empty space" (171).

In parallel, A.'s words vanish into the unknown in front of his eyes; they do not aim at any particular target. Instead, they are nothing but the almost impossible attempt to gain some clarity in spite of the "immense Babel inside him" (136). A. is confronted with the numerous images and voices of the past constantly referring to the present. In particular, when he translates the work of another writer, A. feels, to use Derrida's words, "the confusion of tongues, the irreducible multiplicity of idioms" (Derrida, "Tours de Babel" 250). This task becomes an insoluble problem, a fathomless phenomenon: "Sentences spill out of him at the speed of thought, and each word comes from a different language, a thousand tongues that clamor inside him at once . . ." (Auster, "The Book of Memory" 136). A. is confronted with a fragmentary language differing and deferring itself constantly – or, in short, with the movement of différance itself. He "has trouble deciphering the words" on paper (75) and circles around original meanings without ever reaching them. Hence he concludes what Derrida points out in *Psyché*: that any purity of language remains concealed. The one and only true language with which the book could be translated does not exist. As a result of this experience, A. stops taking care of himself and is not seldom totally unable to work. His journey into himself causes a "self-destructive passion" (Bruckner 28), i.e., he "transforms him[self] into a voluntary castaway" (Bruckner 28):

> He could not work, he could not think. He began to neglect himself, ate only noxious food (frozen dinners, pizza, take-out Chinese noodles), and left the apartment to its own devices: dirty clothes strewn in a bedroom corner, unwashed dishes in the kitchen sink. (Auster, "The Book of Memory" 114)

A.'s neglect of himself is a consequence of his awareness that the more he tries to delve into his almost lost or dismissed memories, the less he will bring back to the surface. It will not need much time until he will have reached the end of his journey: "Sooner or later, he is bound to use himself up" (79). The closer he comes to his last page, the more it seems to A. that he is "hovering like a ghost around his own presence, as if he were living somewhere to the side of himself – not really here, but not anywhere else either" (78). Like the I-narrator's father in "Portrait of an Invisible Man," A. seems to lose his human characteristics – especially when he translates the work of somebody else. Then he feels himself condemned to be nothing but "a kind of ghost of that other man, who is both there and not there" (136).

However, within the dark hole he has brought himself into, within this chasm or desert, he also absorbs "the beauty and extraordinary happiness of feeling [himself] alive, of breathing in the air, the joy of being alive in [his] own skin" (Auster, "Interview with Mark Irwin" 335). The alienation of the self paradoxically means a fountainhead of delight in so far that the confrontation with reality, i.e., the cruelty of the past, helps A. to feel himself again. Everything is turned upside down, or, to use Derrida's words, "différance instigates the subversion of every kingdom" ("Différance" 22):

> Far from troubling him, this state of being lost became a source of happiness, of exhilaration. He breathed it into his very bones. As if on the brink of some previously hidden knowledge, he breathed it into his very bones and said to himself, almost triumphantly: I am lost. (Auster, "The Book of Memory" 87)

Such (paradoxical) optimism can especially be noticed at the end of "The Book of Memory" that is in itself a beginning: A. takes a piece of paper, starts writing and is sure that the future will be different, that it will not repeat the past (172). His words can be referred to the presented fragments of the crimes at the time of the Shoah and also express the hope of a better time. To this extent, they express Liechtenstein's "[belief] in the survival of [his] people and his conviction that "Jews will not be annihilated" (84). Anne Frank also saw a glimmer of hope in spite of all mercilessness, as A. points out:

> '. . . I see the world gradually being turned into a wilderness, I hear the ever-approaching thunder, which will destroy us too, I can feel the sufferings of millions and yet, if I look up into the heavens, I think that it will all come right, that this cruelty too will end. . . .' (157)

On the basis of such optimism the last word of "The Book of Memory" must be understood. It is a logical consequence of the knowledge that "yesterday echoes today, and tomorrow will foreshadow what happens next year" (116). At the same time, it is a moral instruction given to the reader: "Remember" (172). This message is based on the understanding that all men are equal before God. It is conveyed by the biblical story of Jonah retold by Auster in "The Book of Memory." Jonah, who is angry that God has spared the Ninevites, the enemies of Israel, is taught a lesson in the parable of the gourd withering away in one night:

> Then said the Lord, 'Thou hast had pity on then the gourd, for which thou has not labored, neither madest it grow; which came up in a night and perished in a night; And should I not spare Ninevah, that great city, wherein are more than sixscore thousand persons that cannot discern between their right hand and their left hand; and also much cattle?' ("The Book of Memory" 159 and Jon. 4.10-11).

In his essay "The Pact," Lévinas illustrates the Judaic principle of reciprocal responsibility: "His concern is my concern. But is my concern also his? Isn't he responsible for me? And if he is, can I also answer for his responsibility for me? Kol Yisrael 'arevim zeh lazeh,' 'all Israel is responsible one for the other'" (225). According to Lévinas, this concern for the other is not only a Judaic necessity, but, as probably the most important ethical principle, applies to all mankind.

At the end of *The Invention of Solitude*, Auster also points out the concern for the other as an ethical necessity and ideal which includes all human beings:

> These sinners, these heathen – and even the beasts that belong to them – are as much God's creatures as the Hebrews . . . . [T]his, finally, is the essence of what the rabbis have to teach. If there is to be any justice at all, it must be a

> justice for everyone. No one can be excluded, or else there is no such thing as justice. The conclusion is inescapable. This tiniest of books, which tells the curious and even comical story of Jonah, occupies a central place in the liturgy: it is read each year in the synagogue on Yom Kippur, the Day of Atonement, which is the most solemn day on the Jewish calendar. For everything, as has been noted before, is connected to everything else. And if there is everything, then it follows there is everyone. (159)

To sum up, in Auster's autobiographical mosaic the narrators get confused and disoriented on their quest for a father, who has always been absent. They eagerly try to make sense out of their fragmentary memories which disseminate and erase each other constantly. The only answer they get is that the father was a wounded man, too, whose desire to find some stability in life was not satisfied. He became separated from traditional Judaism and had to wander around in different parts of the country without living at one particular place for some longer time. In short, the deep inner wound of separation from Jewish beliefs and customs, which is concealed within Derrida's theory of deconstruction, is here depicted as the effect of the narrators' separation from their father. However, the narrators' hope to get closer to their father is disappointed. Or, in other words, they will not reach the destination of their quest through the act of writing. The movement of différance will always block the end of the search. But at the end, the narrators open up themselves to the exterior world, as they still feel a sense of belonging to Jewish history and culture. With their archive-like writing process, they face up to the Jewish experience of persecution and become able to convey the ethical message of responsibility for the other in Emmanuel Lévinas' understanding.

3.3. *City of Glass* – the development of a hunger artist in a deconstructed detective novel

In an interview with Joseph Mallia, Paul Auster points out that "the *Trilogy* grows directly out of *The Invention of Solitude*" (278). In other words, the three novels *City of Glass*, *Ghosts*, and *The Locked Room* are based on Auster's autobiographical mosaic. Thus it can, as Marc Chénetier remarks, be regarded as some kind of "matrix" or the starting point from which Auster's fiction writing develops (36 and Bruckner 27).

The following analysis will concentrate on the first part of *The New York Trilogy*, *City of Glass*, since the interlocking of Auster's references to (his) Jewishness and his use of the theory of deconstruction can be most clearly recognized in this anti-detective novel. To be more specific, the biblical motive and part of Jewish history, the ardent desire for homecoming or hunger for arrival, which in *The Invention of Solitude* is reflected in the I-narrator's and A.'s ongoing search for the father, is also part of *City of Glass.* At the same time, it is entangled within and transmitted by the deconstruction of the traditional elements of the detective novel.

This inner wound or never-fulfilled desire, the "central" theme of the autobiographical mosaic, is now mirrored by the protagonist, a writer called Daniel Quinn, who is infinitely looking for paternal authority and "author-ity" (Russell 73) by following Stillman, Sr., the "culprit" of the "case."[18] During his search, Quinn does not stop circling around his inner wound and does not understand that neither a case nor a culprit exists in reality. He even needs to maintain his hunger which is clearly foreshadowed and mirrored at the beginning of the novel with regard to his reading mania: "It was a kind of hunger that took hold of him, a craving for special food, and he would not stop until he had eaten his fill" (Auster, *City* 9). However, the more Quinn tries to preserve his hunger, the less he will make out a solution or an end of his "detective search." During his logocentric quest, which is deconstructed from the very beginning,[19] he becomes entangled within the supplementation and dissemination of different signifiers until he feels completely lost. In other words, the movement of différance again blocks any source or origin. Nevertheless, Quinn needs to preserve his yearning and eventually develops into a hunger artist (Rubin 60). Auster must hence be regarded as a Jewish-American writer not only walking in Jacques Derrida's, but also in Franz Kafka's footsteps.

[18] It cannot be really called a case since "[t]here is no crime in the traditional sense, i.e. no murder has been committed" (Holzapfel 29). In other words, the role of the detective, the culprit, and the victim are turned upside down, as this chapter tries to demonstrate.

[19] Alison Russell stresses that "[l]ogocentrism . . . is the 'crime' that Auster investigates in *The New York Trilogy*" (72).

3.3.1. The ardent desire for arrival and the deconstructed elements of the detective novel

Like *The Invention of Solitude*, *City of Glass* starts off from the moment of death. Quinn has lost both his wife and son and is described as someone "living a posthumous life" (6), who has "managed to outlive himself" (6). When Quinn later meets the fictitious Paul Auster and his family, he is directly confronted with his wound, with the deprivation of everything he once loved: "It was too much for Quinn. He felt as though Auster were taunting him with the things he had lost, and he responded with envy and rage, a lacerating self-pity" (121). Quinn sees the only possibility of living with his wound, the experience of death, in leaving his past behind and retreating into complete solitude, into isolation, where he does not seem to be touched by anything anymore. Thus he resembles "the invisible man," the father in the first part of Auster's autobiographical writing or the narrator A. in "The Book of Memory."

Writing mystery novels – the only thing Quinn stays to be able to do – gives him the chance to give up his own identity and take on the name of William Wilson,[20] i.e., he hides himself "behind the mask of his pseudonym" (5) and hence does not need to take responsibility for his works. "He [does] not consider himself to be the author of what he [writes]" (5) – a foreshadowing of the fact that Quinn as the narrator of the red notebook will vanish altogether. Furthermore, he invents Max Work, his private-eye narrator, who becomes a center, but also a double, a twin brother in solitude (7). The longer Quinn keeps on writing his mystery novels, the more he identifies with this narrator until he "stop[s] thinking of himself as real" (10). The detective Max Work serves as a substitute for himself, behind whom Quinn can withdraw into complete isolation.

In other words, Auster depicts his protagonist as a deconstructed subject, a figure who has split up into a "triad of selves" (6). By making use of the Derridean theory, he conveys an identity crisis that is, on a deeper level, marked by a strong hunger for liveliness and sensation.

[20] The passage at the beginning of the novel, when Auster mentions the name of William Wilson for the first time, is one of many examples that clearly demonstrate to what extent the reader is led astray: The claim that "William Wilson, after all, was an invention" (5) is indeed not correct, since it refers to Edgar Allan Poe's story with the very same title. His William Wilson is Auster's double or vice versa. Another hidden "reference to Poe is the quote referring to Dupin, Poe's detective [in "The Murders in the Rue Morgue"], Quinn writes into his notebook" (Holzapfel 50).

Because of Quinn's choice of a hermetic life, this hunger cannot, however, be stilled any more from outside. Hence he feels urged to read mystery novels, sometimes "ten or twelve in a row" (9). He keeps on devouring them as a kind of substitute for being satisfied in true life.

Words have become the most essential sort of food for the protagonist – or better: for the fragmentary identities of a dehumanized figure which Auster illustrates with the image of the ventriloquist and the dummy. He has used it before with regard to A.'s son Daniel who faces death in "The Book of Memory:"[21] "In the triad of selves that Quinn had become, Wilson served as a kind of ventriloquist, Quinn himself was the dummy, and Work was the animated voice that gave purpose to the enterprise" (6). This image makes obvious to what extent Auster connects his books with each other and thus creates a network of ideas, images, and metaphors. One novel springs out of the previous one. Auster depicts Daniel and Quinn as death-like, as vanishing figures. However, repetition, as for Derrida, does not mean repetition of the same. Auster focuses on Daniel's critical physical condition (he falls ill with pneumonia) in contrast to Quinn's death-like psychic condition. Only later will Quinn's body also be affected.

Similar to *The Invention of Solitude*, Auster connects *City of Glass* with other literary works and, as an effect, lets Quinn's identities disseminate. In fact, the protagonist exists as Don Quixote's double from the first page on by having the same initials, as Alison Russell correctly brings to the point: "When Virginia Stillman tells Quinn that she was referred to the Paul Auster Detective Agency by Michael Saavedra (Cervantes's family name) Quinn becomes the quixotic hero, the unknown victim of a strange conspiracy" (74).[22] Besides, Quinn appears

[21] Quinn's first name, which is also Daniel, connects him with the boy as well as with Daniel, the son of the fictitious Paul Auster, in *City of Glass*. The latter and Quinn convert into each other's doubles: "The boy burst out laughing and said, 'Everybody's Daniel!' 'That's right,' said Quinn. 'I'm you, and you're me.' 'And around and around it goes,' shouted the boy, suddenly spreading his arms and spinning around the room like a gyroscope" (Auster, *City* 122).

[22] The protagonist Daniel Quinn mirrors Don Quixote's madness and vice versa. At the same time however, Auster points out that "Don Quixote . . . was not really mad. He only pretended to be. In fact, he orchestrated the whole thing himself. . . . He wanted to test the gullibility of his fellow men" (*City* 119). By identifying Quinn and Don Quixote as each other's doubles, we can maintain that with *City of Glass*, Auster is playing a game with the reader. The question is whether he just wants to find out how far people accept "lies and nonsense" (119).

as Cervantes's double, since the latter equally "goes to great lengths to convince the reader that he is not the author" (Auster, *City* 117) by wearing the mask of Cid Hamete Benengeli.

Auster pushes "the erasure of the borders between one self and the other" (Alford, "Mirrors" 18) and hence the identity crisis of his protagonist even further when the latter ultimately absorbs the role of the fictitious Paul Auster, a writer in New York (Hennings 151). Stillman, Jr., the "victim," has however not looked for him, but for the detective Paul Auster. Quinn eventually thinks of himself as being this detective, a figure standing for "authoritative presence" (Little 155) and is therefore convinced to "[do] good in the world" (Auster, *City* 62). This idea proves to be an illusion when he shortly later understands that "to be Auster mean[s] being a man with no interior, a man with no thoughts" (75). The real Paul Auster ironizes himself in this passage, as Madeleine Sorapure explains: "There is clearly a certain amount of self-conscious play here on the effect of being 'Auster,' as the name of the author is characterized by emptiness and anonymity" (78).

After Quinn has completely absorbed the role of the investigator, the Stillman "case" becomes a never-ending search for a "prelapsarian language," for presence and clarity in speech and writing. This quest is foreshadowed by his strong hunger for words at the beginning of the novel. It turns out to be a "quest for origin and identity" (Russell 72 and Klepper 260) which starts when Stillman, Sr., steps out of his train and Quinn begins to pursue him. Yet from the first encounter of these two figures it is obvious that Quinn's hunger for orientation will never be stilled. Indeed, Stillman, Sr., is deconstructed as a possible paternal authority: at the station Quinn recognizes a second Stillman, a twin brother of the first one whom Quinn is forced not to pay any attention to. From now on, his actions are doomed to failure (Nealon 98):

> There was nothing he could do now that would not be a mistake. Whatever choice he made – and he had to make a choice – would be arbitrary, a submission to chance. Uncertainty would haunt him to the end. (68)

While deconstructing the role of the traditional, finally identifiable culprit, Auster here parodies the rationality normally typical of a detective (Sorapure 79). The second Stillman does not appear on the surface any more, but he "haunts the subsequent proceedings in the form of a continually menacing alternative to Quinn's entire enterprise" (ibid).

Furthermore, Auster does not only deconstruct the role of the detective and the culprit, but also the one of the victim of the "case," Stillman, Jr., who, as a child, was imprisoned by his father in a dark room just as Kaspar Hauser once was. Since then he has acted as "a marionette trying to walk without strings" (Auster, *City* 17), and his face appears to be more that of a ghost than of a human being: "one could see through to the blue veins behind the skin of his face" (18). Furthermore, he is depicted as an extreme embodiment of solitude, as his telling name reveals. He has, similar to the father in Auster's "Portrait of an Invisible Man" and Quinn himself, retreated into total isolation. His language deficit is an effect of this isolation. Since his childhood, he has been forced to live with the creation of his own words as his only company, and, as a consequence, seems to be absent for others while paradoxically being present. He has also splintered up into a variety of different selves: "I am Peter Stillman. That is not my real name. My real name is Peter Rabbit. In the winter I am Mr. White, in the summer I am Mr. Green" (21). Sometimes he does not even think of himself as a grown-up at all, but believes himself to be "the boy who can[not] remember" (19), the baby "born again" (26) every day. In his talk to Quinn, he altogether questions the fact of having an identity and thus mirrors the protagonist's own problem: "My real name is Peter Nobody" (23).

Later, when Quinn becomes absorbed in the "case," he in fact slips into the role of the young Stillman, i.e., he transforms himself into a Kaspar Hauser figure by taking off all his clothes in the Stillmans' apartment and accepting some food from a mysterious, anonymous figure. Auster foreshadows this by letting Quinn imitate Stillman's way of speaking: "'All I can say is this: listen to me. My name is Paul Auster. That is not my real name'" (49).

By taking on so many different identities, Quinn finally comes to the conclusion that "nothing is clear" (49). To the question "who are you?" (49) he does not have any answer. His belief that "he could return to being Quinn whenever he wished" (62) is nothing but an illusion. Auster consequently turns "the role of the detective . . . as an order-establishing centre" (Holzapfel 24) upside down and at the same time depicts a wanderer forever looking for clues on the horizon, for the end of his journey (Rosello 151). Through the deconstruction of the most important features of the traditional detective novel, Auster leads the Old Testament motive of the anticipation of and seemingly endless walk towards a place of homecoming, that is part of *The Invention of Solitude* and his poems, to an extreme. Quinn keeps up his yearning for arrival and develops into a Kafkaesque hunger artist who is ready "to approach absolute zero" (Auster, *City* 136). He in fact "[keeps] the total fast in his mind as an ideal, a state of perfection he could aspire to but never achieve" (136).

In other words, Auster transfers his protagonist's inner condition onto his physical appearance. Quinn becomes a specialist in limiting his bodily needs to almost nothing (Rowen 230 and Shibata 185). He eats and sleeps as little as possible and decides to live in a garbage can, an image of his total immersion into the shattered city. With this decision, he loses all remaining contact to other people, has to fend for himself all alone and thus gets to know "the true nature of solitude" (139). The "ending" highlights this experience of extreme solitude when Quinn sits naked in the Stillmans' empty apartment and thus seems to develop into what Stillman, Jr., was years ago, the innocent child, being ready to speak the prelapsarian language. Quinn in fact clings to his red notebook, his only companion, and suddenly creates "images of such force and quality that they seem able to take their place in the world of objects, to become matter" (Rowen 232): "He wrote about the stars, the earth, his hopes for mankind. He felt that his words had been severed from him, that now they were a part of the world at large, as real and specific as a stone, or a lake, or a flower" (Auster, *City* 156).

However, he is only granted a glimpse into the prelapsarian world and thus does not change reality in any way. Only shortly later will he understand that his hunger for arrival will never be stilled completely, as he reaches the last pages of his notebook: "he realized that the more he wrote, the sooner the time would come when he could no longer write anything" (156). In other words, he keeps up his yearning, but recognizes that on Earth this will never bring him salvation. To this extent, Quinn's story mirrors Jewish experience and Derrida's understanding of the paradoxical nature of human desire, i.e., the continuing attempt to arrive at a particular destination or to get precise answers and the irrefutable prediction that this will never come true (Derrida, "A Testimony Given" 55). In short, it is again the movement of différance which illustrates "the experience of an impossible circle or circulation: the impossibility of closing the circle," as Derrida puts in in "A Testimony Given" (44). On the one hand, the movement of différance is marked by the strong desire to approach a certain destination. On the other hand, this destination, in Quinn's case the hope to get precise answers, remains unattainable. This paradox of différance is paralleled to the contradiction of the personal undertaking of the writing process – or, to put it the other way round, the impossibility of reaching a particular destination hides within itself the movement of différance.

In fact, Quinn's inability to recover his former condition is foreshadowed in the scene when Daniel, the son of the fictitious Auster, shows him his yoyo. Quinn is unable to make the yoyo go up, as the boy observes (121). However, Quinn explains to him that reaching a certain low sometimes encloses its opposite, i.e., the experience of being given fresh impetus or recovering completely: "'A great philosopher once said," muttered Quinn, "that the way up and the way down are one and the same'" (121). By transferring this scene to Quinn's condition at the end, we can say that he almost changes into nothingness but simultaneously merges into a totally different state of being – he seems to develop into a child experiencing its birth for a second time:

> He remembered the moment of his birth and how he had been pulled gently from his mother's womb. He remembered the infinite kindnesses of the world and all the people he had ever loved. Nothing mattered but the beauty of all this. (156)

Auster here clearly deconstructs the closure of death and thus expresses not only his hope in the world, but also one of the most essential beliefs of Judaism: the belief that life lies within death – or, to be more specific, that death is a threshold to a different state of being. At the same time, he is close to Derrida's conviction that "[a]t the moment of death, we can no longer be concerned with anything but the Other in ourselves" (qtd. in Kamuf 203). Lévinas similarly spoke of death as the mysterious or the absolutely ungraspable in "Time and the Other" (43). In *City of Glass*, Quinn is present at his own birth while he is experiencing his own death. Life and death almost fuse – a scary situation that reminds us of Derrida's interview *As If I were Dead* in which he presented "the idea of being dead while being quasi-dead" (20). This includes the fact that Quinn does not change into an active being in the end, but that he watches his birth or death – his crossing from here to there – passively. In other words, Lévinas' conviction that death comes "at a moment we are no longer *able to be able*" ("Time and the Other" 42) and that the subject is reduced to absolute passivity also finds its literary rendition in Auster's novel. In the end Quinn loses control over himself by standing at the threshold between the here and there, and his yearning for arrival in the present is not a question any more.

3.3.2. Infinite wandering in the desert-like labyrinth of New York as Derridean dissemination

Right at the beginning of *City of Glass,* Auster illustrates Quinn's identity crisis with the Old Testament motif of endless wandering through a forlorn, inhuman place where one can become lost from the start. The novel thus mirrors Derrida's interpretation of Edmond Jabès' remarks on the images of the desert and the city in his *Book of Questions* (Derrida, "Edmond Jabès" 69). In *City of Glass*, Quinn's solitary walks through the labyrinth of New York only seem to be an arbitrary, senseless action which in fact reveals his desperate situation:

> By wandering aimlessly, all places became equal, and it no longer mattered where he [Quinn] was. On his best walks, he was able to feel that he was nowhere. And this, finally, was all he ever asked of things: to be nowhere. New York was the nowhere he had built around himself, and he realized that he had no intention of ever leaving it again. (4)

In short, Quinn's roaming through the streets of this metropolitan city, which in his view is nothing but a desolate place lacking any distinguishing marks, mirrors his inner disorientation. At the same time, it makes his actual desire for arrival at a yet obscure destination obvious. The instability of the city reflecting the protagatonist's confusion is intensified with postmodern and neorealistic writing techniques.[23] In a minimalist style resulting from close observation, Auster critically emphasizes the chaos of New York at the end of the 20th century (Hornung, "Postmoderne" 363).

[23] Neorealistic writing is based on a minimalist style resulting from close observation. In particular, Frederick Barthelme, who writes for *The New Yorker*, makes use of it by developing the minimalist style his brother Donald makes use of in his prose. In his short stories, he draws helpless and disoriented figures, who fail in their everyday life as they are not able to communicate with others – a major theme also in Raymond Carver's *What We Talk About When We talk About Love* (1981). Here, the minimalist style based on the depiction of only a few details and the concentration on a minimum of characters underlines the figures' major motives: their aggression and selfishness (Hornung, "Postmoderne" 363).

The desert-like "nowhere" in the sense of a protective wall Daniel Quinn tries to construct around himself can be regarded as a consequence of the depicted chaos. He tries to hide from the outside world and simultaneously yearns to melt with the confusing network of streets spreading themselves out into the infinite. Quinn hopes to become as anonymous as possible (74) and so he seems to be the postmodern man par excellence who is "lost, not only in the city, but within himself as well" (4). To put it even more generally, "space and the self are coeval" (Alford, "Spaced-Out" 631), i.e., the depicted city is suffused with the trace of différance and thus reflects the deconstructed subject.

For Quinn, it is a "hypertextual" area (Rosello 139), "an inexhaustible space, a labyrinth of endless steps" (Auster, *City* 4). Each street of the network points to an infinity of other streets and places similar to the signifiers in space and time. Within this maze, wandering becomes "a kind of mindlessness" (74) in the sense of an inner emptiness. The protagonist's thoughts disseminate into all kinds of directions. The image of the moving, perpetually changing sky at the end of his novel underlines this:

> He [Quinn] saw that, above all, the sky was never still. Even on cloudless days, when the blue seemed to be everywhere, there were constant little shifts, gradual disturbances as the sky thinned out and grew thick, the sudden whitenesses of planes, birds, and flying papers . . . Nothing lasted very long. The colors would soon disperse, merging with others and moving on or fading as the night appeared. (140)

When Quinn eventually follows Stillman, Sr., he exclusively devotes himself to another person's random thoughts and movements. Wandering becomes the only important thing he is preoccupied with until he feels more and more disoriented in this "city of glass, a world of mirrors and multiple reflections, in which signs are purely arbitrary" (Malmgren 190). The glass is of course an image for the transparency of everything, for the fact that anything might be possible (Auster, *City* 4). Hence it is compatible with the images of the sky or the city map by mirroring Derridean dissemination.

However, Stillman's and thus also Quinn's wanderings through the city of mirrors and doubles only appear arbitrary on the surface. The former in fact pursues a more than well-thought out aim, i.e., the creation of "pure logos," which Quinn indirectly becomes dependent on. By merging into the detective Paul Auster and thus emptying himself, Quinn is soon unable to dissociate himself from the urban brokenness surrounding him. Although Stillman, Sr., actively characterizes New York as "the most forlorn of places, the most abject," where the "brokenness is everywhere, the disarray is universal" (94), Quinn paradoxically accepts this shattered state as his inner condition and finally turns into a tramp.

Auster foreshadows this "ending" with the ironized "Hotel Harmony" where Stillman, Sr., stays. It is a place for "winos and vagabonds" (69), marked by the trace of death: "The place stank of cockroach repellant and dead cigarettes. A few of the tenants, with nowhere to go in the rain, were sitting in the lobby, sprawled out on orange plastic chairs. The place seemed blank, a hell of stale thoughts" (104-105). Surprisingly, the creepy, repulsive atmosphere of the hotel does not seem to have any effect on Quinn. This paradox of not being touched by the outside world and at the same time melting into it is also expressed on the last pages of the novel, when Quinn reaches the end of his red notebook. Although the words "no longer [have] anything to do with him" (156), he hopes to keep on writing infinitely. Consequently, the red notebook can be interpreted as an image of the wandering mind, since Quinn's memories disseminate like the different colors of the sky when he fills the empty pages.

Before (or after?) having come to its end, "Quinn literally vanishes" (Russell 75). He is swallowed by the space surrounding him, because his "signifiers are omitted from the printed page" (Russell 75). With his last words "'What will happen where there are no more pages in the red notebook?'" (Auster, *City* 157), Auster stimulates the reader's imagination, i.e., his/her ability to question the plot and to invent new stories of the second Stillman, Sr., or Quinn himself. Hence he fulfills Derrida's demand for "a different writing space [which] must be found, a space which writing has always claimed for itself" (Derrida, "Freud" 222). It is, as in the case of *City of Glass*, a space where the signifiers have the chance to disseminate indefinitely into all directions, where the traces aim at an unlimited number of references. The text consequently opens up an active reading process. According to Derrida, it "must aim at a certain relationship, unperceived by the writer, between what he commands and what he does not command of the patterns of language that he uses" (qtd. in Barry, *Beginning Theory* 69). With Quinn and the other figures suddenly vanishing and with the help of hypertextual references, Auster makes this active reading process possible. The ending of the book is marked by the trace of death, which, however, hints at a yet undiscovered exteriority rooted within the text. It is deconstructed in itself.

3.3.3. The denial of logocentrism or the hopeless attempt to rebuild the Tower of Babel

When Quinn decides to pursue Stillman, Sr. (actually, one of the two), he soon recognizes that Stillman's "eyes [are] permanently fixed on the pavement, as though he [is] searching for something" (Auster, *City* 72). The latter's focus on certain objects on the street, which reminds Quinn of the behavior of an archeologist (72), mirrors his quest for words of a "pure," forgotten language. Soon Quinn becomes fascinated of this pure language. When following each of Stillman's steps, he begins to copy his way of wandering that at first seems to be "a meaningless project" (73). However, with his decision to make notes of each of Stillman's movements, Quinn develops into a second archeologist trying to get to the bottom of certain clues. The red notebook carried around by them both illustrates this sort of doubling.

Furthermore, Quinn's way of recording or archiving reveals his yearning for orientation and is a working against (his own) forgetfulness. In chapter 2.7. of this analysis, Derrida's interpretation of the process of archiving has been depicted. To repeat it briefly, Derrida emphasizes that the process of archiving indeed happens at the moment of forgetting, of amnesia incited by some Freudian death drive: "the archive takes place at the place of originary and structural breakdown of the said memory" (11). He thus calls the archive an "accumulation and capitalization of memory" (12), a home or stockroom for past incidents being at risk of disappearing in man's consciousness. In Auster's *City of Glass*, Quinn also tries to gather material that would otherwise be lost and thus equals Paul Auster himself when he tried to compile his fragmentary memories of his father by writing *The Invention of Solitude*.

On Quinn's walks through the labyrinth of the city, Stillman, Sr., can be interpreted as Quinn's "'father hold[ing] the key to finding a way back to pure logos" by leading him (Russell 74). Although Quinn rightly observes that the objects Stillman is collecting are nothing but broken things, which will not be of any value any more (Russell 72), he does not abandon his belief in this self-proclaimed father of speech. In other words, he is unable to read the clues presented to him and will thus fail as a detective by preserving his hunger for paternal authority. His attempt to archive lost memories by filling the pages of his notebook will not lead him anywhere.

In other words, Auster declares Stillman, Sr.'s, linguistic and theological logocentric theory, which Quinn becomes dependent on, null and void and, by doing so, acts as a spokesman for the Judaic emphasis on diversity and difference. This objective is expressed in the story about the building of the Tower of Babel in Genesis which Auster works into his anti-detective novel. By doing so, he is close to Derrida, who in *Monolingualism of the Other* emphasizes that "there is no such thing as absolute monolingualism" (7). From the beginning of *City of Glass*, Auster turns Stillman's, and later also Quinn's, glorification of the Tower of Babel as an essential logocentric center upside down, as well as their attempt to be a new Adam by giving each thing and living being its proper name (Kierkegaard 168). Hence, like Derrida, he obviously speaks against the imposition of a single, universal language – and indirectly against any politics aimed at uniformity.

Auster, for example, ironizes Stillman in the scene when he presents him as the intellectual successor of (the fictitious) Henry Dark, seemingly the private secretary of John Milton, who spoke in favor of the possibility of establishing the center of truth and innocence within language (Auster, *City* 57). Quinn however does not have a clue who this Henry Dark is: "'Nineteen sixty,' he said aloud. He tried to conjure up an image of Henry Dark, but nothing came to him. In his mind he saw only fire, a blaze of burning books" (59) – a foreshadowing of the fact that Stillman's own book, "The Garden and the Tower: Early Visions of the New World," will vanish with him altogether.

In his book, Stillman tries to show that after the fall of man, "[n]ames became detached from things; words developed into a collection of arbitrary signs; language had been severed from God" (52). Adam, in his view, did not fulfill God's directions and must consequently be held responsible for the splitting up of signifier and signified – in short, for "the fall of language" (52). Stillman now sees the sense of his life in undoing this division, in searching for the unity which once seemed to have existed. He tries to make the signifier correspond to the signified (Holzapfel 45 and Nealon 100), to weed out the arbitrariness of the sign and thus the "impure" state of language in general. The destination of his wanderings is a pre-Saussurean point in time where a "prelapsarian language" (Auster, *City* 57) based on the total concurrence of things and names might hopefully be implemented (Malmgren 192):

> 'A new language?'
>
> 'Yes. A language that will at last say what we have to say. For our words no longer correspond to the world. When things were whole, we felt confident that our words could express them. But little by little these things have broken apart, shattered, collapsed into chaos. And yet our words have remained the same. They have not adapted themselves to the new reality. Hence, every time we try to speak what we see, we speak falsely, distorting the very thing we are trying to represent. It's made a mess of everything. . . . (92-93)

According to this passage, Stillman, Sr., and later also his "son" Quinn represent the old Babylonian dream of being united by one language forever. By glorifying the Tower of Babel as the symbol for complete understanding, they do not only speak for the suppression of every diversity, but also support human hubris on the whole. In fact, they ignore the Judaic interpretation of this Old Testament parable which is completely opposed to their way of thinking: God's act of confusing the Semites' language was not only unavoidable, but essential, since it went along with the necessary evocation of differences between men.

By letting Stillman, Sr., finally vanish out of the text, Auster clearly declares himself in favor of this Judaic interpretation. He, as well as Derrida, perhaps *the* postmodern spokesman for the complex nature of language and a necessary, radical skepticism about words ("White Mythology" 248), find themselves corroborated by the story of the Tower of Babel. For the philosopher, "this story recounts, among other things, the origin of the confusion of tongues, the irreducible multiplicity of idioms . . ." ("Des Tours de Babel" 253). He also emphasizes that God here "interrupts . . . the colonial violence or the linguistic imperialism" (253) signified by the Semites' dedication to a universal tongue and their decision to "bring the world to reason" (253).

Similarly, Auster speaks against colonization when Stillman's attempt to create a map based on the letters of the three words "Tower of Babel" comes to nothing. The "culprit's" undertaking of inserting one specific concept of truth or of order into space (Rosello 130 and Holzapfel 39) ends abruptly when Stillman commits suicide. To be more precise, Stillman's identification with Henry Dark is turned upside down. The latter seemingly saw America as the ideal country for the "paradisiacal" erection of "the new Babel" (Auster, *City* 59), as "a symbol for the resurrection of the human spirit" (59). Yet Stillman's wanderings, which can be compared to the early settlers' move to the New World, will not lead him anywhere.

With this "ending," Auster indirectly criticizes the 17th-century Puritan conviction of being the newly "chosen people" for the creation of the "promised land." To put it more generally, he speaks out against any colonial intention of occupying another country on the basis of a philosophy of superiority. At the same time he declares himself in favor of the Judaic understanding of the promised land as "a mythical Israel, held up as a model and ideal" (Atlan, "Chosen People" 56) one needs to keep on looking for, and not as a definite, static, and irrevocable reality. "The election is one of duty, not of rights or attributes" (56), as Henry Atlan emphasizes.[24] This ethical necessity is also expressed by Derrida in "A Testimony Given." Here, he points out that the Judaic belief in being the chosen people means, above all, to be responsible for one's behavior and thus for the other (41).

The Judaic understanding of homecoming, of reaching the promised land is most clearly expressed in chapter 26 of Deuteronomy, which "speaks in the future perfect tense of blessings made palpable, promises fulfilled, covenantal relations of justice and harmony with one's fellows" (Eisen 221). The declared predictions will, however, only come true if one sticks to the law: chapter 28 is about the certainty that God will put a (renewed) curse on His people if it disobeys Him. Home thus means "an affair of the imagination" (Eisen 221), a destination that remains to be desired forever.

Auster expresses this belief in the promised land as an unobtainable place on Earth by making use of Jacques Derrida's concept of dissemination. Stillman, Sr.'s, multiple associations of Quinn's name foreshadow that their attempt to construct a new promised land by creating presence in language will finally dissolve or "fly off" into space and time:

[24] Similarly, Arnold Eisen points out that "Home, for Jews, would always mean far more than conquest, which in any event could never establish absolute ownership. It is rather a state of being, which land makes possible but cannot in and of itself establish; it is a sacred order of commandment in which the curses pronounced in the Garden of Eden are in large measure reversed" ("Exile" 221).

> 'Hmmm. Very interesting. I see many possibilities for this word, this Quinn, this . . . quintessence . . . of quiddity. Quick, for example. And quill. And quack. And quirk. Hmmm. Rhymes with grin. Not to speak of kin. Hmmm. Very interesting. And win. And fin. And din. And gin. And pin. And tin. And bin. Hmmm. Even rhymes with djinn. Hmmm. And if you say it right, with been. Hmmm. Yes, very interesting. I like your name enormously, Mr. Quinn. It flies off in so many directions at once.' (Auster, *City* 90)

In parallel, Quinn's diagrams of Stillman's walks "look like a map of some imaginary state in the Midwest" (Auster, *City* 82) and thus illustrate the attempt of mastering space – but at the same time are an image of paths arbitrarily running into each other and forming a network in which the wanderer yearns for orientation. Thus they also reveal forgetfulness (Alford, "Spaced-Out" 627-28), since Quinn is unable to connect Stillman's walks in the city with certain buildings. The "culprit's" steps, and, with them, the whole project of building a new Tower of Babel, are not clearly taken down anywhere and will hence neither be remembered by Quinn, nor by anyone else: "It was like drawing a picture in the air with your finger. The image vanishes as you are making it. There is no result, no trace to mark what you have done" (Auster, *City* 86).

However, Quinn "disbelieves the arbitrariness of Stillman's actions" (83) until the fictitious Paul Auster tells him that the latter has jumped off Brooklyn Bridge. He does not accept that he is caught in a desert-like place, a maze of ideas and things where "[t]he center is everywhere" (9). He is unable to give up his dependence on paternal authority and talks himself into the clarity of signs – the worst thing a detective can do. After he has had his conversation with the fictitious Paul Auster, he calls, for example, Virginia, Stillman, Jr.'s wife, several times and clings to the busy signal which paradoxically stands for stability and hope: "The busy signal, he saw now, had not been arbitrary. It had been a sign, and it was telling him that he could not yet break his connection with the case, even if he wanted to" (Auster, *City* 132).

Quinn's missing sensitivity for a suitable interpretation of signs finally leads to the failure of his project of tracking down logocentric ideas. His attempt to complete a jigsaw puzzle with certain fragments by walking in Stillman's footsteps will not lead him anywhere but into extreme solitude and isolation. This, of course, means that his desire to come closer to a father-figure remains unfulfilled. The anonymity between "father" and "son" goes hand in hand with the protagonist's loss of the past and his forgetfulness and also mirrors itself in the deconstruction of God's name, as the following chapter will show.

3.3.4. The deconstructed God on Earth and the Judaic belief that life lies within death

Stillman, Sr.'s, role as Quinn's father-figure doubles itself in the relationship between Stillman, Sr., and his "real" son Peter – with the difference that Quinn chooses this "father of logos" of his own free will, whereas Peter, as a child, was abused by his father for the paradoxical aim of finding God's language. This quest is deconstructed from the beginning, while Stillman, Jr., distorts the meaning of God as man's father. When he talks to Quinn, the name of God is a randomly chosen word that could stand for anything in a variety of different contexts:

> This is what my wife says. She says the father talked about God. That is a funny word to me. When you put it backwards, it spells dog. And a dog is not much like God, is it? Woof woof. Bow wow. Those are dog words. I think they are beautiful. So pretty and true. Like the words I make up. (*City* 23)

Similarly, when Quinn has become part of Stillman, Sr.'s, logocentric undertaking of constructing the Tower of Babel for a second time, he will regard God's name as nothing but a word fragment, a scrap of conversation that suddenly appears on the surface, but that does not have any deeper meaning. It is only a signifier of the past hinting at Quinn's (and others') separation from religion in the postmodern present time:

> The last two letters remained – the 'E' and the 'L.' Quinn's mind dispersed. He arrived in a neverland of fragments, a place of wordless things and thingless words. Then, struggling through his torpor one last time, he told himself that El was the ancient Hebrew for God. (87)

This passage could also be interpreted in the way that Quinn, while being surrounded by fragments, scraps, or remnants only, suddenly filters out some significance to the extent that God's name seemingly corroborates his attempt to pinpoint the clues given to him by Stillman, Sr. What we can, however, definitely argue is that Quinn's sudden recognition of God's name will not have any consequences for him. On the contrary, the following two lines anticipate the ending, while they also hint at the connection of Quinn's and Stillman, Jr.'s, past experiences: "In his dream, which he later forgot, he found himself in the town dump of his childhood, sifting through a mountain of rubbish" (87).

To sum up, in Quinn's logocentric quest, his ongoing search for definite meaning and truth which will arrive at nothing, his inner wound, the unfulfilled desire to come closer to a self-chosen father-figure, is entangled. This unsatisfied yearning also reflects itself in the depiction of God's name: it seems to be nothing but a fragment of thought flying off into all sorts of imaginable directions. Within the postmodern world, the reality of mirrors and doubles, a definite concept of God cannot be made out, as the image of the sky also shows: "the sky would remain hidden, inaccessible even at the farthest limit of sight" (152).

After Quinn has developed into some sort of hunger artist, he no longer has interest in himself and changes into nothingness. However, he momentarily reaches purity by passively watching the moment of his death and of his birth at the same time. With this deconstruction of the closure of death, Auster hints at the Jewish belief in a "cycle of an eternal return to the Garden of Eden, which began personally with the birth of the individual and mythically with the expulsion from paradise" (Abramovitch, "Death" 134). Quinn seemingly fulfills what Stillman, Sr., tried to explain to him: "We exist, but we have not yet achieved the form that is our destiny. We are pure potential, an example of the not-yet-arrived" (Auster, *City* 98). However, we do not find out whether Quinn has indeed reached any original source or afterlife. Auster lets his protagonist mysteriously vanish out of the text into space and time. Thus he also expresses Jewish modern thought which emphasizes man's inability to foresee what will happen to the soul at the threshold between life and death (Abramovitch 132). A definite answer is not given, and the reader is left alone or even lost.

3.4. *In the Country of Last Things* – an apocalyptic vision at the end of the 20th century

In an interview with Larry McCaffery and Sinda Gregory, Paul Auster emphasizes that he began writing his epistolary novel *In the Country of Last Things* (1987) in the early 1970s, when he was publishing his first poems. Until the middle of the 1980s, he felt compelled to work on his idea to draw an apocalyptic scenery and to depict its effects on man from a woman's perspective. For years, this writing process, which again connects postmodern with neorealistic techniques, was extremely challenging for Auster, and so difficult that he almost gave up:

> In many ways, writing that book was like taking dictation. I heard her voice speaking to me – and that voice was utterly distinct from my own. In that sense, there was almost no difficulty at all.
>
> But when you consider that I first heard that voice in 1970 and didn't finish the book until 1985, it's safe to conclude that it was a very difficult book to write. I didn't want to do it. (319)

In the Berg Collection at the New York Public Library, very early typescripts of Auster's apocalyptic novel,[25] titled "Letters from the City" and "Dead Letters," can be found, next to "City of Words" analyzed in chapter 3.1.1. of this investigation.[26] Some of them are very similar to certain passages of the published novel and show the interconnection of Jewishness with a deconstructive style of writing at a very early stage. They also illustrate that Auster's prose writing refers to his poetry and vice versa. Indeed, the Jewish motive of becoming separated from one's roots and of perpetually yearning to arrive at a yet indistinct, but nevertheless promising destination again appears in Auster's 1987 novel.

[25] Auster's 1987 novel refers to Jewish-Christian apocalyptic literature, for example to *The Book of Daniel* (150 B.C.E.) (Glatzer 20). Here, Daniel interprets Nebuchadnezzar's dream of four world empires succeeding each other. The last terrible pagan empire will be destroyed by God, who Himself will rule in eternity (Dan. 2.29-45). In a similar vision, four animals representing four kingdoms rise from the sea, whereas the fourth one is the most dreadful one (Dan. 7.1-15). This beast or empire will devour and crush the Earth. However, it is defeated at court, and eventually "one like a human being [comes] with the clouds of heaven" (Dan. 7.14). This Messiah resembling man rings in a new era, an everlasting one that will rescue the pious ones, but dooms the suppressors "to reproaches, to everlasting abhorrence" (Dan. 12.1-2). Another example of apocalyptic literature is the third part of *The Book of Isaiah*. Here, different words of salvation are loosely connected that culminate in the description of Zion, the City of God, where only the just and peaceful will rule (Isa. 60.1-23). The end of *The Book of Isaiah* finally celebrates the expected redemption and renewal in the last days (Isa. 65.16-25). In *In the Country of Last Things,* Paul Auster does not hint at the salvation of man in the future. But with his heroine Anna Blume struggling in this world of decay and doing her utmost for those who suffer even more than herself, he clearly expresses "Jewish hopes for better days to come" (Glatzer 22). Moreover, he gives a detailed description of her apocalyptic surroundings. By doing so, Auster acts similarly to the visionaries of the Old Testament, speaking in allegories, allusions, or dreams (Glatzer 19).

[26] Paul Auster kindly looked over the early typescripts used here and gave me permission to quote from them.

It is the paradoxical act of circling around this wound that Derrida speaks of in "A Testimony Given" and that Auster also refers to in his 1987 novel. Indeed, the Jewish protagonist Anna Blume,[27] who tries to find her brother in a nightmarish urban place, hopes to cope with her present situation by writing a letter to an anonymous friend in her intact past (Washburn 62).[28] She tries to depict what she sees and feels in this apocalyptic world as precisely as possible and thus indirectly confronts herself with her inner wound of having become separated from everything she was used to in her intact past. However, the more Anna faces the present reality, the less she is able to grasp the consequences of her decision to have left her past behind and instead live in a city of decay. Her letter is an attempt to cope with the effects of her separation from home; yet she can hold onto her words only temporarily as nothing can be taken for granted any more:

> Bit by bit, the city robs you of certainty. There can never be any fixed path, and you can survive only if nothing is necessary to you. Without warning, you must be able to change, to drop what you are doing, to reverse. In the end, there is nothing that is not the case. (Auster, *In the Country* 6)

In other words, the act of circling around the wound of separation, which Jacques Derrida emphasizes in "A Testimony Given," encloses a paradox in *In the Country of Last Things*, too. On the one hand, Auster stresses the desire to face this inner wound courageously; on the other hand, he points out the inability to grasp its effects in detail. At the same time, this paradoxical undertaking seems to be connected with the

[27] The name is taken from Kurt Schwitters' poem "Anna Blume." By using it, Auster praises his protagonist's heroic behavior similar to the lyrical I in Schwitters's poem singing of the woman he admires. However, with Anna Blume's attempt to write a coherent letter to her friend, he also distances himself from the Dadaistic writing aiming at an aesthetics of absurdity.

[28] In contrast to most of his poems, *The Invention of Solitude*, and also some passages of *City of Glass*, Auster now stresses the confrontation with the external world and the turn to the other. In Auster's unpublished, early poem "Land's End" and its prose version "City of Words," which was actually the title he first had in mind for *In the Country of Last Things,* this development is already traced out. The image of the "message in a bottle" in "Land's End" exemplifies the attempt to get in touch with an other. This undertaking is, however, doomed to failure since it is unlikely that the addressed person will ever get the written lines as is the case of Anna Blume's friend.

playful movement of signifiers which is marked by spacial and temporal difference. The more words the protagonist tries to put on paper, the more often she is confronted with a network of supplemented signifiers which are able to postpone any notion of 'presence' to a later time. Or, in short, it is the movement of différance that in Auster's 1987 novel seems to be linked with the impossibility of comprehending the consequences of an inner wound, i.e., of being uprooted and yearning for a better place to live.

Moreover, the protagonist's division from her Jewish roots is mirrored by a language that is in constant danger to dissolve: "The story starts and stops, goes forward and then loses itself, and between each word, what silences, what words escape and vanish, never to be seen again" (38). Because of the dissemination and disappearance of words, ideas, and memories, Anna Blume will not get any answer to the question where her brother has gone to or why she cannot leave the nightmarish city any more. In more general terms, she will not get any closer to the origin of her wound. The playful movement of signifiers blocks the way towards it, as Derrida puts it in "A Testimony Given" (55). Consequently, Blume does not only feel separated from her roots, but also from language itself, similarly to the I-narrator of *The Invention of Solitude* or Quinn in *City of Glass*. In his early unpublished piece "City of Words," Auster already emphasized the instability and indefiniteness of language from the perspective of a third-person narrator:

> There is no word. Only the many words that stand in the place of silence. For the city is all that cannot be said, and it is each word that drowns in the sea of words . . . . The words come, therefore, at the moment there are no more words. And they belong to no one. She writes the words from the city and then vanishes back into the city. There is no city except for the evidence of her words. And her words have been lost from the very beginning – from the moment she began to write. Nevertheless, she writes.

Very often, Anna Blume cannot think at all or does not "know how to act" (20). Her memory is a trap, it is blurred. Hence, she "stray[s] from the point" (38) when she is writing, although she is trying hard to "[read] between the lines and . . . to fill in the gaps herself" (48). Until the end, Blume makes every effort to put her fragmentary memories and words together as if doing a jigsaw puzzle, although she is sure that she finally has to surrender. In other words, her letter seems like a "fragile tent of words erected in the desert," as Derrida puts it in his analysis of Edmond

Jabès' writing ("Edmond Jabès" 69). "Death strolls between [the] letters" (71) similarly to Jabès' *Book of Questions*. It is an existential experience of desolation that is at the core of Auster's apocalyptic novel and connected with the protagonist's struggle to capture what she experiences and remembers with words. However, Blume will not get any definite answers. The idea of an unequivocal truth fades away from the very beginning of her letter. Until the last page, her writing process is a constant questioning of human existence, an ongoing search for answers.

Moreover, with Blume's uprooting and her walk into a country of decay, Auster indirectly refers to the history of Judaism, too, which is marked by the experience of dispersion, torture, and death. In his essay on Jabès, Derrida calls it an "ageless wound" from which Jabès' writing seems to grow ("Edmond Jabès" 64). In parallel, Anna Blume starts writing out of an inner necessity. Her experience of having become separated from her past becomes the prerequisite of her writing which is, however, doomed to failure. She is forced to stay in the city, where she aimlessly wanders around, such as Daniel Quinn in *City of Glass,* and incessantly looks for a possibility to escape. Like Jabès, Auster replaces the Jewish image of old age, the desert, with the city as an image of modernity, which stands for separation, alienation, and yearning. Besides, it is characterized by supplementation and spacing. By walking through the confusing street-network, the protagonist can get lost easily. As with his anti-detective novel *City of Glass,* Auster is close to Derrida again, who depicts the city as a "labyrinth" by quoting Jabès. In this labyrinth, as Derrida points out, "*we will go over the same way ten times, a hundred times . . . And all these pathways have their own pathways. – Otherwise they would not be pathways*'" ("Edmond Jabès" 69).

In short, with Anna Blume, who is separated from home and her Jewish past and incessantly walks through a desert-like urban labyrinth, Auster seems to refer to Jewish experience in a wider sense. "Every writer in some way experiences the Jewish condition," Jabès emphasizes in the interview with Paul Auster, in the sense that that the book becomes "a kind of exile" for the writer (Auster, "Providence" 149). By continuing to fill the pages of her notebook in spite of the decay and violence threatening her, Anna Blume seems to experience the "Jewish condition" which Jabès speaks of. At the same time, she is, in contrast to Daniel Quinn in *City of Class*, ready to face her surroundings realistically. With her strong will and ability to open herself up to complete strangers, Auster portrays her as a heroine contrasted to all apocalyptic portents.

3.4.1. Writing out of wounds and the deconstruction of writing

The longer Anna Blume lives in the city, the more she understands that she will not be able to get out of it. In her letter, she tells about the government's "Sea Wall Project," a political measure which prevents the urbanites to flee into a neighboring country. On a more existential level, the Sea Wall can be interpreted as an image for the protagonist's inability to reach home. The way to her intact past will always be blocked: "Just because you are able to get in, that does not mean you will be able to get out" (85). Similar to *The Invention of Solitude*, the lasting separation from Jewish roots is underlined by the dissemination of signifiers, which constantly change their meaning:

> Entrances do not become exits, and there is nothing to guarantee that the door you walked through a moment ago will still be there when you turn around to look for it again. That is how it works in the city. Every time you think you know the answer to a question, you discover that the question makes no sense. (85)

To use Jacques Derrida's words, it is the movement of 'différance' that again "bars the origin," as he puts it in "A Testimony Given" (55). Anna Blume's desire to get closer to her origin will not be satisfied, since the origin is constantly differed and deferred and thus divided from itself. Moreover, she tries hard to remember details of her idyllic childhood, "to store [them] up for later," "to hold on to [them]" for the possibly even more disastrous future:

> Sometimes, when I find myself groping for a thought that has eluded me, I begin to drift off to the old days back home, remembering how it used to be when I was a little girl and the whole family would go up north on the train for summer holidays. . . . It was always so beautiful to me, so much more beautiful than the things in the city, and every year I would say to myself, Anna, you have never seen anything more beautiful than this – try to remember it, try to memorize all the beautiful things you are seeing, and in that way they will always be with you, even when you can't see them anymore. (88)

Yet Blume must admit that, as a child, she did not succeed in remembering the things she was astonished of or even overwhemed by. The beauty she was surrounded by did not become a part of herself for any longer time, so that now, as an adult, she cannot fall back on it: "But the odd thing was that none of it ever stayed with me. I tried so hard, but somehow or other I always wound up losing it, and in the end the only thing I could remember was how hard I tried" (88). In other words, Blume's present situation, her imprisonment at a disastrous place and her inability to flee from it, can be referred back to her childhood when she already lost contact to her family. It is not only a present, but a lifelong inability to hold onto past moments that the protagonist writes about in her letter. Her memories have always been disseminating and erasing each other; the result is a feeling of emptiness, an inner void which she cannot ignore:

> The things themselves passed too quickly, and by the time I saw them they were already flying out of my head, replaced by still more things that vanished before I could see them. The only thing that remains for me is a blur, a bright and beautiful blur. But the trees and the sky and the water – all that is gone. It was always gone, even before I had it. (88)

The disastrous happenings in the city mirror Blume's dilemma, i.e., her desire to get hold of her intact past, which, however, eludes itself over and over again. In parallel, she needs to observe her surroundings as precisely as possible and, at the same time, to distance herself from them in order to survive. But since her inner self is already wounded, she is unable to grasp what she sees. At the same time, she cannot separate herself from the dead bodies lying in the streets or the buildings being destroyed daily. She is affected by what she is surrounded by, but cannot do anything about it – just as little as she can change anything about her lost past:

> That is what I mean by being wounded; you cannot merely see, for each thing somehow belongs to you, is part of the story unfolding inside you. It would be good, I suppose, to make yourself so hard that nothing could affect you anymore. But then you would be alone, so totally cut off from everyone else that life would become impossible. (19)

Besides, Anna Blume is, more or less than all urbanites, forced to hunger, to "eat as little as [she] can" (*In the Country* 2). This hunger is not an aesthetic, self-chosen one like Daniel Quinn's in *City of Glass*, but, first and foremost, a literal, existential one. Actually, Blume tries to avoid meeting men like Quinn, Kafkaesque hunger artists, "who eat without ever filling themselves" (4). In contrast to them, she only tries to get those portions that keep her from dying. However, her hunger helps

Blume not to give up. It becomes a hunger for survival that paradoxically keeps her going. At the same time, her hunger will never be stilled completely since her life is constantly threatened. Moments of hope in which she finds food, shelter, and love, in particular by meeting Sam, Isabel, and Victoria, are often followed by disastrous experiences:

> This much is certain. If not for my hunger, I wouldn't be able to go on. You must get used to doing with as little as you can. By wanting less, you are content with less, and the less you need, the better off you are. That is what the city does to you. It turns your thoughts inside out. It makes you want to live, and at the same time it tries to take your life away from you. (2-3)

Since her hunger for food and security cannot be stilled, she begins to write. Words become, as in *City of Glass* and *The Invention of Solitude*, an existential necessity, a means to survive. By writing her letter to her undisclosed friend, Anna Blume tries to cope with her calamitous, ruinous surroundings and with the fact that she is a wounded being: "if I don't quickly write it down, my head will burst" (3).

Furthermore, Anna hopes to prevent her thoughts from vanishing with the help of writing. She tries hard to compile all details of her past which are at risk of becoming lost. Her aim is to reveal what has already been covered or hidden in her mind and to save her present impressions from vanishing. In short, she tries to fight against her own forgetfulness with a piece of writing that is directed towards the past, the present, and the future (Kiely 32). In this way, her letter becomes a kind of archive in the Derridean sense of the term, a "home" or "stockroom" for present experiences and past memories of the private and the public sphere. According to Derrida, the death drive, which affects man's memory, is the prerequisite for every archive. "There is no archive fever without the threat of this death drive," he maintains (*Archive Fever* 19). In other words, the possibility that memories and impressions might get lost awake the yearning for an archive. In parallel, Anna Blume's letter is an archive-like piece of writing that is more than necessary because of the disappearance of thoughts at the moment of death:

> It's not just that things vanish – but once they vanish, the memory of them vanishes as well. Dark areas form in the brain, and unless you make a constant effort to summon up the things that are gone, they will quickly be

lost forever. I am no more immune to this disease than anyone else, and no doubt there are many such blanks inside me. (87)[29]

Because of these blanks in her mind, Anna Blume faces the probability of a permanent wound, i.e., that she will lose her memory of her past altogether. Consequently, she tries hard to make sense of her disseminating thoughts similar to Daniel Quinn. She creates "islands of intactness" (36), accumulations of idyllic memories, and tries to connect them with each other like the unbroken objects she finds on the street. Her aim is "to store [them] up for later" (88). This future moment may be a time when she will need her memories even more than she does now, or it may be a time when the letter will possibly be found. Whatever happens, the act of writing expresses Anna's will to survive in this ruinous world causing and mirroring her inner wounds.

In an interview with Larry McCaffery and Sinda Gregory, Paul Auster points out that while he was working on *In the Country of Last Things*, he thought of "Anna Blume walking through the twentieth century" (320). This quotation can be understood in the way that he connected his theme of the wound, i.e., the separation from (Jewish) roots, with the depiction of present realities, including the pollution of capital cities and the destruction of certain ecosystems. In particular, he aimed at referring to disasters of the immediate past, the Shoah and the battles of the Second World War (Little 147):

> There are specific references to the Warsaw ghetto and the siege of Leningrad, but also to events taking place in the Third World today – not to speak of New York, which is rapidly turning into a Third World city before our eyes. The garbage system, which I describe at such great length in the novel, is loosely based on the present-day garbage system in Cairo. All in all, there's very little invented material in the book. ("Interview with McCaffery and Gregory" 321)[30]

[29] Katharine Washburn calls Anna Blume a "rare agent of memory" and relates the style of her letter to "the tone and urgency of Anne Frank's *Diary of a Young Girl*" (1949). In addition to their similar names, the girl and the young woman are connected by the "intolerable present" they are forced to face (65).

[30] With his vision of an intolerable state, Auster intertextually includes 19th- and 20th-century literature in his novel which circles around the same theme. Nathaniel Hawthorne's short story "The Celestial Railroad" (1846) for instance contributes an epigraph to *In the Country of Last Things*: "Not a great while ago, passing through the gate of dreams, I visited that region of the earth in which lies the famous City of

By alluding to the effects of fascism and to present Western politics creating class differences and racial conflicts, Auster circles around death as the essence of 20th-century life and links it with his protagonist's struggle not to lose contact with her past. Like *The Invention of Solitude* and *City of Glass,* the epistolary novel starts off from the moment of death. As Auster's mouthpiece, Anna Blume begins her letter to her undisclosed friend from her intact past in the following way: "These are the last things, she wrote. One by one they disappear and never come back" (1). With her archive-like piece of writing, Blume revolts against this seemingly given fact. However, the more she yearns to accumulate her disseminating present impressions and past memories, the more often she must admit that she cannot prevent them from vanishing. She circles around her origins and wounds, but in contrast to Daniel Quinn in *City of Glass* or the I-narrator of "Portrait of an Invisible Man," she is far more realistic. She sees through the fact that the longer she keeps on writing, the less she will be able to hold onto her senses and remembrance. From the moment she arrived in the "country of last things," she has been conscious of the fact that her writing is, like Quinn's notebook, doomed to failure.

In an unpublished early typescript, Auster stresses that the act of writing a letter can only substitute the necessity of food for a while. The writer's thoughts disappear into the unknown so that he will lose his taste for words altogether: "This letter is a gradual process of starvation, it will end on the day I can't eat another morsel, at the moment I've lost taste for food." In *In the Country of Last Things*, Anna similarly understands that she has been infected by "the process of erasure" (89) from the early beginning, by the "illness" of letting thoughts slip through the network of memory. Although she starts her writing project, she knows that she will remain unable to get to the bottom of herself by raising her forgotten memories up to the surface: "I can't help it if there are gaps in my memory. Certain events refuse to reappear, and no matter how hard I struggle, I am powerless to unearth them" (125). In short, Anna's desire to approach her roots by accumulating her memories and present impressions will not be satisfied.

Destruction." In parallel, the reader is prompted to think of George Orwell's *Nineteen Eighty-Four* (1948). Auster, however, does not deal with the structures or prerequisites of dictatorship and corrupted politics, but with the effects on the people, foremost with the phenomena of homelessness, hunger, and death.

Besides, Samuel Farr, the former colleague of Anna's brother William and her later partner, is equally affected by the erasure of consciousness. The stories he tells Anna after the library, his home, has burnt down, lack coherence. He can neither remember certain past events nor unravel his thoughts that run freely into each other (161). As a consequence, Anna and Sam defend themselves against any metaphysical illusion of ever coming to a clear solution of their present situation. At the end, they try to flee from the "country of last things," but they know that anything might happen on their way. They understand that they will repeatedly fail in their attempt "to read the signs" (6), or, in other words, to regard the city as a text that has to be analyzed carefully (Woods, "'Looking for Signs in the Air'" 115). This necessity is deconstructed from the beginning, since the signifier and the signified constantly change their meaning, supplement, and erase each other. Until the end, everything remains uncertain and confusing:

> But everything happens too fast here, the shifts are too abrupt, what is true one minute is no longer true the next. I have wasted much time looking for signs in the air, trying to study the atmosphere for hints of the clouds, the speed and direction of the wind, the smells at any given hour, the texture of the sky at night, the sprawls of the sunset, the intensity of the dew at dawn. But nothing has ever helped me. (Auster, *In the Country* 25)

This "process of erasure" (89) does not only have a great impact on Anna's way of thinking, but on her words as well that "tend to last a bit longer than things, but eventually they fade too, along with the pictures they once evoked" (89). Nevertheless, she keeps herself from speaking "the language of ghosts" (10), words which might trick her into believing in wishes and apparitions only. Instead, Anna gets close to people who face reality, too, by speaking a language marked by shifts and turns. One of these people is Boris Stepanovich, who uses words "as an instrument of locomotion – constantly on the move, darting and feinting, circling, disappearing, suddenly appearing again in a different spot" (146). For him, no word has a fixed meaning. Language appears as a "shifting course" (146), unstable and unpredictable. Precisely because of this movement of words, Anna's yearning to survive will never be stilled. The fragmentation of language will make her realize that her actions, including her writing, are arbitrary, a submission to chance. Although she tries hard to "[read] between the lines and . . . to fill in the gaps herself" (48), her letter remains "a series of broken recollections" (Woods, "'Looking for signs in the Air'" 119), a struggle with itself.

Paradoxically, Blume eagerly keeps on filling the pages of her notebook like Quinn, since she knows that sooner or later she will be forced to stop: “But now it is the one thing that matters to me: to have my say at last, to get it down on these pages before it is too late” (Auster, *In the Country* 79). Her writing process thus mirrors what Edmond Jabès expresses in the interview with Paul Auster (Auster, “Providence” 149). It is a never-ending search for truth of existential necessity, an incessant defense of human needs against the background of disaster and devastation. Besides, Anna does not give up her hope of finding her brother William and of leaving the apocalyptic country with her friends. She does not stop believing in finally reaching a home-like place in spite of her realistic attitude, her “hard calculation” (Auster, *In the Country* 11).

To sum up, the protagonist’s wound of having lost contact to her past is mirrored by the deconstruction of words and thoughts. Her desire to get closer to her Jewish roots is not satisfied, since her memories have always been eluding themselves. The separation from her past set in when, as a girl, she was unable to memorize the people and things she was surrounded by, when many of her experiences and impressions did not stay with her. By beginning to write, Blume hopes to lift her hidden memories up to the surface and to cope with the decay of urban life. Eagerly, she tries to accumulate her thoughts and, thus, to prevent them from vanishing. In other words, her letter resembles an archivist’s undertaking in the Derridean sense of the term. From the moment Blume begins to write, she is, however, aware that she will fail with her attempt “to store [her memories] up for later” (88) and to prevent the disintegration of language. By continuously wandering through the confusing street-network and by filling the pages of her notebook, she does not arrive at any desired destination. Consequently, the ending of her letter is deconstructed in itself. It is depicted as being “only imaginary, a destination you invent to keep yourself going, but a point comes when you will realize you will never get there” (*In the Country* 183). In other words, Anna might never reach the end of her journey, i.e., neither of her actual journey out of “the country of last things,” nor of her writing process. However, the few white unwritten pages of the novel underline its open ending, the unceasing circulation of ideas. In the reader’s imagination, Anna’s future writing might again be a “screaming into a vast and terrible blankness” (183), but she keeps on walking, hopefully into a better time.

3.4.2. *Infinite wandering as the condition of the (Jewish) writer*

Right from the beginning of *In the Country of Last Things*, Auster again makes use of the Old Testament motif of endless wandering through a desert-like, inhuman place where one can become lost from the start. The novel thus reflects, similar to *City of Glass,* Edmond Jabès' *Book of Questions* and Derrida's interpretation of it. The images of the city and the desert again refer to each other and so connect the situation of the writer with Jewish experience. Anna Blume's walks through the city of decay in fact reveal her struggle for survival. The whole object of her wandering is to find food or intact, usable things to sell: "I put one foot in front of the other, and then the other foot in front of the first, and then hope I can do it again" (2). Already around 1970, Auster indeed outlined this essential sort of wandering in a detailed unpublished typescript:

> To keep moving is the only alternative. And so it goes, from morning till night. Up and out, on my feet, from one place to the next. It's easier that way. If you can keep up the illusion of activity, a steady smile on your face, an air of agitation and purpose, there is little interference from the police, and people don't talk behind your back. Since the first day, I have been moving. I have been moving. I arrived at night, and wandered without purpose through the streets, not daring to stop, and too tired to look for a room.

In Auster's 1987 novel, Anna needs to adapt herself to her surroundings as well as she can. For weeks, her only intention is to find her way through the streets, to orientate herself by things and places she might have seen before. In other words, the metropolis is, similar to *City of Glass*, again depicted as a text suffused with the trace of différance that requires great concentration to read (Woods 115). It is a confusing network of streets spreading themselves out into the infinite, an inexhaustible space that perpetually changes (Auster, *In the Country* 2). Like Quinn or the I-narrator of "Portrait of an Invisible Man," Anna understands that she is in constant danger to feel lost: "I wandered around like a sleepwalker, not knowing where I was, not even daring to talk to anyone" (43). Anna's wandering thus leads to her inner emptiness which is paradoxically, as Isabel teaches her, the prerequisite for survival:

> Never think about anything, she said. Just melt into the street and pretend your body doesn't exist. No musings; no sadness or happiness; no anything but the street, all empty inside, concentrating only on the next step you are

> about to take. Of all the advice she gave me, it was the one thing I ever understood. (57)

Anna's thoughts often deviate from her intention to take care of herself; they disseminate like the streets themselves (77). Sometimes she becomes totally unable to keep an inner distance to the decay and suffering she is daily confronted with. In order not to melt completely with the confusing street network, she continues writing her letter with the utmost concentration. With her notebook, she hopes to hold onto her thoughts, to produce coherent sentences, and thus to keep her humanity intact. This is also true for Sam who is trying to write a long journalistic report about the city of decay. His book is of existential necessity for him because with it, he is, like Anna, able to look at himself from a distance:

> The book is the only thing that keeps me going. It prevents me from thinking about myself and getting sucked up into my own life. If I ever stopped working on it, I'd be lost. I don't think I'd make it through another day. (104)

By wandering though the city and by filling the pages, Anna, as well as Sam, develop into "object hunter[s]" (33), not only in the literal, but also in the poetic sense of the word. Both try to find unbroken, useful things on the street and, in parallel, try to think of words which express their feelings and ideas most suitably. In fact, Anna Blume meets Otto Frick, who works at Woburn House to help the homeless and also regards words as a material, i.e., as if they were "physical objects [or] literal stones" (133) (Woods 118). This material is full of paradoxes and contrasts since the signifier is divided from the signified or "sounds [are] divorced from their meanings" (Auster, *In the Country* 133). Nevertheless, words might convey a fragmentary message serving to explain the world. Otto, for example, uses his and Anna's name, both palindromes, to describe the basis of différance – that there is no end, that everything starts again:

> 'Words be what tells me how to know,' he once explained to me. 'That's why I got to be such an old man. My name is Otto. It go back and forth the same. It don't end nowhere but begin again. I get to live twice that way, twice as long as no one else. You too, miss. You be named the same as me. A-n-n-a. Back and forth the same, just like Otto myself. That's why you got to be born again. It's a blessing of luck, Miss Anna.' (133)

Besides, Anna stumbles on suitable words unintentionally: "The words come only when I think I won't be able to find them anymore" (38). Her letter reflects her wandering, uncontrollable mind as well as her often arbitrary movements through the streets of the city. By walking around, she comes across buildings, things, and people by accident and loses them again without having expected this. When she writes, meaningful passages come to her mind that she cannot, however, hold onto for a long time: "The story starts and stops, goes forward and then loses itself, and between each word, what silences, what words escape and vanish, never to be seen again" (38).

Nevertheless, by wandering aimlessly through the city, Anna trips over most useful things or accidentally meets people who give her new hope. In parallel, by filling the pages of her notebook she produces a coherent text consisting of phrases that she has partly not used before (Barone, "Introduction" 8). The intact remains of objects as well as the fragments of words connect themselves with each other to form something new: "And yet, very strangely, at the limit of all this chaos, everything begins to fuse again" (35). With the ending of her letter, Anna underlines her hope of the improbable occurring in the future. She will keep on walking to a yet unclear destination on the horizon that she will, as she is convinced, reach together with her friends. At the same moment, she is sure that she will then continue her letter. In short, writing is connected with Derrida's understanding of the Jewish image of wandering as a past, present, as well as future phenomenon: "Once we get to where we are going, I will try to write you again, I promise" (188).

3.4.3. The allusions to the Shoah and the invisible God as present realities

In *The Invention of Solitude*, both narrators remind us of past crimes, the Shoah in particular, so that they will not be committed again. For *In the Country of Last Things*, this is true as well, but now the effects of past crimes on the present are emphasized: "It is a book about our own moment," Auster stresses in an interview with Joseph Mallia (284). With this statement, he obviously means that he understands past memories of extreme suffering, for example of the Warsaw ghetto he alludes to in his novel, as a reality of our present time. They determine the world we are living in now.

With his vivid, detailed description of Anna Blume's surroundings, Paul Auster raises past memories to the surface to make the reader aware of his world, as he makes it clear in the interview: ". . . the country Anna goes to might not be immediately recognizable, but I feel that this is where we live. It could be that we've become so accustomed to it that we no longer see it" (285).

In other words, Auster indirectly hints at the need of the other, just as in *The Invention of Solitude.* According to Emmanuel Lévinas, this responsibility for the need of the other is grounded within Judaism, as he, for example, points out in his essay "The Pact" (225/26). In Auster's apocalyptic novel, Blume's ongoing struggle for survival and her readiness to help others are linked with historical facts of the Shoah and with the present situation of certain metropolises. Hence, the ethical Judaic message of responsibility concerning the past, the present, and the future is conveyed between the lines. In particular, different points of time refer to each other, when Anna Blume accidentally enters a Jewish library. Here, the Rabbi tells her of the ongoing Jewish experience of living under constant threat:

> Every Jew . . . believes that he belongs to the last generation of Jews. We are always at the end, always standing on the brink of the last moment, and why should we expect things to be any different now? (Auster, *In the Country* 112)

Indeed, after this talk, Anna will not see the Rabbi again. He has already lost academy status, like the German Jews in the 1930s, and he will probably be deported to a labor or concentration camp, as the Rabbi's successor in the library, the criminal Henry Dujardin, tells Anna (112). To Anna's question, where the Rabbi has been taken exactly, he replies sarcastically: "[He is] on the way to the promised land" (113). With the figure of Dujardin, who will even lure Anna into a human slaughterhouse, Auster not only works historical facts into his novel, he also indirectly criticizes present-day anti-Semitic behavior. This is also true for the ending of the novel, when Otto Frick's burial site has been defiled. Anna writes about this event resignedly: "The order of things had been smashed, and no amount of talk from me would ever set it right" (179).

However, when Anna meets the Rabbi for the first time, he gives her hope for the future and points out that Jews will always be able to survive persecutions and murder: "It's not easy to get rid of us" (95).

Moreover, he stirs up Anna's memories of her intact past and revives her buried belief in other people:

> It was strange what had come over me in the presence of this man, but the more I talked to him, the more I sounded like a child. Perhaps he reminded me of how things had been when I was very young, back in the dark ages when I still believed in what fathers and teachers said to me. I can't say for sure, but the fact was that I felt on solid ground with him, and I knew that he was someone I could trust. (96)

The same is true for Isabel who is rescued by Anna. Out of gratitude for Anna's selflessness, Isabel gives her shelter, food, and the advice she needs. Besides, Isabel confirms her belief in God in spite of her living conditions and gives Anna, who has lost faith, new hope: "I know that people don't talk about God anymore, but I can't help myself. I think about him every day, I pray to him at night . . ., I talk to him in my heart all the time" (49). Isabel regards Anna as an angel-like being, fallen from the sky to rescue her. This idea underlines her innocent thinking and at the same time her strong belief in the spiritual that motivates her to help others, foremost Anna: "You are the dear, sweet child that God has sent to me, and now I am going to take care of you, I am going to do everything I can for you" (49). Auster indeed portrays Isabel as a highly religious person who believes in the unexplainable in spite of a God who sometimes does not show His face. In short, in spite of her strong belief, Isabel mirrors Derrida's interpretation of the absent God in Exodus (Derrida, "Edmond Jabès" 67): "I know he is very busy and doesn't have time for an old woman like me, but God is a gentleman, and he has me on his list" (Auster, *In the Country* 49).

The Rabbi in the library also regards God as hiding Himself in a different sphere, remote from earthly decay and hunger. The tone of his speech is philosophical and realistic: "We talk to him. But whether or not he hears us is another matter" (96). Indeed, God seems to have ceased to exist in the apocalyptic world. Anna has stopped believing in God, and even the Rabbi admits that "[i]t's best not to expect miracles" (95). When Anna shows him her photograph of Sam, he does, however, recognize Sam's face and tells her that he lives just a few rooms away from where they are right now. Similar to the encounter of Anna and Isabel, this is again a miraculous, almost spiritual scene contrasted to all cruelty.

At the end of the novel, Auster emphasizes that religious rituals or ceremonies do not exist any more in the "country of last things" and so alludes to the missing or very liberal religious practices and diminished religious communities, foremost Jewish ones, in the 20th century. The burial of Otto Frick, for example, is depicted as "a primitive ceremony at best – no prayers, no songs . . . " (173). However, everybody who has known Frick over the last years attends it. In short, the ethical necessity of being present for the other is stressed again. With her writing, Anna expresses her hope of humane behavior and so, generally speaking, of the future, in spite of the memories of the Shoah, as the following chapter will show in greater detail.

3.4.4. The double-bind nature of death and the hope of the "humanity of human beings"

In her fascist surroundings, Anna Blume constantly has to live with her anxiety of facing death. But in spite of the detailed, most pessimistic depiction of the city of decay, Auster does not depict death as something absolute which determines every single aspect of life. With Anna's realistic writing, which is also an attempt to look at the different faces of death more closely, Auster circles around the question of how we react when we are confronted with death. He looks at his heroine and her friends from the outside. In parallel, Jacques Derrida looks at himself from the outside in the interview "As if I were Dead." He observes himself as someone else and tells about his experiment of taking on the role of a corpse (16 ff.).

Death is here, as much as in Auster's apocalyptic novel, depicted as being characterized by a "double bind." On the one hand, it is the finite itself, an absolute mark inherent in life, behind which nothing seems to exist anymore. With this concept, Auster and Derrida partly cover the Judaic notion of death, i.e., the necessity to accept mortality as an undeniable fact of human existence (Abramovitch, "Death" 131). They both concentrate on this knowledge of our mortality and the anxiety connected with it. Anna Blume writes about the finality of death in the following way:

> Close your eyes for a moment, turn around to look at something else, and the thing that was before you is suddenly gone. Nothing lasts, you see, not even the thoughts inside you. And you mustn't waste your time looking for them. Once a thing is gone, that is the end of it. (Auster, *In the Country* 2)

On the other hand, the Judaic notion that the awareness of our mortality brings us closer to life is also stressed. Anna Blume indeed must treat every day as if it were her last, since otherwise she would be lost: "Even it is for the hundredth time, you must encounter each thing as if you have never known it before. No matter how many times, it must always be the first time. This is next to impossible, I realize, but it is an absolute rule" (7). In *Psyché*, Derrida moreover emphasizes that "at the moment of death, we *can* no longer be concerned with anything but the other *in ourselves*" (qtd. in Kamuf 203). In parallel, Lévinas argues that at the moment of death "we are in relation with something that is absolutely other" ("Time and the Other" 43), that man is then able to open up himself to the ungraspable, to the mysterious. Auster's protagonist Anna Blume also faces the mysterious while being present for Isabel, who is almost run over by a group of people. With her passive behavior, Isabel would have died. She is no longer in possession of her powers, or, to hint at Lévinas' elaborations in "Time and the Other" (41), she has lost her virility and her ability to react. But Anna intuitively takes responsibility for an absolute stranger and rescues her (Auster, *In the Country* 44-45).

This shared experience of death leads to reciprocal responsibility and helpfulness, until the two women become dependent on each other. Moreover, with Anna's spontaneous decision to save Isabel, a new period of time sets in for her. The moment of death does not appear as a standstill, but as a transition to different, more positive experiences, above all to her writing process within the four walls of Isabel's room. She is conscious of the fact that because of Isabel's helplessness at a most critical moment, she has been given a new chance:

> For better or worse, my true life in that city began at that moment. Everything else is a prologue, a swarm of tottering steps, of days and nights, of thoughts I do not remember. If not for that one irrational moment in the street, the story I am telling you would not be this one. Given the shape I was in at the time, I doubt there would have been any story at all. (45)

Later, after Isabel has finally died, Anna is able to write even more fluently than before. She knows that if she had not been present at Isabel's death, she would never have been able to take down her memories. In other words, Anna's archive-like writing process comes into being at the moment of death: "If Isabel hadn't lost her voice, none of these words would exist. Because she had no more words, these other words have come out of me" (79). At another moment, Anna goes through a similar experience of death followed by a different period of time. She loses her shopping cart, the only necessity to do her "job" properly, to go on scavenging. Without it, she first seems to be lost (82). But after a while she understands that the apparently disastrous experience gives her the opportunity to lead a different life, to change her daily routine by taking other possibilities into consideration: "It was a part of a life that had ended for me, and here was my chance to set out on a fresh course, to take my life in my own hands and do something about it" (83).

In parallel, Anna meets Sam by chance at a moment when she is sure of dying soon. Because of this awareness, she again opens herself up to a complete stranger and is ready to take responsibility. Extremely realistically, she faces Sam with the facts: "We're going to die, and it's stupid to die when you don't have to" (105). On account of their similar experiences with death, Anna and Sam decide to help each other. They, to put it differently, fulfill what Lévinas explains in "Time and the Other":

> ". . . only a being whose solitude has reached a crispation through suffering, and in relation with death, takes its place on a ground where the relationship with the other becomes possible" (43).

The protagonists' ability to get involved with each other rescues them, at least for a while, and shortly later, Anna even describes her time with Sam as "the best days of [her] life" (107). The book they write together keeps them believing in "a possible future" (114), and when Anna gets pregnant, Sam is absolutely convinced that they have managed to thwart the moment of death and to determine their future: "The child meant that we had been spared, he said. We had overturned the odds, and from now on everything would be different. By creating a child together, we had made it possible for a new world to begin" (117).

This conviction of a new start in spite of all adversities will not last very long, since Anna gets caught in a trap, loses her child, and almost dies. However, the moment of death is again followed by a moment of hope. Anna is rescued by Victoria, who behaves in the same way as Anna herself does when she saves Isabel. With these three women who are ready to take responsibility without knowing each other and to develop deep friendships, Auster conveys his ethical message that was already part of *The Invention of Solitude*. In his 1987 novel, he develops it by again linking his protagonists' personal experiences of death with allusions to Jewish history, foremost to the Shoah.

Indeed, Woburn House, where Anna, Sam, and Victoria try to do their utmost at the end of the novel, is contrasted as an idyllic sort of refuge against the burnt-down library, from where the Rabbi and other Jews are driven away. In spite of "the fact . . . that Woburn House [is] on the verge of going under" (167), the three friends work together as long as possible for the needs of others. They do not accept the finality of death, but arouse other people's hopes.[31] Thus they fulfill the ideal Emmanuel Lévinas speaks about in "The Pact," i.e., his vision of "the humanity of human beings" (226). In "A Testimony Given," Jacques Derrida also stresses the necessity of a universal responsibility against the backdrop of the Jewish religion:

> 'I am Jewish,' which means: I am testifying to the humanity of human beings, to universality, to responsibility for universality. 'We are the chosen people' means: We are par excellence, and in an exemplary way, witnesses to what a people can be, we are not only God's allies, God's chosen, but God's witnesses, and so on.' (41)

With his Jewish protagonist, Auster indirectly conveys the religious connotations of a responsible form of behavior. In the interview with Larry McCaffery and Sinda Gregory, he stresses the ethical dimension of his novel more than directly (Kiely 32). Even his words are similar to Derrida's or Lévinas', when he depicts Anna's behavior in the sense of a *pars pro toto*, standing for the indispensable responsibility of all human beings, especially with regard to future times to come:

> I find it the most hopeful book I've ever written. . . . Even in the midst of the most brutal realities, the most terrible social conditions, she [Anna Blume] struggles to remain a human being, to keep her humanity intact. I can't imagine anything more noble and courageous than that. It's a struggle that millions of people have had to face in our time, and not many of them have been tenacious as she is. I think of Anna Blume as a true heroine. (321)

[31] Anna Blume's readiness to help others as a cause for hope is again part of Paul Auster's most recent novel *Travels in the Scriptorium* (2006). Here, she is depicted as an almost supernatural being by patiently looking after Mr. Blank, the main character, who sits in a locked room with almost no contact to the outside world and who awakes each day with no memory: "So Mr. Blank allows Anna to feed him, and as she calmly goes about the business of scooping out portions of the poached eggs, holding the teacup to his lips, and wiping his mouth with a paper napkin, Mr. Blank begins to think that Anna is not a woman so much as an angel, or, if you will, an angel in the form of a woman" (16).

3.5. *The Book of Illusions* – a novel about facing wounds and figments on the way to realistic observation

With *The Book of Illusions* (2002), Auster does not continue his depiction of apocalyptic sceneries, but devotes himself to an extreme family situation and its effects at the present time. His focus is now the development of the I-narrator David Zimmer, who, like the I-narrator of "Portrait of an Invisible Man," secludes himself from his surroundings after he has lost his wife and his two sons in a plane crash. Generally speaking, the question is now how a human being behaves after an unlikable, but possible catastrophe in the Western everyday world. In his grief, David Zimmer accidentally comes across a Jewish silent comedian called Hector Mann, who was separated from his family as a child and later disappeared after committing a crime in 1929. In other words, the topic of the wound is again at the heart of the text.

In order to distract himself, Zimmer decides to write about the actor. He travels around Europe and the United States to watch Hector's films in different libraries and finally pays him a visit in his hiding place in New Mexico. With his attempt to find out as much as possible about the mysterious Hector Mann and to analyze his films in detail, he equals Daniel Quinn in *City of Glass,* who obsessively follows Stillman, Sr. With his intensive research work and writing process, Zimmer also tries to get to the bottom of another person's hidden secrets and simultaneously circles around his own wound of having lost his family. Like Quinn, he eventually becomes haunted by ghost-like appearances, unsolved mysteries, and split-up identities. Films and stories mirror themselves, figments, and realities cannot be distinguished until Zimmer feels utterly confused.

In short, *The Book of Illusions* is marked by the movement of différance, too, that blocks the origin or source the I-narrator hopes to reach. The more he indeed wanders around the world to put the fragmentary truths about Hector together, the more he becomes unsure of who Hector Mann really was and what happened to him. All sorts of ideas and theories that he develops about him tend to supplement and erase each other as soon as they come up: "To think one thought meant thinking the opposite thought, and no sooner did that second thought destroy the first thought than a third thought rose up to destroy the second" (4).

But, in contrast to Daniel Quinn, David Zimmer slowly learns to see through his and other people's illusions resulting from sorrow and grief. With the help of Alma Grund, who is the link between David's and Hector's story, he will eventually be able to cope with his wounds. By raising the hidden memories of a Jewish artist to the surface, Zimmer begins to look at his surroundings more realistically. His archive-like writing process is, as a consequence, characterized by a detailed depiction of everyday realities, the persons he meets, and of a scattered, partly unpublished work of art. It seems to be even clearer in *The Book of Illusions* than in *In the Country of Last Things* that Auster has begun to get past the deconstructive way of thinking with the help of a more realistic style based on precise observation. His I-narrator will, after finishing his book about Hector Mann, stop secluding himself. With this ending, Auster clearly emphasizes the necessity to accept one's memories and to turn towards the exterior world.

3.5.1. Opening up oneself towards the exterior world by trying to get at the bottom of one's wounds

Like *The Invention of Solitude* and *In the Country of Last Things*, *The Book of Illusions* starts off with the moment of death. While still mourning for his wife and his two sons, the I-narrator David Zimmer gets more and more interested in the Jewish silent movie comedian Hector Mann, who vanished without a trace about sixty years ago. He is fascinated by a man of whom "everyone thought he was dead" (1) – not primarily because of Hector's films, but because of his own experiences. In particular, before beginning to write about the comedian, Zimmer is an almost "dead" man, too. He gives up his teaching position at the university and excludes himself from all social life. In his solitude he tries to be as close as possible to the dead by walling himself off in his house similar to the I-narrator in *The Invention of Solitude*, as his surname, the German word for "room," alludes at. For weeks he does not do anything except walking from room to room and playing with his sons' toys. In a ghost-like way, he "[carries] on their little phantom lives for them by repeating the gestures they had made when they still had bodies" (8). Watching silent comedies makes Zimmer laugh again for some rare moments and at the same time ties him to the dead, since the films are "a dead art" (15) in themselves.

With the invention of sound, as Zimmer points out, the genre has not been practiced any more since Hector Mann vanished. Zimmer concentrates on an almost unreal, past phenomenon and thus distracts himself from his grief. He watches the films "from across a great chasm of forgetfulness" (15) and is deeply moved by their dream-like, poetic plots. He tries to bridge this chasm by beginning to write about the films in a small apartment in New York. Besides, he collects the fragmentary information about Hector Mann, who has vanished, and puts it together like a jigsaw puzzle.

In short, Zimmer's writing process "[is] born out of a great sorrow" (5), as he himself emphasizes. In the course of time, he analyzes one film after the other and so continues circling around his wound. At the same time, he tries to prevent himself from being thrown off balance. The title of his book, "The Silent World of Hector Mann," refers to the comedian's disappearance, to the genre of his films, and of course to Zimmer's own solitude. In particular, while watching and writing about the still moments of Hector's films, contrasted to the multitude of jokes, he apparently sees himself "as if in a mirror" (30). He identifies with the actor more and more, whom he tries to rediscover with his book. He hopes to bring him back to life, but foremost to rescue himself.

However, the more Zimmer writes about the silent comedian in his little room in New York, the more he begins to resemble him. The more films Zimmer watches, the more he hides from his surroundings. Indeed, Hector Mann does not only vanish in (the fictional) reality, but also as a film character. In "Mr. Nobody," as the narrator elaborates, he becomes invisible after having swallowed a poisonous drink (42). With the detailed depiction of the film plot, Auster reflects both the stories of David Zimmer and Hector Mann and alienates them. As "Mr. Nobody," Hector "[is] invisible to everyone around him, but his body can still interact with the world" (45); whereas Zimmer is visible to everyone around him, but stops interacting with other people.

For all three characters it is true that the rules of their former lives do not apply any more: "[t]he world has been turned upside down, and everything in it has broken" (44). Under these circumstances, they can choose to do whatever they want to; they can do good or evil. The movie character first commits a crime and then develops into a ghost-like figure which "has been reduced to nothing" (50), hovering about its former house. Hector Mann makes himself invisible by leaving his former life behind to take on different identities at a different place. David Zimmer vanishes for a longer period of time first by traveling across the United States, where Hector Mann's movies are stored in different libraries, then by seeking solitude through his writing process. In his small apartment, he lives the life of a hermit, not being able to get into contact with anybody. He concentrates on nothing but the book (and indirectly, without consciously being aware of it, on his own wounds), since he fears that he would otherwise go mad (55-56). Finally, his experiences seem to fuse with Hector Mann's story:

> I was in the book, and the book was in my head, and as long as I stayed inside my head, I could go on writing the book. It was like living in a padded cell, but of all the lives I could have lived at that moment, it was the only one that made sense to me. I wasn't capable of being in the world, and I knew that if I tried to go back into it before I was ready, I would be crushed. So I holed up in that small apartment and spent my days writing about Hector Mann. (55)

After Zimmer has finished writing the book, he looks for "another project to work on, another ocean to drown [himself] in" (57). He decides to move back to Vermont, not into his former house that he shared with his wife, but into a little, empty mental hospital, a house "for the living dead" (57). With the depiction of the creepy, "depersonalized interiors" (57), Auster realistically mirrors Zimmer's inner state and reminds the reader of the I-narrator's father in "Portrait of an Invisible Man" and his ghost-like surroundings ("Portrait" 10). In the former hospital, David Zimmer isolates himself completely, not speaking to anybody except Alex Kronenberg, a former classmate and at present a lecturer at Columbia University, who asks him to translate Chateaubriand's autobiography *Memoires d'outre-tombe* (1848).

Chateaubriand needed thirty-five years to complete the book, as Auster explains in the voice of his I-narrator, and he wanted it to be published not earlier than five years after his death. "'It's literally written in the voice of a dead man,'" Zimmer tells Kronenberg on the phone (62). In the introduction to the autobiography, Chateaubriand underlined that he "prefer[red] to speak from the depths of [his] tomb" (67). Zimmer therefore calls it "Memoirs of a Dead Man" (62), another hint at his present mental instability. Besides, Chateaubriand's book can be interpreted as a sort of archive of past experiences from his childhood to the last moments of his death and can thus be referred to Derrida's elaborations on human remembrance as "*internal* archivization" in *Archive Fever. A Freudian Impression* (13). Moreover, the book reflects Hector Mann's fictional life story. In both cases, life and death cannot be clearly distinguished. As Chateaubriand writes in his introduction, they create a "mysterious unity": "My cradle recalls something of my tomb, my tomb something of my cradle" (67).

With the help of the intertextual reference, Auster emphasizes Zimmer's inner state, his continuing seclusion in a kind of vacuum. Translating Chateaubriand turns out to be a mechanical job which he is willing to do as long as he can. At least for a few years, he decides to be nothing but "the servant of the text" (70). What Zimmer however likes about the work is that it creates a distance between himself and his nightmarish memories. Hence it prevents him from completely falling into grief and self-pity (70). When he gets a letter from Frieda Spelling, Hector's wife, telling him that Hector is still alive and wants to get in contact with him, he needs to think over his decision to keep away from friends, relatives, and colleagues. But not before Alma Grund, the daughter of Hector's cameraman, threatens him with a pistol in his house, will he agree to follow Frieda's invitation. Together with Alma, whose courage and determination fascinates him, he travels to New Mexico to fulfill the wish of the dying Hector.

On their journey and on Hector's ranch in the desert, Alma's openness brings about the turning point in David Zimmer's life, the understanding that he needs to face up to his inner wounds. By telling him that Hector disappeared because he had helped his fiancée to bury the corpse of his lover and by revealing some intimate details of her own life, Alma makes Zimmer realize that he needs to accept the past in order to go on living. Otherwise, as she unintentionally teaches him, he "wouldn't be allowed to have a future" (117). Alma's telling name, "the feminine form of *almus*, meaning nourishing, bountiful" (116), underlines her ability to change Zimmer's way of thinking and feeling. Moreover, it is a four-letter name beginning and ending with an "a" like "Anna," the heroine in Auster's *In the Country of Last Things*. Their surnames ("Grund" and "Blume") are both German and have got five letters each. We can thus argue that Auster connects the two female characters with each other to emphasize their courage and staying power as a cause for hope. Indeed, "Grund" means "cause" or "reason" in English, as well as "land" or "ground," possibly referring to the desert of New Mexico, where Zimmer's life changes.

Besides, Alma has got a birthmark on the left side of her face covering half her cheek. This birthmark was the reason for her feeling of inferiority when she was little, but has finally taught her to accept who she is. Thus, just as in Nathaniel Hawthorne's short story "The

Birthmark" (1846), Alma's favorite story, it is a sign of humanity: "That was the difference between me and everyone else. I wasn't allowed to hide who I was. Every time people looked at me, they were looking right into my soul" (121). Alma is, to put it differently, a wounded human being like David Zimmer. Therefore she has the impression that she is looking into a mirror when she meets him for the first time: "I looked at you, and for a couple of moments it was almost like looking at myself. That's never happened to me before" (122). In contrast to David's sorrow, Alma's wound is clearly visible to everybody. This congruence of her outer appearance with her inner self made her an easy target when she was young, but has finally helped her to realize whom she can trust (121). Vice versa, Alma is the first person Zimmer begins to have confidence in.

During their drive to New Mexico, Alma acts in an exemplary fashion by making Zimmer aware of his limitations, by making him face reality. What he primarily has to learn in the desert is that the more he tries to find out the truth about Hector's past and to accept his own, the more confused he might become. The real and the unreal can often not be distinguished, as he soon understands. When he meets Hector for the first and only time, he is, on the one hand, surprised that Hector is not an illusion, a figment of his imagination, but a real human being:

> It stunned me to acknowledge that Hector had hand and eyes, fingernails and shoulders, a neck and a left ear – that he was tangible, that he wasn't an imaginary being. He had been inside my head for so long, it seemed doubtful that he could exist anywhere else. (222)

On the other hand, Zimmer does not hear much about Hector's mysterious disappearance or the reason why he is eager to get to know him. The morning after Zimmer speaks to Hector, the latter is dead, and only much later will Zimmer understand that Frieda killed him. Since she neither wants the truth about Hector's life, nor the films they made together published, she needs to get rid of Zimmer. The easiest way for her to do this is to deprive Zimmer of his motivation to stay longer on the ranch, i.e., she must get rid of her husband and his work (319). In other words, through Frieda's violent actions, the crime Hector committed in 1929 is doubled, whereas Zimmer soon feels guilty of neither having prevented the death of his family, nor the destruction of Hector's movies.

Moreover, with the burning films a form of extreme, absurd aestheticism is depicted: "It was about making something in order to destroy it" (279). The I-narrator clearly distances himself from this radical artistic approach, when Frieda becomes insane and Alma commits suicide. Zimmer understands that it is based on nothing but illusions, as a key passage about the ranch in one of Hector's notebooks tells him. Hector once named it after a "blue stone" he had apparently found on the street in a dark, misty night. When he touched it, it turned out to be "a gob of human spit" (286).

Foremost, David distances himself from the temptation of annihilating the past: "All I can remember is saying no to the idea of cremation. No more fire, I said, no more ashes" (311). This sentence hints at the wounds aroused by the Shoah and is, similar to the ending of *The Invention of Solitude*, an indirect, urgent appeal not to repeat the crimes of the past. The renunciation of violence as well as the active turn to past realities are at the "center" of *The Book of Illusions*. "This is a book of fragments, a compilation of sorrows and half-remembered dreams," Zimmer writes at the end of the novel (316). The writing process is, in other words, an attempt to get to the bottom of one's wounds and the illusions coupled with them. In spite of his courage, concentration, and cleverness, Zimmer will not be able to solve every mystery. But he, in contrast to Daniel Quinn in *City of Glass*, does not let himself be lured into building up a life on apparitions alone. With Alma's help, he manages to face reality, i.e., his wounds of the past as well as his future:

> . . . and in order to tell the story, I have to confine myself to the events of the story itself. I will simply say that I live in a large city now, somewhere between Boston and Washington, D.C., and that this is the first piece of writing that I have attempted since *The Silent World of Hector Mann*. I taught for a while again, found other work that was more satisfying for me, then quit teaching for good. I should also say (for those who care about such things) that I no longer live alone. (316)

3.5.2. Being separated from Jewish roots and the change of identity

In his analysis of Hector Mann's films, Zimmer brings to light what has been buried similar to the I-narrator of "Portrait of an Invisible Man." He finds out that Hector seemingly "stepped out for a short walk," but actually "vanished from the face of the earth" (1). Nobody has seen the comedian, since he decided to pay for his guilt by breaking off contact with everyone he felt closely attached to. Like the father in "Portrait of an Invisible Man," he appears as a ghost-like figure, a man who has stopped living without having died. Without revealing his true identity, he hovers about people he was once indirectly related to, such as his lover's sister. But for almost everybody, he remains unattainable, a person who has especially become alienated from his Jewish family background.

Auster, in other words, again depicts a figure that has always been absent and developed into "a block of impenetrable space in the form of a man" ("Portrait" 7). It is a character that has withdrawn into some kind of inner exile, who has entered, figuratively spoken, a no-man's land. Auster indeed stresses this language that is reminiscent of Derrida: "By 1932 or 1933, Hector belonged to an extinct universe, and if there were any traces of him left, it was only as a footnote in some obscure book that no one bothered to read anymore" (*The Book of Illusions* 2).

During the years following Hector's disappearance, different stories seem to have developed. They disseminate in the I-narrator's mind without giving him any plausible answer as to why Hector suddenly vanished. They do not tell him what Hector decided to do afterwards, either. Like in *The Invention of Solitude*, the idea of an accessible truth fades away, as Zimmer is aware from the beginning of his writing process: "[f]or several years following his disappearance, various stories and rumors circulated about what had happened to him, but none of these conjectures ever amounted to anything" (2). The multitude of these different realities is reflected by Hector's contradictory roles in his silent films: "he is both a populist and an aristocrat, a sensualist and a closet romantic, a man of precise, even punctilious manners, who never hesitates to make the grand gesture" (35). While splitting up into such various characters, Hector apparently ironies himself, as Zimmer thinks. On the one hand, the comedian demonstrates his acting talent; on the other hand he always looks at himself from a distance or, in a slapstick-like manner, ridicules his roles (35).

The contradictory "code of images" (30) in the comedies underlines the impossibility of discerning Hector's true identity. His black moustache and the white suit are the most important images, whereas "[t]he moustache is the link to his inner self, a metonym of urges, cogitations, and mental storms. The suit embodies his relation to the social world" (31). In fact, the suit gets dirty in each of Hector's comedies and thus seems to anticipate that he will later lose his innocence. As “a sign of Hector’s vulnerability,” the suit shows that both in his films and in “real” life “he is achieving the opposite of what he has intended. He isn’t protecting himself against potential blows, he is turning himself into a target” (31). With this parallel between the different layers of text, Auster mirrors his I-narrator’s inevitable fate, namely his unintended participation in a criminal action, the destruction of Hector’s films. At the same time, however, Auster deconstructs the similarities between his two male characters, as he does not depict Hector just as a vulnerable comedian, but also as a man who is well-known for his “steadfastness” and “spiritual calm” (33). Hector’s character thus seems to be as obscure as the stories circulating about his past.

Furthermore, Hector’s disappearance and the different identities he later takes on are not only reflected by the film scenes Zimmer depicts in detail, but they are also foreshadowed by his childhood experiences. When Zimmer works on the newspaper articles and interviews with Hector, he realizes that Hector’s statements about his past contradict each other. In one of them, Hector tells that he comes from Germany, in another he stresses his Polish background and speaks about the time he spent in Argentina. By putting these different family stories together, Zimmer thus comes to the conclusion that “you wind up with nothing” (83), that Hector “is reduced to a pile of fragments, a jigsaw puzzle whose pieces no longer connect” (83). In spite of his confusion, Zimmer tries to find out the reason for Hector’s contradictory statements that erase each other. He assumes that beneath them lies Hector’s secret about his Jewish identity which he tried to hide from his surroundings:

> If Hector was indeed hiding something, and if that something turned out to be the religion he had been born into, then all I had uncovered was the most pedestrian kind of social hypocrisy. It wasn’t a crime to be a Jew in Hollywood back then. It was merely something that one chose not to talk about. (86)

Although Zimmer condemns Hector’s decision to renounce his Jewishness, he tries to understand the psychological reasons for his break with religion: “[b]eing Jewish might have been a burden to Hector. He might have suffered from it, and he might have been ashamed of it . . .” (86). After a while Zimmer finds out that from Hector’s childhood onwards, he has been separated from any Jewish religious and cultural life. Indeed, he “was born Chaim Mandelbaum – on a Dutch steamship in the middle of the Atlantic" (127). Moreover, his mother died shortly later, and anti-Semitic actions in Buenos Aires in 1919 also separated Hector from his father, who "was nearly beaten to death" (127). This separation from both his parents and the lack of a native country seem to have made Hector an alienated human being, who later led the life of a disoriented, guilt-ridden wanderer. Making silent comedies becomes a means for Hector to protect himself against his grief. It is an antipodal world that takes his mind off his worries and makes him live in seclusion, too. In short, Hector is later "trapped in his psycho-religious battle between desire and self-abnegation" (279). His films paradoxically serve as an attempt to both get in contact with his inner self and to simultaneously free himself of it.

This contradictory desire caused by Hector's uprooting later leads to his transformation. After he has helped bury the corpse of his murdered lover, he arbitrarily takes on different names and identities. First he changes into a man called Herman Loesser. The double meaning of the name – "[s]ome would pronounce it *Lesser*, and others would read it as *Loser*" – helps him "to get rid of himself for others, but to remember who he was for himself" (144). Moreover, he changes his outward appearance by getting rid of his moustache, his most distinctive mark, and by wearing a cap. "The two operations [cancel] him out," the I-narrator emphasizes. They transform him into an ordinary person, an average man without any noticeable features (144).

By taking pronunciation lessons Hector additionally gets rid of his accent and, with it, his last distinctive characteristic. In annihilating every trace of his past, they "[have] the deepest and most lasting effect. . . . they [remain] in his body for the rest of his life" (157). Later, Hector takes on Frieda Spelling's second name and thus makes it even more difficult for others to track down his true identity. Eventually, Hector becomes a human being whose characteristics supplement and erase each other constantly. He appears "as a collection of random particles of matter, and finally as a single speck of dust" (147). Indeed, Hector is well aware of the overall aim of his transformations, as he clearly puts it in one of his journals: "*If I mean to save my life, then I have to come within an inch of destroying it*" (154). This absurd motivation will later lead to Hector's dream-like, pathological perception of reality. He looks at his everyday actions as if he were constantly delirious: "Life was a fever, he discovered, and reality was a groundless world of figments and hallucinations, a place where everything you imagined came true" (163).

In Hector's imagination, nothing seems to be stable, everything can change into its opposite at any time: "*The earth is the sky, the sun is the moon, the rivers are mountains*" (172).

This threatening sense of reality reflects Zimmer's own dream-like perception, his ghost-like experiences when revealing more and more of Hector's secrets. He is haunted by déjà vus, and past memories seem to mix up with present events. When Zimmer enters Hector's study, for example, he notices Chateaubriand's *Memoires d'outres-tombe* on one of the bookshelves, the autobiography he has been translating for some time. This coincidence is "another point of contact . . ., another link in the chain of accidental encounters" (238) between the two men. It tells Zimmer that Hector "ha[s] entered the same labyrinth of memories that [he has] been wandering in . . ." (238). Besides, Zimmer gets to know that Hector's son Tad died like his son Todd. The similarity of the two events and of the names is another creepy coincidence that draws Zimmer even closer to the comedian: "No mental gymnastics required to understand the situation. Tad and Todd. It can't get any closer than that, can it?" (206). Most importantly, this parallel makes the I-narrator aware of his own uprooting, the fact that his life also crumbled to pieces with the death of his family.

Like every other experience following his lover's death, Hector regards his son's accident from a religious point of view and thus judges himself. To him, it has always seemed to be "a form of divine punishment" for the crime he once committed (206). Besides, Alma passes judgment on herself by committing suicide after she has unintentionally killed Hector's wife. The farewell letter she writes Zimmer indeed looks as if "sent from the ancient past: half of a Torah, or a message delivered from some Etruscan battlefield" (308). This letter, as well as Hector's experiences, connect Zimmer with his deepest wounds and force him to get in contact with them. The parallels help him to accept the past, but also to distance himself from it. In contrast to Hector or Alma, he will not judge himself from a religious perspective, but he will decide to go on living by writing another book. Before he is able to do this, he has to learn to see through his uncanny experiences, the hallucinations, and figments he is confronted with when getting at the bottom of Hector's life-story. It's a long path he has to follow until he finally leaves the silent comedian behind and, with him, his grief as well.

3.5.3. Constantly wandering right into the desert, a place of deceptions

Right from the start of *The Book of Illusions*, Auster underlines Zimmer's necessary learning process to eventually face up to his inner wounds with the Old Testament motif of constant wandering. After the death of his family, the I-narrator "[chooses] to wander around the world looking at silent comedies" (13). He hopes to distract himself by traveling to well-known libraries in six different American and European cities where twelve of Hector Mann's films are stored. The long distances he needs to cover form some kind of network, which reminds the reader of the street network in *City of Glass*. While becoming part of it, Zimmer's aim is to bring the different films in connection with each other and to make sense out of the fragmentary knowledge of Hector's past. By exclusively preoccupying himself with another person and his art, he above all tries to distract himself from his grief.

In other words, Zimmer's postmodern kind of wandering is the consequence of his inner wound of having lost his family. He is driven by his desire to get to know the truth about Hector Mann's life story and to analyze his films in detail. This yearning for arrival at a yet obscure destination primarily connects him with Daniel Quinn. Both protagonists try to construct a protective wall around themselves by constantly being on the move. They distance themselves from the outside world and simultaneously hope to get to the bottom of another person's secrets.

On his journeys, Zimmer is afraid of becoming lost or of losing his temper, as he tells his doctor: "'I don't trust myself anymore, I'm afraid I'll lose control'" (22). His fear of flying reflects what indeed happens to Daniel Quinn in *City of Glass*: "'If I loosened my grip now, I'd fall apart. I'd fly off in a hundred different directions, and I'd never be able to put myself together again'" (25). Only a drug makes it possible for him to go on these journeys, but, as he soon learns, it also increases what he hoped to prevent, namely his anxiety of getting out of touch with reality. It obliterates every memory of the flights so that Zimmer has the impression that he "[has] never lost track of [himself] so thoroughly" (27).

In Europe, Zimmer nevertheless stays much longer than intended since his project "[is] taken to a new level of intensity, a single-mindedness that verge[s] on obsession" (27). Writing the book becomes a means "to think about one thing and one thing only," to live "the life of a monomaniac" (27). But while exclusively preoccupying himself with the films and by wandering around the world, Zimmer gets more and more confused about Hector's roles. As an actor, Hector is "[u]npredictable in his behavior, full of contradictory impulses and desires" (35). Besides, the strange jokes in Hector's films do not entertain Zimmer very much, but foremost add to his uncertainty: "Hector's gags unfold like musical compositions, a confluence of contrasting lines and voices, and the more the voices interact with one another, the more precarious and unstable the world becomes" (38).

Moreover, Hector's unstable existence caused by his constant traveling around the globe mirrors Zimmer's wandering. The comedian moves from Europe to South America and then goes to North America where he lives at different places, too. His nomadic life remarkably ends in the desert of New Mexico, where, in the first years, he loses every ambition and does nothing but plant trees (205). In parallel, Zimmer's research work ends in the desert, too. Here he finds the former quite famous actor, who is separated from everything he was once connected with. In short, the desert is depicted as a place of seclusion and alienation, where Hector, again under a different name, tries to hide his true identity, and the crime he committed, from society. Besides, the lack of life in the area underlines his absurd action, the production of films destined to be burnt.

With the metaphor of the desert, Hector's alienation and David Zimmer's yearning to reveal a secret is stressed. To use Derrida's words, it is especially the I-narrator's learning and writing process that Auster describes as a "way through the Desert" ("Edmond Jabès" 68), "while the desired destination will keep out of sight" (66). When arriving at Hector's ranch in the desert, Zimmer only seems to have reached the place that he was striving to get to for a long time. The extraordinary scenery indeed emphasizes his expectations, his vigilance, and agility:

> Now we were in the desert, walking under a sky without clouds, breathing in the thin, juniper-scented air. . . . I felt hyper-alert, filled with a kind of mad resolve, a jumbled-up state of fear, expectation, and happiness – as if I had three minds, and they were all working at once" (Auster, *Book of Illusions* 238-239).

However, his desire to get as close as possible to the truth about Hector will be thwarted, as he is only allowed to speak to Hector for a few minutes and to watch not more than two of his films. Thus the desert is not only depicted as a place of seclusion but of deceptions, too, as the title of the novel makes clear. Shortly after he has arrived at the ranch, Zimmer becomes haunted by creepy appearances, by figments, and lies. He is, for example, utterly confused about Conchita and Juan, two "[s]trange little people who cannot talk" (253). The I-narrator describes them as ghost-like or shadow figures underscoring the mysterious, uncanny atmosphere. Most of the time, they are not clearly visible, and Zimmer has difficulties in recognizing them (223). Later they become Frieda's accomplices in blurring every trace of Hector's work and then disappear like Hector, who also covered up the tracks of his crime.

When Frieda begins to destroy Hector's movies he has shot on the ranch, Zimmer eventually realizes that he went down to New Mexico not to become acquainted with Hector, but "to participate in a crime" (270). At the end of his journey, he needs to learn that he has not arrived where he hoped to get to. He he has been led only by his subjective impressions and talked himself into a false assumption. Besides, Auster emphasizes this learning process by quoting Immanuel Kant, the most significant German philosopher of the Enlightenment: "*Things which we see are not by themselves what we see . . . so that, if we drop our subject or the subjective form of our senses, all qualities, all relations of objects in space and time, nay space and time themselves, would vanish*" (264).

Auster furthermore embeds a fictitious movie, "The Inner Life of Martin Frost," in his novel to underline the I-narrator's confusion. He depicts the plot in detail as if it had really been shot. When Zimmer watches it before Frieda destroys it, he has the feeling that it "was filmed with such deadpan realism, such scrupulous attention to the particulars of everyday life" (242) that he becomes unable to perceive it as a work of art. Since the film is shot on Hector's and Frieda's ranch and their real names are mentioned, Zimmer is extremely irritated and cannot see through Hector's intention of doubling his life story:

> Until the film began to play out on the screen in front of me, all those things had been real. Now, in the black-and-white images of Charlie Grund's camera, they had been turned into the elements of a fictional world. I was supposed to read them as shadows, but my mind was slow to make the adjustment. Again and again, I saw them as they were, not as they were meant to be. (243)

The writer Martin Frost intends to take a rest in the desert, "to live the life of a stone" (245). However, he is soon haunted by the mysterious, secretive Claire, whose surname is the same as his first name. By falling in love with her, Martin loses ground since Claire refuses to reveal any of her secrets. He will have the same impression as Zimmer, namely that as soon as he finds an answer to a question, another mystery turns up: "And yet, Martin continues, speaking after another long pause, by eliminating one kind of confusion, you only create another" (253). At the end, Martin surprisingly burns his short story in order to rescue the dying Claire. Auster here turns the destructive element of fire upside down and transforms it into a life-saving means. He depicts Martin as an artist who, by burning the pages he has written, makes a great sacrifice in order to turn the tables (268).

In parallel, Hector tries to "rescue" Brigid O'Fallon, his lover, and indirectly himself, too, by making films that will later be burnt. With an act of destruction, he paradoxically confesses his guilt; he hopes to clear his conscience (278). However, Zimmer's research work and his journeys seem to become senseless, when all of Hector's films made at the ranch turn into ashes, together with Hector's corpse. Zimmer even becomes unintentionally involved in the destruction of the movies. Auster here deconstructs the expected ending, i.e., that his I-narrator will find out the truth about the comedian's mysterious life and his work. On the whole Zimmer has to learn that Hector's "central aim was nothingness" (279), that the films were merely self-centered to the extent that the spectator did not play any role in Hector's aesthetic understanding. With Frieda's invitation, Zimmer is enticed into supporting this form of art lacking any reference to the outside world. After his extremely active research around the world, he is now condemned to inactivity and does nothing except "[continuing his] aimless travels around the house" (282). Hence he remains unable to prevent Frieda from becoming obsessive and violent and Alma from committing suicide.

With the depiction of Zimmer's following return to Vermont, Auster underlines the destructive urge which entraps his I-narrator. Everywhere he walks, he sees signs of death or "instances of decay: the . . . bark fragments moldering on the trails, . . . the mildew stains on the walls of the house" (296). At the end of his postmodern wandering Zimmer has apparently arrived where he once started out from. He has been wandering in circles, as Alma's farewell letter suggests: "*You start from somewhere, and no matter how far you think you've traveled from that place, you always wind up there in the end*" (309).

However, Zimmer has gained some new, more realistic insight. With Alma's help, he has become sensitive towards his surroundings and realizes details he was not aware of beforehand. The destruction of Hector's work has taught him to sharpen his senses and thus to see through what happens around himself: "After a while, I understood that I was looking at these things through Alma's eyes, trying to see them with a new clarity . . ." (296). To this extent, Auster performs what he already had in mind when writing the transitional piece *White Spaces* or his poem "Credo" from his collection "Facing the Music." It is the necessary turn towards the real objects surrounding ourselves that Auster emphasizes. The wish to become one with the external world seems to come true after his I-narrator is able to leave the desert behind and stop his wandering.

3.5.4. The fragmentary hints at pogroms at the end of the 19th century and the moment of hope

David Zimmer's ability to see through deceptive appearances at the very end of *The Book of Illusions* is foreshadowed by his precise investigations of Hector's family background and the analysis of his films. Right at the beginning of his tour through Europe and across the States, he finds out that Hector's constant efforts to hide the truth about his Jewish roots has been the result of his family's persecution in the province of Galicia at the end of the 19th century. The wound of having experienced anti-Semitic actions at an early age influenced Hector to the extent that he has avoided telling any details of his family. As the narrator puts it more generally, the erasure of memory goes back to "Russian pogroms in the 1880s" that forced "hundreds of thousands of Yiddish-speaking immigrants [to fan] out across western Europe and the United States. Many of them went to South America as well" (85).

By working this event into his 2002 novel, Auster indirectly connects *The Book of Illusions* with his autobiographical mosaic *The Invention of Solitude* and his apocalyptic novel *In the Country of Last Things*. Between the lines the reader is again asked to remember anti-Semitic crimes and thus to link the past with the present. His I-narrator tells a story of a family that was once torn apart and emphasizes the psychic consequences of this experience. The narrative tone is more sober than in Auster's previous books, but the fragmentary character of the fictive story that might really have happened, is quite similar. In just one passage embedded in

Zimmer's investigations of Hector's disappearance, the I-narrator tells about Hector's childhood experience of the anti-Semitic mobs in Galicia. It is indeed the reader's task to place this event in connection with Hector's later decisions. He/she will then understand that Hector's aimless wandering has been the consequence of something that deeply influenced him in his early childhood. Estranged from his roots, his adult life ends in a constant flight, a run from what once formed his identity.

The indirectly conveyed, almost imperceptible instruction to remember crimes of the past is, moreover, based on an optimism that reminds the reader of *The Invention of Solitude* and *In the Country of Last Things,* too. Shortly before he dies, Hector indeed says goodbye to Zimmer with the words "'Until tomorrow'" or "'To be continued'" (226). In spite of his wound of having lost his family, the comedian believes in a future up to the end of his life (226). At the beginning of the novel, this optimism is reflected by Zimmer's denial to give up after he has lost his wife and sons. With the help of his writing process, he becomes more and more able to open himself up to new opportunities instead of secluding himself. In London he has the impression that "[his] life start[s] again" (27), and with Alma's help he later learns that "something [is] still in front of [him]" (200). When Alma dies and Zimmer, for the second time, loses the person he loves the most, he is even strong enough to carry on: "I had been planning to fall apart, to slip into my old routine of hapless sorrow and alcoholic ruin, but in the light of that summer morning in Vermont, something in me resisted the urge to destroy myself" (313-314).

With these passages, as well as with the open ending of *The Book of Illusions*, the moment of hope is emphasized just as in *In the Country of Last Things*. Indeed, the I-narrator does not know whether Hector's missing films will ever be found, but he "live[s] with that hope" (321). It is the belief that life will not end in a destructive, violent way, but that it can always go on with new confidence. We can argue that Zimmer's understanding of hope comprises a "Judaic spiritual attitude" which is also part of Jacques Derrida's work (Vernoff 417).[32] It is "a self-concerned, direct, and often specific volition towards a redeeming good, engendered by humans out of their pressing concrete needs" (418). In short, hope includes active behavior.

[32] This Judaic attitude has its basis in "the covenant relation between God and Israel" (Vernoff 417). The original covenant means the "faithful performance of actions – God's faithful leading, Abram's faithful following" (418).

Man's responsibility as the basis of the Jewish understanding of hope is part of Derrida's and Lévinas' philosophy and runs like a thread through Auster's work as well. In *The Book of Illusions*, the I-narrator looks after others and, for example, believes that "Hector's films haven't been lost" (321). In other words, he hopes that in the future people will not resign themselves to the destruction of a work of art and, by doing so, will not consign Hector's experience of persecution to oblivion. The hidden truth about Hector's films and his life will, as Zimmer is sure, be brought to the surface: ". . . and sooner or later a person will come along who accidentally opens the door of the room where Alma hid them, and the story will start all over again. I live with that hope" (321). With this topic of the concern for the other that shows itself in unearthing buried memories, the novel reflects the ethical ideas of Emmanuel Lévinas' philosophy. For him, it is a Judaic necessity that will never be completely fulfilled. In *The Book of Illusions*, the hope of a person's responsibility for an artist's work and his life is also an ideal, a state of perfection in the imagination that might possibly be achieved at some future point in time.

In his 2002 novel, Auster deals with, generally speaking, man's curiosity and resolution to bring the past in connection with the present. His I-narrator does not stop putting the fragmentary hidden memories together and making sense of them. By opening himself up to other people, especially to Alma Grund, he learns to recognize the ethical necessity of his undertaking, i.e., the search for buried truths about a Jewish artist who was once persecuted and, as a consequence, forced to take on different identities. In seeing himself mirrored by Hector Mann, a wanderer, the I-narrator manages to face up to his own past instead of repressing it. He courageously meets the experience of death and his own uprooting and thus gains a more realistic view of his surroundings. Through Zimmer's eyes, Auster looks at an American writer's everyday-world, his thoughts, and impressions, and at the fictitious work of a Jewish artist in particular. It is a writing process that still uses postmodern techniques, but simultaneously hints at how they can be overcome. In particular, Auster's 2002 novel is characterized by a plain, simple style which avoids any elaborations and embellishments. Close observation of familiar surroundings in our Western world also seems to be a poetic necessity which Auster puts into practice. It is possibly the attempt to leave the depiction of confusion and inner turmoil behind which is at the heart of *The Book of Illusions*. Its ending remains open while the I-narrator strongly emphasizes his hope of a pleasant future.

4. Conclusion

This analysis of selected texts by the Jewish-American author Paul Auster, including some published and unpublished early poems as well as certain prose texts, has tried to demonstrate that references to Jewish teaching and history lie at their heart and are interconnected with the development of a deconstructive style of writing which he later left behind. During Auster's intensive study of modern and postmodern European-Jewish, especially French-Jewish, philosophy and literature in the early 1970s, his own writing began to take shape. By reading and analyzing Jacques Derrida, Edmond Jabès, Franz Kafka, Paul Celan, Charles Reznikoff, and others, Auster indirectly turned to address his own Jewish identity. Similar to Auster's analysis of Edmond Jabès, we can thus argue that he "found himself as a [postmodern] writer in the act of discovering himself as a Jew" ("Book of the Dead" 114).

However, Auster does not deal with (his) Jewishness as openly as Jabès or as, for example, the Jewish-American writer Jonathan Safran Foer[33] has done so just recently. Old Testament motives, such as the seemingly endless walk through the desert, the collapse of the Tower of Babel, or the invisible, unreachable God, run like a red thread through his texts, but are often hidden between the lines. The biblical allusions disseminate and supplement each other in Auster's writing and ask for

[33] In his first novel *Everything is Illuminated* (2002), Foer deals with his family's involvement in the Shoah. The fictional alter ego Jonathan Safran Foer travels to the Ukraine in order to find a woman who apparently saved his grandfather from the Nazis. Together with the Ukrainian translator Alex Perchov and his grandfather, he travels through Eastern Europe to the old Jewish shtetl Trachimbrod. A series of letters written by Alex and Jonathan are linked with a narrative of an imagined shtetl of the 18th century which was destroyed during the Shoah. With the help of Alex's grandfather, who is ready to face up to his past, Jonathan becomes able to guess what concretely happened to his family more than fifty years ago (Hornung, "Postmoderne" 383).

the reader's unrestricted concentration to make out the connections they draw between the poems and the prose texts.

By making use of poststructuralist literary means and by metaphorically including aspects of Jewish experience, Auster fulfils what Derrida or Jabès demanded, namely the necessity to "put [writing] into question," as Auster himself emphasized in his essay "Book of the Dead" on Jabès (114). If the writer confronts himself with the boundaries of language, especially by playfully dealing with them, he needs to understand that he might never get precise answers, since "his words are [nothing] more than 'grains of sand' thrown to the wind" (112-13). By regarding deconstructive theory as a literary tool, Auster, in other words, has got the chance to express what is deeply rooted in Judaism, i.e., the tradition of constantly questioning in the sense of a search for truth. At the same time, he transfers a Judaic necessity onto the condition of the writer in general and thus opens up his writing. His incessant questioning with the help of writing is a personal Jewish experience, but also an existential one that every writer needs to come to terms with. When being interviewed by Paul Auster, Edmond Jabès brought this to the point: "And the questioning of the book for the Jew, as you know, is a search for the truth. And this truth is also the writer's truth. When the writer questions the book, it is solely in order to enter the truth of the book, which is his truth" (Auster, "Providence" 149).

Furthermore, Auster pushes writing to its limits and hides the fragmented references to Jewish teaching and experience between the lines. Hence we can argue that his texts cannot be interpreted on the basis of a strict adherence to traditional Jewish life. They must rather be read against the background of Auster's distance to Jewish law and customs. In this respect, he is very close to Jacques Derrida, the father of the theory of deconstruction, who, in "A Testimony Given," admits that because of his ignorance of Hebrew and his unfamiliarity with Jewish history and culture, he turned to "the metaphorical, rhetorical, allegorical dimension of Judaism" (43).

The reason for the rift Derrida felt between himself and Judaism is different to the one we can assume in Auster's case. In *Monolingualism of the Other,* Derrida expands on the wound of having been persecuted because of his Jewish identity, first by having been expelled from school in Algeria in El-Biar in 1942, and then when he was deprived of French citizenship. He became, as he points out, "cut off . . . from Jewish memory" (55), from Jewish religious, historical, and cultural knowledge.

This alienation from Jewish tradition caused Derrida to write about his Jewish identity only indirectly, mainly by analyzing other Jewish philosophers or writers such as Jabès or Lévinas, and then to circle around images or metaphors in Jewish culture and history. In particular, he expanded on the Jewish ritual of circumcision and transferred it onto the field of language.

In her *Portrait of Jacques Derrida as a Young Jewish Saint* (2001), Hélène Cixous explains what it meant for Derrida to be "circumcised" by language. She points to his Jewish first name, which is "Elie" (French for Elijah), his "no-name, . . . the one that will remain hidden" (13). It is an example of a word illustrating the wound existing within language: "*Elie* is there then, always has been, as soon as he begins to write, as a repeated scar, the wound, the word, the word for the wound" (14). In other words, Derrida turns the traditional ritual of circumcision into an image for man's inner wounds and for the "circumcised language" with which man is confronted in general. By doing so, Derrida opens up the religious meaning of "circumcision" and is hence close to the Russian poet Marina Tsvetaeva and her phrase "All poets are Jews" ("A Testimony Given" 68). "This equation is located at the exact center of Jabès's work, is the kernel from which everything else springs," Paul Auster points out in his essay "Book of the Dead" (114). Both Derrida and Jabès underline the "universal mark" of circumcision (Derrida, "A Testimony Given" 40) and, in particular, the writer's separation from language, his inability to express what he wants to say. The poetic experience of language as an "experience of circumcision" (68) can also be detected in Auster's poetry and his prose texts as they are marked by a fragmentary style, by gaps, and omissions.

In his early poetry collections *Unearth* (1970-1972) and *Wall Writing* (1971-1975), Auster depicts writing as a process emerging out of a wound. It is a death-like experience which the impersonal "you" in the first poem of *Unearth*, for example, needs to face up to. It is the feeling of being exiled, imprisoned, or utterly left alone that Auster circles around like Edmond Jabès in his *Book of Questions*. However, it remains impossible for the lyrical I to get to the bottom of its wounds, to explore their hidden reasons. In *Unearth*, Auster already points out the paradox that the more one tries to get close to one's wounds, the more unlikely it becomes to finally reach and understand them (57). Derrida maintains exactly the same, namely the contradiction between the obsession with a wound on the one hand, and the inability to pinpoint it on the other hand.

"Circling around a wound" will always remain a hopeless undertaking, as he emphasizes in "A Testimony Given" (40). Moreover, he connects it with the meaning of "différance," the playful operation that avoids any centeredness or fixation on an origin. Since every source or origin becomes differed and deferred against itself in Derrida's philosophical project, it is impossible to get to the bottom of it. In short, the movement of "différance" blocks every wound by distancing it from itself ("A Testimony Given" 44). This includes the act of remembering, the attempt to get hold of almost forgotten past experiences by heaving them to the surface. As Derrida stresses, memories are always at risk of being forgotten (51); they slip through the network of present impressions and dissolve into the unknown.

The I-narrator of Auster's autobiographical memoir "Portrait of an Invisible Man," the first part of *The Invention of Solitude*, tries to gather his memories of his father after the latter has died. With the help of his writing process, he hopes to satisfy his inmost "hunger," his desire to understand who his father really was. He tries to cope with his inner wound, the fact that his father was always an "invisible man," and indirectly yearns to get close to his Jewish roots. This "hunger" he needs to maintain for a long time, since he knows that if he stops looking for his father, the latter would vanish altogether ("Portrait" 6). However, the more details the I-narrator tries to gather about his father's life, the more confused he becomes. His memories of his father disseminate, displace, and erase each other, until he understands that his hunger will never be stilled completely. Hence he produces a fragmented autobiographical piece of writing which consists of short, independent paragraphs loosely connected with each other. The breaks within the text reflect the I-narrator's old sores which have been opened by the father's death. Until the end he remains unable to draw a coherent picture of the father, and the only answer he gets is that his father's absence is the cause of his alienation from Jewish roots.

With "The Book of Memory," the second part of *The Invention of Solitude*, Auster also creates a fragmentary piece of writing, in which disseminating thoughts displace each other permanently. The shift is to a third-person narrator called A., with whom Auster emphasizes the general necessity to turn away from oneself to the other. In doing so, he presents a more distanced picture of himself. In some early published and unpublished poems, Auster's approach to the other and the surrounding ordinary things can already be seen. The necessary turn toward the real lies, for example, at the center of "Interior," a poem from *Wall Writing*. Here, the influence the Objectivists such as George Oppen, Charles Reznikoff, or William Carlos Williams have had on Auster can be detected, as Auster puts the emphasis on the attempt of the lyrical I to depict the surrounding things most exactly (67). Indeed, in his essay "The Decisive Moment" on the Jewish-American Charles Reznikoff, Auster comes to the conclusion that at the bottom of the Objectivists' attempt to stay on the surface of life and to describe nothing but concrete details, there lies the Jewish experience of being exiled (39). The Objectivists, according to Auster, need to look at the world like "an outsider" or "a stranger," while the observing eye "vanishes" (3). Otherwise they would not be able to depict a thing as precisely as they wish to. Both attempts – to open up oneself to the real and to describe a particular object as exactly as possible – are part of Auster's early poems. Especially in his unpublished poem "Land's End," Auster underlines the necessity of finding purity and precision in language, which Stéphane Mallarmé demanded with his "oeuvre pure."

However, as Auster's writing turns to prose, an interesting shift occurs. Auster now points out the writer's inability to approach one particular thing and grasp it with words. In the prose version of "Land's End," "City of Words," he describes a modern urban scenery and, with it, distances himself from concentrating on the internal world of a lyrical I. To this extent, "City of Words" foreshadows what Auster later illustrates in his novels. In *City of Glass*, the protagonist Daniel Quinn yearns to take down every of Stillman, Sr.'s steps by following and observing him everywhere. In parallel, Anna Blume in *In The Country of Last Things* also tries to describe her apocalyptic surroundings as exactly as possible in order to keep her memory intact. Both characters will, however, learn that this attempt is doomed to failure, since their, and other people's, thoughts and words incessantly disseminate, supplement each other, and disappear. In short, Auster's valediction from poetry and his turn to deconstructive prose writing goes along with his denial of finding perfection or purity in language. In particular, the transitional piece *White Spaces* underlines the impossibility of finding a word that sums up a specific atmosphere or situation.

This extreme skepticism of language goes along with the insight that the attempt to circle around one's wounds will always be a paradoxical and thus disturbing undertaking. Auster already outlined this in some poems of *Unearth* and develops it in his prose texts. In "Portrait of an

Invisible Man," the I-narrator does not only fail to put the fragmentary, contradictory memories of his father together, to capture the "man hidden inside the man who was not there" (20). He is also unable to come to terms with the different stories of his grandfather's death, and can hence only assume why he himself and his father have lost any deeper contact to their Jewish background.

In parallel, Daniel Quinn in Auster's anti-detective novel *City of Glass* tries to cope with the death of his wife and son by first retreating into complete isolation and writing mystery novels, then by taking on the role of a detective and following Stillman, Sr., who is apparently a criminal, through the street network of New York. When becoming obsessed with the "case," Quinn constantly circles around his inner wound without understanding that the pursuit of Stillman, Sr., will not give him any answer. He cannot imagine that the idea of the Stillman case has probably been nothing but a figment of his imagination, that there is no culprit or victim in reality. With the deconstruction of the main features of the detective novel, Auster, in other words, underlines the impossibility of tracking down a specific center, origin, or the end of a search.

The Jewish protagonist Anna Blume in the epistolary novel *In the Country of Last Things* has not only been wounded in the sense that she has lost her brother from the moment she arrived in an apocalyptic, nightmarish world of decay. Moreover, she already lost contact to her family when she was still living at home. In her letter to her friend, she admits that she has never been good in remembering details of her everyday-life. It is not a temporary, but a permanent inability to hold onto past moments which the protagonist suffers from. Her memories have always been disseminating and erasing each other; the result is a feeling of emptiness, an inner void that Anna Blume cannot ignore. She knows that she might never return home or see her brother again and admits that she will repeatedly fail in her attempt "to read the signs" (6), to prevent signifiers from vanishing. In fact, her desire to get hold of her intact past and to memorize her present experiences by taking down as many words as possible will not be satisfied until the end. However, her view of her surroundings is far more realistic than Daniel Quinn's, and she is consequently able to write about the dissemination and erasure of her memories and impressions in a down-to-earth manner.

With Anna Blume's attempt to complete a coherent letter, Auster clearly distances himself from the Dadaistic approach which aims at an aesthetic of absurdity. At the same time, he hints at possibilities how the poststructuralist writing methods can be overcome. Observing one's surroundings as precisely as possible is one of the possibilities that Anna tries to pursue in order to survive. Auster depicts this necessity of close observation, which he already hints at in "Interior," as well as in other early poems, in a minimalist, neorealistic style. This style which he connected with the use of poststructuralist techniques in *City of Glass*, he now develops by focusing on the violent and destructive forces of the postmodern metropolis.

In *The Book of Illusions,* Auster continues the interconnection of deconstructive and neorealistic writing methods to depict the consequences of an extreme family situation (Hornung, "Postmoderne" 384). To overcome his grief after the loss of his family, David Zimmer, the I-narrator, analyzes the films of the vanished Jewish silent comedian Hector Mann and tries to depict his life story in detail. Only with his powers of observation and his growing sensitivity towards the actor's past experiences will he eventually see through his own and other people's illusions. Until Zimmer will be able to do so, he needs to gather and then put together the contradictory, fragmentary information about the comedian as if doing a jigsaw puzzle, similar to the I-narrator of "Portrait of an Invisible Man."

By trying to get to the bottom of Hector Mann's wounds, i.e., the separation from his family, Zimmer is, similar to Daniel Quinn, haunted by doubles, ghost-like apparitions, and figments. Simultaneously, he circles around his own wound, the loss of his family, in his solitude without being able to get in contact with reality until he finally meets Hector Mann. In other words, the movement of différance, this "strategy without finality," as Derrida calls it in his essay and lecture "Différance," runs through Auster's 2002 novel and the above mentioned prose texts by preventing wounded characters from getting answers, solving mysterious, disturbing riddles, or from reaching any long-desired destination.

Jacques Derrida and Edmond Jabès both depict man's struggle to cope with his inner self and the surrounding world with the Old Testament metaphor of the desert. In particular, the writer incessantly yearns to reach the "promised land," a place of fulfillment, a moment of precision in language. However, this yearning will never be stilled; he remains separated from any epistemological truth and from the purity of words. By experiencing this "form of exiled speech" (67), it is only a "vague estate" the writer can reach, often nothing but a "non-place" (69). In "Portrait of an Invisible Man," Auster also parallels the writing process with the walk through the desert. By arduously trying to put his memories of his Jewish family, especially his father, into words, the I-narrator becomes sure "that the path towards [his] object does not exist" (32). His "feeling of moving around in circles, of perpetual back-tracking" (32) prevents him from getting the desired answers and from producing a coherent, traditionally structured piece of writing.

This utter state of desolation is equally emphasized with biblical, metaphorical language in Auster's poetry. In poem No. 2 of *Unearth*, Auster, for instance, expresses the impossibility of taking hold of what the desired place of homecoming seems to assure: "Flails, the whiteness, the flowers / of the promised land: and all / you hoard, crumbling at the brink / of breath" (38). In poem No. 17 of the same collection, Auster highlights the difficulty of the writing process by describing the walk towards the promised land as one filled with brutality and suffering: ". . . this path of tallied cries, and grain / after grain, the never-done-with / desert, burning on your lips / that jell in violence" (53). The tone in Auster's collection *Fragments from Cold* becomes softer, but in his poem "Quarry," the lyrical I is also certain that the imagined destination of an inner search will repeatedly elude: "The world / that walks inside me / is a world beyond reach" (138).

In the transitional prose piece *White Spaces*, Auster depicts the lack of any desired destination even more plainly by making use of the metaphor of the city that he compares with the desert as well as the sea. All three places express the self-contradictory undertaking of trying to hold onto disappearing thoughts on a journey ad infinitum: "It is a journey through space, as if into many cities and out of them, as if across deserts, as if to the edge of some imaginary ocean, where each thought drowns in the relentless waves of the real" (159).

Edmond Jabès, as Derrida points out, also replaces the image of the desert with the image of the city. With both of them, Jabès seems to capture the writer's situation, his alienation, and his yearning, and simultaneously relates the history of Judaism to the situation of the modern writer and vice versa. In Derrida's analysis, the desert and the city appear as a "labyrinth" as their pathways space up themselves into the infinite ("Edmond Jabès" 69). In poem No. 7 of *Disappearances*, Auster also makes use of the metaphor of the city and places the emphasis on the unsuccessfulness of the writer's efforts. His search for the individual, very personal and thus precise word will be in vain: ". . . For the city is monstrous, / and its mouth suffers / no issue / that does not devour the word / of oneself" (113).

With Daniel Quinn's pursuit of Stillman, Sr., in *City of Glass,* Auster develops his use of both the metaphor of the desert and the city to illustrate the inner disorientation of the postmodern writer. Like Derrida, Auster depicts the city as a "labyrinth of endless steps," a confusing network of streets spreading themselves out into the unknown. By slipping into the role of a detective and by arbitrarily wandering through the street network of New York, Quinn erases his true identity and becomes dependent on Stillman, Sr.'s, linguistic and theological project, the creation of "pure logos" (Russell 74). First, Quinn's decision to follow Stillman wherever he walks does not have any deeper meaning, but after a while he behaves like an archivist trying to record each of "the culprit's" steps that would otherwise be invisible. With Quinn's manner of recording, Auster is close to Derrida's topic of the process of archiving that comes into being at the moment of forgetting (Derrida, *Archive Fever* 11 ff.). By gathering material that would otherwise be lost, the archivist, according to Derrida and Auster, hopes to prevent memories from slipping through the network of consciousness, and hence to satisfy his desire for orientation.

Daniel Quinn tries to satisfy his yearning for stability by walking in the steps of his self-proclaimed "father" of speech. The latter declares himself as a new Adam by undoing the "fall of language" (Auster, *City of Glass* 52), i.e., the arbitrariness of the sign, the splitting up of signifier and signified (Holzapfel 45 and Kierkegaard 168). Both Quinn and Stillman, Sr., hope to revive the old Babylonian dream of being united by one unmistakable, "pure" language. With their belief in one absolute truth, they regard the Tower of Babel as a symbol of power underlining the necessity to achieve complete "understanding" between men. By wandering through the desert-like metropolis, they, as a consequence, do not only search for the total correspondence between signifier and signified, but also hope to suppress any form of diversity. However, with the "ending" of their logocentric undertaking – Stillman, Sr. commits suicide and Quinn literally vanishes out of the text – Auster speaks, like Derrida, in favor of the Jewish-Christian interpretation of the Old Testament parable, i.e., God's unavoidable decision to confuse the Semites' language and evocate diversity between men.

In his essay "White Mythology," Jacques Derrida also points out that in the story of the Tower of Babel, God "interrupts . . . the colonial violence or the linguistic imperialism" (253) of the Semites' readiness to introduce one universal language. In parallel, Auster criticizes colonization indirectly by deconstructing Stillman's attempt to "draw" a map for the erection of the "new Babel" in America (Auster, *City of Glass* 59). He especially speaks against the 17th-century Puritan conviction of being the newly "chosen people" for the creation of the "promised land." In fact, Stillman's plan to recreate the "prelapsarian language" in America, which was apparently spoken in Eden (57), will not have any consequences. The letters of the four words "The Tower of Babel" he tries to draw into space will remain invisible; they vanish as soon as Stillman begins to walk through the streets.

As a result, Quinn's desire for paternal authority and "author-ity" (Russell 73) will not be satisfied. With his continuing logocentric quest, his search for definite meaning and truth, he does not stop circling around his wound of having lost what he once loved. By arduously maintaining his yearning, he develops into a Kafkaesque hunger artist and finally vanishes out of the text like Stillman, Sr.'s, double noticed by Quinn at the beginning of his pursuit. *City of Glass* is, in short, a novel about the attempt to reach a particular destination or origin by continuously "tracking down the signs of its disappearance," as Derrida puts it in "Ellipsis," another essay on Jabès's *Book of Questions.* In other words, "it is an origin by means of which nothing has begun" (295).

In the apocalyptic novel *In the Country of Last Things,* Auster also uses the Old Testament motif of endless wandering through an inhuman, desert-like place to underline the impossibility of ever reaching a desired destination by putting words on paper. It is the non-existence of "the promised land" on the horizon of the writing process that Auster already focused on in his poem "Late Summer" of his collection *Wall Writing* (118). In his 1987 novel, the protagonist Anna Blume does not only hope to collect as many "broken things" as possible on her roams through the streets, but also to find words that may express her feelings and observations most precisely. Spoken words are indeed depicted as a material, "as though they were physical objects, literal stones" (133). The signifier is compared to a material substance being separated from the signified. The disappearance of objects in Auster's apocalyptic novel thus reflects Derrida's renunciation of any presence in language.

By writing her letter, Anna Blume struggles against the disintegration of words. She hopes to hinder the signifiers from vanishing into the unknown, to stop them from getting lost in time and space. However, she continually needs to admit that she fails with her project of keeping the written language intact, of searching her mind for words she has not used for a long time. This uncertainty of the future of language is underlined by the motif of wandering at the very end of the novel. Anna does not know where she will head towards on her flight out of "the country of last things," nor is it clear whether her friend will ever get her letter. However, with Anna's belief that she will continue her writing as soon as she reaches her destination, Auster expresses his hope of the future in spite of all present adversities.

In *The Book of Illusions,* the desert is depicted as the place where the turning point in Zimmer's, the I-narrator's, life occurs. Here, he has to face his limitations before he is able to write a coherent text about Hector Mann's films and his own experiences. He has to understand that the more eagerly he tries to track down the truth, the more confused he might become. Indeed, Zimmer's postmodern way of wandering by flying around the globe, which reflects Mann's restless existence and vice versa, makes him uncertain of Mann's true character. Like the I-narrator of "Portrait of an Invisible Man," he does not get the desired answers when he meets him. The only definite answer Zimmer finally gets is that Mann chose the desert, a place of complete isolation, of his own free will after having led a nomadic way of life. Here, in a kind of inner exile, Mann can shoot films destined to be burnt. By depicting the film plots in detail, Auster doubles Mann's life story and thus heightens his I-narrator's confusion, also concerning Mann's radical aesthetic approach. This approach is, as Zimmer learns, based on Mann's illusion of being able to continue his life as an artist by cutting himself off from society and by wiping out any possible effect of his work on the future. The uncanny apparitions and déjà-vus Zimmer needs to cope with after arriving in the desert of New Mexico underline the absurdity of Hector's art, but foremost turn the idea of a clearly perceptible destination upside down. Again, it is the absence of any center or fixed idea of truth that Auster writes about. As Derrida puts it in "Edmond Jabès or the Question of the Book": "the Land always keeps itself beyond any proximity" (66).

In this essay, Derrida also describes "the moment of the desert as the moment of Separation" (68) between man and God as a consequence of “a rupture within God” Himself (67). The biblical key passage for Derrida is the one in Exodus, when God keeps silent and hides His face after Moses has broken the Tables (EX 32,7 – 33,23). In *The Book of Questions,* Jabès depicts the invisibility of God by connecting it with the suffering of the Israelites: “’God is the absence of God. Exile within exile’” (272). Because of God’s silence, man becomes, as both Derrida and Jabès point out, responsible for his own actions, his own words, and consequently for writing itself: “Writing is, thus, originally hermetic and secondary. Our writing, certainly, but already His, which starts with the stifling of his voice and the dissimulation of his Face” (Derrida, “Edmond Jabès” 67). This responsibility expressing itself in writing is not only the consequence of the absence of God, but of original sin, too. As man was unable to obey God’s commands, he has had to live a life of constant questioning by writing. In *The Book of Questions,* Jabès summarizes this in the following way: “The garden means speaking, the desert, writing. In every grain of sand, a sign surprises us” (149).

The traditional Jewish image of the invisible, unattainable God also appears in Auster’s poetry, for example in “Song of Degrees” from *Wall Writing* (94). Here, God remains absent while man is praying on his walk through the desert. In his poem “Covenant” of the same collection, Auster, however, emphasizes that God can be present although he might not be seen or heard. He is visible and invisible at the same time (83). When being interviewed by Paul Auster, Jabès also points to the possibility of God’s presence in spite of his absence:

> In other words, when you say ‘invisible,’ you are pointing to the boundary between the visible and the invisible: there are words for that. But when you can’t say the word, you are standing before nothing. And for me this is even more powerful because, finally, there is a visible in the invisible, just as there is an invisible in the visible. And this, this abolishes everything. (Auster, “Providence” 160)

In parallel, the invisibility of God is made visible through the writing process in Auster’s poem “Wall Writing.” Here, the “whiteness of a word,” i.e., its “invisible” connotations, is “scratched into a wall” and connected with God’s absence (81). In “Ecliptic. Les Halles,” God also remains invisible, but speaks indirectly, with the voice of the prophet Ezekiel (74). Auster’s poems consequently do not neglect the possibility of God’s existence, but instead confirm it by hinting at the ungraspable. By showing “the visible in the invisible” (“Providence” 160) they also fulfill Derrida's demand to track down the hidden meanings "between the margins" of a text.

In Auster's prose writing, the self-concealment of God is linked with the I-narrator's or protagonist's unsatisfied desire to receive a definite answer or reach a specific source by putting words on paper. The depiction of God as the absent, unattainable origin in "Portrait of an Invisible Man" reflects the I-narrator's continuous search for the father and his Jewish roots. As a consequence, Auster is close to Derrida's renunciation of "logocentrism," the metaphysical dependence on a center, or, more precisely, on God's original voice, His spoken words. The theory of deconstruction subverts the traditional hierarchy between speech and writing by treating writing as a signifying process and links it with the self-concealment of God.

In *City of Glass*, Auster also clearly connects the depiction of God as the non-present origin with the failure of his protagonist's logocentric quest. Daniel Quinn's unsuccessful pursuit of Stillman, Sr., his new "father of logos" who hopes to find God's language, goes hand in hand with God's absence. In contrast to the poems, Auster here deconstructs God' name; he depicts it as a signifier of the past reflecting the break of the postmodern man with traditional religious practice. Quinn's fragmentary thought of God's existence flies off into all kinds of imaginable directions similarly to the words "Tower of Babel" that Stillman, Sr., tries to implant in time and space by walking through New York. Quinn's recognition of God's name – "El", the two last letters of the word "Babel," is the Hebrew word for God – will not have any consequences for him.

In *In the Country of Last Things*, Auster does not deconstruct God's name, but depicts God as the One who does not show His face. Both Isabel, Anna's friend, and the Rabbi, whom Anna meets in the library, believe that God is hiding in a different sphere, remote from all the destruction and suffering they experience daily. God seems to have ceased to exist in this apocalyptic world, and most urbanites, including Anna, have stopped believing in Him. The lack of religious rituals or ceremonies in the "country of last things" reminds the reader of the missing or very liberal religious practices and the diminished communities and parishes, foremost Jewish-European ones after World War II. However, Isabel innocently accepts the unexplainable, and the Rabbi helps Anna by telling her where Sam, her brother's colleague, lives. Auster thus contrasts the apocalyptic cruelties with miraculous, almost spiritual scenes and expresses his hope of humane behavior.

With Auster's turn to prose, the moment of hope lights up over and over again in spite of the absence of truth in a desolate world. Most of the early poems, with the exception of "Pastoral" from *Wall Writing* and a few others, are however "taut and furious" texts (Finkelstein, "Introduction" 10), sinister or ominous lines rebelling against injustice and violence, often in a coded, symbolically condensed language. When the poetry "was beginning to change, beginning to open up," as Auster explains in an interview with Larry McCaffery and Sinda Gregory (301), he apparently confronted the "stony exterior world" more directly (Finkelstein, "Introduction" 12). His references to crimes of the past and their effects on the present gradually become more distinct, until Auster unmistakably faces the Shoah in his autobiographical memoir *The Invention of Solitude.*

With those poems that deal with extreme suffering by emphasizing the infinity of the desert and the non-existence of the promised land, Auster also confronts the Shoah, however indirectly. His subsequent writing in prose gradually becomes more pointed. In "The Book of Memory," the second part of *The Invention of Solitude,* Auster underlines that the sadness he felt when standing in Anne Frank's little room in Amsterdam was one major cause for writing this text. The feeling of identification he connects with a multitude of fragmentary quotations from other Jewish writers as well as passages from stories and reports on the time of the Shoah. All these quotations do not only refer to each other, but point to those novels by Auster that also deal with the Shoah. By reflecting each other, the texts connect present personal experiences of death with Jewish history and thus make clear that the present can only be understood in relation to the past. Above all, Auster transports the Jewish ethical principle of responsibility with the poststructuralist means of intertextuality. By reminding the reader of the past, he emphasizes the need of the other so that the future will be more peaceful.

The ethical component in Jacques Derrida's philosophical project of deconstruction shows the influence the French-Jewish philosopher Emmanuel Lévinas has had on him. Indeed, Lévinas's restriction of the Greek similarity principle based on the same or the autonomous with the help of the Otherness principle pointed the way to Derrida's denial of "logocentrism." The "absolutely Other," as Lévinas explains in *Totality and Infinity* (33), remains separated from, or foreign to, the I and can thus never be possessed (39). However, Lévinas develops an ethics based on a metaphysical desire that turns toward this "absolutely other," toward the ungraspable or mysterious (33): ". . . it appears as a movement going forth from a world that is familiar to us, . . . from an 'at home' ['chez-soi'] which we inhabit, toward an alien outside-of-oneself [*hors-de-soi*], toward a yonder" (33). It is the necessity of presenting oneself to the face of the other in the way Abraham presented himself to God by saying "hineni" ("here I am") (Putnam 38). The unrestricted openness to the divine command is paralleled to the ethical demand of offering oneself to the other. At the same time, the I needs to understand that the distance to the other can never be fully overcome. As much as God hides His face, the other remains "an exteriority that does not call for power or possession" *(Totality and Infinity* 51).

The necessary approach to the other can also be detected in Paul Auster. In his poetry, it seems to be more an aesthetic phenomenon, whereas it develops into an ethical necessity in his prose. The desire to get in contact with the surrounding world to depict the inner state most precisely is one of the most crucial themes of Auster's poetry. Norman Finkelstein sees it similarly: "The strange meetings with an other which inspire poem after poem . . . are the accounts of a restless young man, formidably intelligent, who is determined to make lasting contact with the world outside his own head" ("Introduction" 12/13). Quite often, the lyrical I addresses an impersonal "you" to find the most suitable words for expressing its loneliness and desperation, excitement and resistance.

However, "the urgency of the communication, combined with an innate respect (honor *and* fear) of language" is not, as Finkelstein claims, "such that he finds himself" (13). The inner self will rather remain inaccessible, as well as the other whom the writer approaches to overcome the inadequacy of his words. In spite of all efforts, the other is separated from the searching subject: "And in the nethermost / lode of whiteness – a memory / that adds your steps / to the lost. / Endlessly / I would have walked with you" (Auster, "Effigies" 154/155).

In *City of Glass,* the approach to the other is of existential necessity. With Stillman, Sr., Quinn unconsciously hopes to satisfy his hunger for paternal authority, for orientation, and stability. By recording or archiving each of Stillman's movements as exactly as possible, he tries to cope with his own forgetfulness. However, Quinn preserves his hunger even after Stillman has already vanished out of the text. "Father" and "son" will remain separated from each other.

With Anna Blume's readiness to help absolute strangers in *In the Country of Last Things*, the approach to the other becomes an ethical necessity. According to Emmanuel Lévinas, the concern for the other is grounded within Judaism: "*Kol Yisrael 'arevim zeh lazeh*, 'All Israel is responsible one for the Other'" ("The Pact" 226). In recent years, Derrida has similarly outlined the ethical necessity of a universal responsibility against the background of a religious, especially Jewish-Christian, context. In his 1987 novel, Auster conveys the principle of reciprocal responsibility foremost with his female characters (Anna, Isabel, and Victoria) rescuing each other. He contrasts their heroic behavior against the background of an apocalyptic scenery, the Shoah, and present-day anti-Semitic thinking. Thus he indirectly expresses his hope of a better, more humane future. The reader's task is not only to remember the crimes of the past, as Auster stresses in "The Book of Memory," but to become active by taking responsibility for the other, the one unknown to oneself.

With David Zimmer's, the I-narrator's, preoccupation with the mysterious Hector Mann, Paul Auster also expresses an existential as well as ethical necessity. In order to live with the disastrous experiences he made, Zimmer needs to get as close as possible to the uprooted actor, who, like Zimmer, has separated himself from the exterior world. His intensive investigations of Mann's background reveal buried truths about the actor's decision to hide his Jewish roots. Because of his childhood experience of Russian pogroms at the end of the 19th century, Mann became separated from his family and estranged from any religious practice, as the I-narrator finds out.

When Mann eventually dies, Zimmer learns that not only the other always stays to be a stranger, but that he will never completely understand himself, either. When leaving Mann's ranch, Zimmer is, however, able to distance himself from the actor's and filmmaker's paradoxical aesthetic theory to create a work of art by destroying it. Moreover, Zimmer's decision to refuse "the idea of cremation" (311) is also an indirect, but urgent appeal not to repeat the crimes of the Shoah and of other times in history. The active turn to past realities is demanded to overcome present illusions and to do what one can for a more tolerable future. Connected with this ethical necessity is an aesthetic one that connects *The Book of Illusions* with Auster's poetry.

The demand to leave behind the absolute concentration on one's inner self and to turn to the other leads to the decision to observe and then to depict the exterior world as exactly as possible. By opening up himself to Alma Grund, and by accurately describing Mann's surroundings and his films, Zimmer becomes able to face up to his own past and to produce a coherent narrative text.

In spite of the deconstructive ideas that find its literary rendition in *In the Country of Last Things*, Auster does not dissolve the epistolary form of the novel. It lacks chapters and headings, but there is a clear beginning of the letter, as well as a clear end. With his more recent novel *The Brooklyn Follies* (2005) Auster seems to have distanced himself from Jacques Derrida's philosophical ideas even further. Clearly structured and subdivided into chapters of almost equal length, it tells about the experiences of Nathan and Tom, an uncle and his nephew, before September 11, 2001. With its ending, the collapse of the Twin Towers, Auster continues his depiction of present-day disasters which he, often marginally, refers to in his novels. Moreover, the language he uses reminds the reader of the Shoah and thus links the novel with Auster's former prose texts and his poems: "Just two hours after that, the smoke of three thousand incinerated bodies would drift over toward Brooklyn and come pouring down on us in a white cloud of ashes and death" (*Brooklyn Follies* 304).

The reason why Auster has apparently turned toward a more realistic and structured way of writing may lie in the theory of deconstruction itself. Indeed, Derrida's texts "are conducted at the highest level of sustained analytical grasp" (Norris 151). They in fact have to be, since there is no point in simply not creating an "intentionalist ground of appeal" (ibid.) In other words, Derrida creates a well thought-out, extremely polished line of argumentation based on his key "concept" of différance. (Norris 152).[34] Consequently, deconstruction cannot be regarded as a species of all-licensing sophistical 'freeplay'" (Norris 151), offering an inexhaustible supply of indefinite, obscure possibilities.

[34] However, this has been critized as an inconsistency by a number of philosophers and literary critics. In spite of Derrida's explanation that the movement of différance cannot be regarded as a newly established origin (Derrida, "Différance" 64), Christopher Norris and others have stressed that it can indeed be interpreted as a new center, from which Derrida develops his ideas.

Although Auster does not adher to deconstructive ideas in T*he Brooklyn Follies* any more, the motive of the remote, inaccessible place of homecoming is also present at the end. Nathan, the I-narrator, feels "happy as any man who [has] ever lived" at eight o'clock on 9/11, just some minutes before the first plane is supposed to crash into the World Trade Center. Nathan's happiness will not last any longer, so he will probably become a seeker for some meaning in life again, just like Daniel Quinn, Anna Blume, or David Zimmer. In an unpublished part of the interview with Larry McCaffery and Sinda Gregory, which can be found in the Berg Collection of The New York Public Library, Auster emphasizes his intention of continuously leading his characters to a boundary, where they realize that the place of homecoming they have been looking for does not exist:

> They are all seekers . . . they are seeking for the moment of truth. But, you see, I don't believe that moment is possible. There's no promised land, it's not going to happen. . . . that point of extremity is where the truth is, and that's the place I seemed to be compelled to push my characters toward to see how they will react.

With the collapse of the World Trade Center at the end of *Brooklyn Follies*, Auster again depicts the city as a place where man can never be safe, where his yearning to find rest will not be satisfied. Surprisingly, the image of the destruction of towers, that is here an actual, not a fictional, point of reference, already appears in an early unpublished holograph. In this holograph, it can be understood in more general terms, i.e., as an image for any lost guidance in life, or it can be referred to the biblical image of the Tower of Babel: "The city has never been ours. / Banished by the stones we hoisted, / We wait where wolves bleed. / The tower is finished." The lyrical I is wounded, driven away, and possibly forced to live in exile. However, it might leave its devastating present and start walking into a more pleasant future. Another quest might begin.

5. Cited Works

5.1. Primary Literature

Auster, Paul. *The Art of Hunger. Essays, Prefaces, Interviews, and The Red Notebook.* 1992. New York: Penguin, 1997.

- - -. "The Art of Hunger." *The Art of Hunger* 9-20.

- - -. "Between the Lines." *Collected Poems* 147.

- - -. "Book of the Dead." *The Art of Hunger* 107-14.

- - -. *The Book of Illusions.* New York: Henry Holt and Company, 2002.

- - -. "The Book of Memory." *The Invention of Solitude* 71-171.

- - -. *The Brooklyn Follies*. London: Faber and Faber, 2005.

- - -. "Choral." *Collected Poems* 70.

- - -. *City of Glass*. 1985. *The New York Trilogy*. New York: Penguin, 1990. 1-158.

- - -. *Collected Poems*. Woodstock, New York: The Overlook Press, 2004.

- - -. "Covenant." *Collected Poems* 83.

- - -. "Credo." *Collected Poems* 141.

- - -. "The Decisive Moment." *The Art of Hunger* 35-53.

- - -. *Disappearances*. 1975. *Collected Poems* 105-14.

- - -. "Ecliptic. Les Halles." *Collected Poems* 74.

- - -. *Facing the Music.*1980. *Collected Poems* 141-52.

- - -. *Fragments from Cold.* 1977. *Collected Poems* 123-38.

- - -. "Hieroglyph." *Collected Poems* 86.

- - -. "Interior." *Collected Poems* 67.

- - -. *In the Country of Last Things.* 1987. London: Faber and Faber, 1989.

- - -. "Interview with Joseph Mallia." *The Art of Hunger* 327-40.

- - -. "Interview with Larry McCaffery and Sinda Gregory." *The Art of Hunger* 287-326.

- - -. “Interview with Mark Irwin.” *The Art of Hunger* 327-40.

- - -. *The Invention of Solitude*. 1982. New York: Penguin, 1988.

- - -. *Leviathan*. 1992. New York: Penguin, 1993.

- - -. “In Memory of Myself.” *Collected Poems* 148.

- - -. *The Music of Chance*. 1990. London: Faber and Faber, 1991.

- - -. *The New York Trilogy. City of Glass, Ghosts, The Locked Room*. London: Faber and Faber, 1988. New York: Penguin, 1990.

- - -. “Notes from a Composition Book.” *Collected Poems* 201-205.

- - -. “Pages for Kafka. On the Fiftieth Anniversary of His Death.” *The Art of Hunger* 23-25.

- - -. “Pastoral.” *Collected Poems* 92.

- - -. “Portrait of an Invisible Man.” *The Invention of Solitude* 1-79.

- - -. “Private I. Public Eye.” *The Art of Hunger* 115-19.

- - -. “Providence. A Conversation with Edmond Jabès.” *The Art of Hunger* 144-69.

- - -. “Pulse.” *Collected Poems* 68.

- - -. “Quarry.” *Collected Poems* 138.

- - -. “Scribe.” *Collected Poems* 69.

- - -. “Search for a Definition.” *Collected Poems* 145-46.

- - -. “Song of Degrees.” *Collected Poems* 94-95.

- - -. *Timbuktu*. London: Faber and Faber, 1999.

- - -. *Travels in the Scriptorium*. London: Faber and Faber, 2006.

- - -. *Unearth.*1974. *Collected Poems* 35-61.

- - -. *Wall Writing*. 1976. *Collected Poems 63-103.*

- - -. “Wall Writing.” *Collected Poems* 81.

- - -. “White.” *Collected Poems* 87.

- - -. “White Nights.” *Collected Poems* 65.

- - -. *White Spaces*. 1980. *Collected Poems*. 153-62.

Benjamin, Walter. “Die Aufgabe des Übersetzers.“ 1923. *Sprache und Geschichte. Philosophische Essays.* Comp. Rolf Tiedemann. Stuttgart: Reclam, 1992. 50-64.

- - -. “Über Sprache überhaupt und über die Sprache des Menschen.” 1916. *Sprache und Geschichte. Philosophische Essays.* Comp. Rolf Tiedemann.

Stuttgart: Reclam, 1992. 30-49. Derrida, Jacques, and Pierre Jean Labbarière. *Altérités*. Paris 1996.

Derrida, Jacques. *Acts of Religion*. Ed. Gil Anidjar. New York: Routledge, 2002.

- - -, and Pierre Jean Labbarière. *Altérités*. Paris 1996.

- - -. *Apories. Mourir – s'attendre aux 'limites de la vérité.'* Paris : Éditions Galilée, 1996.

- - -. *Archive Fever. A Freudian Impression.* Trans. Eric Prenowitz. Chicago, London: U of Chicago P, 1996. Trans. of *Mal d'Archive: une impression freudienne*. 1995.

- - -. *As if I were Dead. An Interview with Jacques Derrida.* Ed. Ulrike Oudée Dinkelsbühler and Thomas Frey. Wien: Turia und Kant, 2000.

- - -. "At this very Moment Here I Am." *Re-Reading Lévinas.* Ed. Robert Bernasconi and Simon Critchley. Bloomington: Indiana UP, 1991. 11-51.

- - -. "Circumfession. Fifty-nine periods and periphrases written in a sort of internal margin, between Geoffrey Bennington's book and work in preparation (January 1989 – April 1990)." Trans. Geoffrey Bennington. *Jacques Derrida.* Chicago: U of Chicago P, 1993. 3-315. Trans. of *Circonfession.* Paris: Seuil, 1991.

- - -. "Différance." *Margins of Philosophy* 1-27.

- - -. *Dissemination*. Trans. Barbara Johnson. Chicago: The University of Chicago Press, 1981. Trans. of *La Dissémination*. 1972.

- - -. "The Double Session." Abr. Kamuf, *A Derrida Reader* 171-99.

- - -. *The Ear of the Other. Otobiography, Transference, Translation.* Lincoln: U of Nebraska P, 1985.

- - -. "Edmond Jabès and the Question of the Book." *Writing and Difference* 64-78.

- - -. "Ellipsis." *Writing and Difference* 295-300.

- - -. "The Ends of Man." *Margins of Philosophy* 109-36.

- - -. "Faith and Knowledge: The Two Sources of 'Religion' at the Limits of Reason Alone." *Religion* 1-78.

- - -. "Freud and the Scene of Writing." *Writing and Difference* 196-231.

- - -. *Glas*. Paris: Éditions Galilée, 1974.

- - -. "Of Grammatology." Abr. Kamuf, *A Derrida Reader* 34-58.

- - -. "Implications: Interview with Henri Rose." *Positions* 1-14.

- - -. "Interpretations at War: Kant, the Jew, the German." *New Literary History* 22 (1991): 39-95.

- - -, and Geoffrey Bennington. *Jacques Derrida.* 1991. Chicago: U of Chicago P, 1993.

- - -. *Khora.* Paris: Éditions Galilée, 1993.

- - -. "Living On: Border Lines." Abr. Kamuf, *A Derrida Reader* 256-68.

- - -. *Margins of Philosophy.* Trans. Alan Bass. New York: Harvester Wheatsheaf, 1982. Trans. of *Marges de la philosophie.* 1972.

- - -. *Monolingualism of the Other; or, The Prosthesis of Origin.* Stanford: Stanford UP, 1998. Trans. of *Le Monolinguisme de l'autre: ou la prothèse d'origine.* 1996.

- - -. *Positions.* Trans. Alan Bass. London: The Athlone Press, 1987.

- - -. "Positions: Interview with Jean-Louis Houdebine and Guy Scarpetta." *Positions* 37-96.

- - -. "Préjugés. Devant la loi." *La faculté de juger.* Paris 1985. 87-139.

- - -. *Psyché. Inventions de l'Autre. Paris: Galilée 1987.*

- - -, and Gianni Vattimo, eds. *Religion.* Stanford: Stanford UP, 1998.

- - -. *Schibboleth pour Paul Celan.* Paris: Éditions Galilée, 1986.

- - -. "Semiology and Grammatology: *Interview with Julia Kristeva.*" *Positions* 15-36.

- - -. "Signature, Event, Context." *Margins of Philosophy* 307-30.

- - -. "Speech and Phenomena." Abr. Kamuf, *A Derrida Reader* 8-30.

- - -. "Structure, Sign, and Play in the Discourse of the Human Sciences." *Writing and Difference* 278-93.

- - -. "A Testimony Given. Interview with Elizabeth Weber." Weber 39-58.

- - -. "Des Tours de Babel." Abr. Kamuf, *A Derrida Reader* 244-53.

- - -. "Of an Apocalyptic Tone Recently Adopted in Philosophy." *The Oxford Literary Review* 6, 2 (1984). 3-37.

- - -. "Violence and Metaphysics: An Essay on the Thought of Emmanuel Lévinas." *Writing and Difference* 79-153.

- - -. "White Mythology: Metaphor in the Text of Philosophy." *Margins of Philosophy*. 207-71.

- - -. *Writing and Difference.* Trans. Alan Bass. Chicago: The University of Chicago Press, 1978. Trans. of *L'écriture et la différance.* 1967.

Foer, Jonathan Safran. *Everything is Illuminated.* 2002. New York: Penguin, 2003.

Frank, Anne. *Diary of a Young Girl.* Trans. of *Das Tagebuch der Anne Frank.*1949.

Habermas, Jürgen. *Der philosophische Diskurs der Moderne. Zwölf Vorlesungen.* Frankfurt: Suhrkamp Taschenbuch 1988.

Hand, Seàn, ed. *The Lévinas Reader.* Oxford: Blackwell, 2002.

Jabès, Edmond. *The Book of Questions.* Trans. Rosmarie Waldrop. Hanover and London: Wesleyan UP, 1991. Trans. of *Le Livre de Questions*. Paris: Éditions Gallimard, 1963.

Joyce, James. *A Portrait of an Artist as a Young Man*. 1916. London: Penguin, 1996.

Kafka, Franz. "Before the Law." Trans. of "Vor dem Gesetz." *Die Erzählungen und andere ausgewählte Prosa.* Ed. Roger Hermes. Frankfurt a.M.: Fischer Taschenbuch, 2001. 162-63.

- - -. *Der Prozeß.* 1925. Frankfurt a.M.: Fischer Taschenbuch, 1991.

Kamuf, Peggy, ed. *A Derrida Reader: Between the Blinds.* New York: Harvester Wheatsheaf, 1991.

Lévinas, Emmanuel. "Ethics as First Philosophy." Hand 75-87.

- - -. "God and Philosophy." Hand 166-89.

- - -. "Martin Buber and the Theory of Knowledge." Hand 59-74.

- - -. *Otherwise than Being or Beyond Essence.* The Hague: Martinus Nijhoff, 1981. Trans. of *Autrement qu'être ou au-delà de l'essence*. 1974.

- - -. "The Pact." Hand 211-26.

- - -. "Revelation in the Jewish Tradition." Hand 190-210.

- - -. "Time and the Other." Hand 37-58.

- - -. *Totality and Infinity: An Essay on Exteriority.* Trans. Alphonso Lingis. Pittsburgh: Duquesne University Press, 2004. Trans. of *Totalité et Infini.* 1961.

Mallarmé, Stéphane. *Corréspondances 1862-1871*. Paris: Gallimard, 1959.

- - -. "Hérodiade." *Sämtliche Dichtungen.* Trans. Carl Fischer and Rolf Stabel. Ed. F.-H. Hausmann and E. Gräfin Mandelsloh. München: Deutscher Taschenbuch Verlag, 2000. 40-59.

Orwell, George. *Nineteen-Eighty Four*. 1949. London: Penguin, 1990.

Ozick, Cynthia. *The Shawl*. New York: Vintage International, 1990.

Rosenzweig, Franz. *The Star of Redemption.* Trans. William W. Hallo. Boston: Beacon, 1964. Trans. of *Der Stern der Erlösung.* 1921.

Roth, Philip. *Portnoy's Complaint.* 1967. London: Vintage, 1999.

Schwitters, Kurt. *Anna Blume und ich: Die gesammelten Anna Blume-Texte.* Ed. Ernst Schwitters. Zürich: Arche, 1996.

Weber, Elisabeth. *Questioning Judaism: Interviews by Elisabeth Weber.* Standford: Stanford UP, 2004.

5.2. Secondary Literature

Abramovitch, Henry. "Death." Cohen and Mendes-Flohr 131-35.

Ackermann, Christiane. "'It flies off in so many little directions at once.' Das Subjekt als Hyperstruktur in Paul Austers *City of Glass*." Lienkamp and Werth, "*As Strange as the World*" 99-117.

Alford, Steven E. "Spaced-Out: Signification and Space in Paul Auster's *The New York Trilogy*." *Contemporary Literature* 36.4 (1995): 613-32.

- - -. "Mirrors of Madness: Paul Auster's The New York Trilogy." *Critique: Studies in Contemporary Fiction* 37.1 (1995): 17-33.

Atlan, Henri. "Chosen People." Cohen and Mendes-Flohr 55-59.

Azria, Regina. "The Diaspora-Community-Tradition. Paradigms of Jewish Identity: A Reappraisal." Krausz and Tulea 21-32.

Barone, Dennis. "Auster's Memory." *The Review of Contemporary Fiction* 14.1 (1994 Spring): 32-34.

- - -, ed. *Beyond the Red Notebook. Essays on Paul Auster.* Philadelphia: U of Pennsylvania P, 1995.

- - -, "Introduction. Paul Auster and the Postmodern American Novel." *Beyond the Red Notebook* 1-26.

Barry, Peter. *Beginning Theor: An Introduction to Literary and Cultural Theory.* Manchester: Manchester UP, 1995.

- - -. "Introduction." *Issues in Contemporary Critical Theory: A Selection of Critical Essays*. Ed. Peter Barry. London: Macmillan, 1987. 2-18.

Barthes, Roland. "The Death of the Author." *Image – Music – Text*. Ed. S. Heeath. London: Fonatana, 1977. 142-148.

Bawer, Bruce. "Doubles and More Doubles." *The New Criterion* 7.8 (1989):67-74.

Baxter, Charles. "The Bureau of Missing Persons: Notes on Paul Auster's Fiction." *The Review of Contemporary Fiction* 14.1 (1994 Spring): 40-43.

Bennington, Geoffrey. "Acts (The Law of Genre)." *Jacques Derrida.* Jacques Derrida and Geoffrey Bennington 317-401.

- - -. "Derridabase." *Jacques Derrida*. Chicago: U of Chicago P, 1993. 3-316.

Birkerts, Sven. "Reality, Fiction, and *In the Country of Last Things*." *The Review of Contemporary Fiction* 14.1 (1994 Spring): 66-69.

Bruckner, Pascal. "Paul Auster, or the Heir Interstate." Barone, *Beyond the Red Notebook* 27-33.

Caputo, John D., ed. *Deconstruction in a Nutshell: A Conversation with Jacques Derrida.* New York: Fordham UP, 1997.

Chametzky, Jules and John Festiner, eds. *Jewish American Literature: A Norton Anthology.* New York, London: W.W. Norton & Company, 2001.

Chénetier, Marc. "Paul Auster's Pseudonymous World." Barone, *Beyond the Red Notebook* 34-43.

Cixous, Hélène. *Portrait of Jacques Derrida as a Young Jewish Saint.* New York: Columbia UP, 2004.

Cohen, Arthur A., and Paul Mendes-Flohr, eds. *Contemporary Jewish Religious Thought: Original Essays on Critical Concepts, Movements and Beliefs*. New York: Free Press, 1988.

Creeley, Robert. "Austerities." *The Review of Contemporary Fiction* 14.1 (Spring 1994): 35-39.

Eisen, Arnold. "Exile." Cohen and Mendes-Flohr 219-25.

Enck, J. "John Hawkes: An Interview." *Wisconsin Studies in Contemporary Literature* 6 (1965): 149.

Fackenheim, Emil L. "Holocaust." Cohen and Mendes-Flohr 399-408.

Finkelstein, Norman. Introduction. *Collected Poems.* By Paul Auster. New York: The Overlook Press, 2004. 9-17.

- - -. *The Ritual of New Creation: Jewish Tradition and Contemporary Literature.* Albany: State U of New York P,1992.

Fisch, Harold: "Fathers, Mothers, Sons and Lovers: Jewish and Gentile Patterns in Literature." *Midstream, a Monthly Jewish Review* 18 (1972): 37-45.

Glatzer, Nahum. N. "Apocalypse." Cohen and Mendes-Flohr 19-22.

Hauck, Johannes. "Nachwort." Mallarmé 333.

Hennings, Terri Jane. "Writing Against Aesthetic Ideology: Tom Sharpe's the Great Pursuit and Paul Auster's *City of Glass.*" *Dissertation Abstracts International, Section A: The Humanities and Social Sciences* 57.1 (1996): 136-52.

Herweg, Rachel Monika. *Die jüdische Mutter: Das verborgene Matriarchat.* Darmstadt: Wissenschaftliche Buchgesellschaft, 1995.

Holzapfel, Anne M. *The New York Trilogy: Whodunit? Tracking the Structure of Paul Auster's Anti-Detective Novels.* Frankfurt a.M., Berlin: Peter Lang, 1996.

Hornung, Alfred. "Autobiography." *International Postmodernism: Theory and Literary Practise.* Ed. Hans Bertens and Douwe Fokkema. Amsterdam: Benjamins, 1997. 221-33.

- - -. "Hungerkünstler und die jüdisch-amerikanische Literatur: Kafka, Roth, Ozick, Auster." *Identität und Gedächtnis in der jüdischen Literatur nach 1945.* Ed. Dieter Lamping. Berlin: Erich Schmidt Verlag, 2003. 116-126.

- - -. "Postmoderne bis zur Gegenwart." *Amerikanische Literaturgeschichte.* Ed. Hubert Zapf. Stuttgart: Metzler, 2004. 306-86.

Ickstadt, Heinz. "Die unstabile Postmoderne oder: Wie postmodern ist der zeitgenössische amerikanische Roman?" *Poststrukturalismus – Dekonstruktion – Postmoderne.* Ed. Klaus W. Hempfer. Stuttgart: Franz Steiner, 1992. 39-51.

Jacobs, Louis. "God." Cohen and Mendes-Flohr 291-98.

Kiely, Robert. *Reverse Tradition: Postmodern Fictions and the 19th Century Novel.* Cambridge, MA: Harvard UP, 1993.

Kierkegaard, Peter. "Cities, Signs, and Meaning in Walter Benjamin and Paul Auster, or: Never Sure of any of it." *Orbis Litterarum: International Review of Literary Studies* 48.2-3 (1993): 161-79.

Kimmerle, Heinz. *Jacques Derrida zur Einführung.* Hamburg: Junius, 2000.

Klepper, Martin. *Pynchon, Auster, De Lillo. Die amerikanische Postmoderne zwischen Spiel und Rekonstruktion.* Frankfurt a.M.: Campus Verlag, 1996.

Lavender, William. "The Novel of Critical Engagement: Paul Auster's *City of Glass.*" *Contemporary Literature* 34.2 (1993): 219-39.

Little, William G. "Nothing to Go On: Paul Auster's *City of Glass.*" *Contemporary Literature* 38.1 (1997): 133-63.

Lawlor, Leonard. "The Relation as the Fundamental Issue in Derrida." Mc Kenna and Evans 151-84.

Malmgren, Carl D. "Detecting / Writing the Real: Paul Auster's *City of Glass.*" *Narrative Turns and Minor Genres in Postmodernism.* Ed. Theo D'haen and Hans Bertens. Amsterdam: Rodopi, 1995. 177-98.

Mertens, Heinrich A. *Handbuch der Bibelkunde: Literarische, historische, archäologische, religionsgeschichtliche, kulturkundliche, geographische Aspekte des Alten und Neuen Testaments.* Düsseldorf: Patmos, 1989.

Nealon, Jeffrey T. "Work of the Detective, Work of the Writer: Paul Auster's *City of Glass.*" *Modern Fiction Studies* 42.1 (1996): 91-110.

Niebylski, Dianna C. *The Poem on the Edge of the Word: The Limits of Language and the Uses of Silence in the Poetry of Mallarmé, Rilke, and Vallejo.* New York: Peter Lang, 1993.

Norris, Christopher. *What's Wrong with Postmodernism: Critical Theory and the Ends of Philosophy.* New York: Harvester Wheatsheaf, 1990.

Ofrat, Gideon. *The Jewish Derrida.* Syracuse UP, 2001.

Putnam, Hilary. "Lévinas and Judaism." *The Cambridge Companion to Lévinas.* Ed. Robert Bernasconi and Simon Critchley. Cambridge: Cambridge UP, 2002. 33-62.

Robinson, George. *Essential Judaism. A Complete Guide to Beliefs, Customs, and Rituals.* New York, London: Pocket Books, 2000.

Rosello, Mireille. “The Screener’s Maps: Michel Certeau’s Wandersmänner’ and Paul Auster’s Hypertextual Detective.” *Hyper/Text/Theory.* Ed. George P. Landow. Baltimore: The Johns Hopkins UP, 1994. 121-58.

Rowen, Norma. “The Detective in Search of the Lost Tongue of Adam: Paul Auster’s City of Glass.” *Critique: Studies in Contemporary Fiction* 32.4 (1991): 224-34.

Rubin, Derek. “’The Hunger Must Be Preserved at All Cost’: A Reading of *The Invention of Solitude*.” Barone, *Beyond the Red Notebook.* 60-70.

Russell, Alison. “Deconstructing *The New York Trilogy*: Paul Auster’s Anti-Detective Fiction.” *Critique: Studies in Contemporary Fiction* 31.2 (1990): 71-84.

Selden, Raman. *A Reader’s Guide to Contemporary Literary Theory.* Brighton: Harvester Press, 1985.

Shibata, Motoyuki. “Being Paul Auster’s Ghost.” Barone, *Beyond the Red Notebook* 183-88.

Shiloh, Ilana. *Paul Auster and the Postmodern Quest. On the Road to Nowhere.* New York, Washington: Peter Lang, 2002.

Sorapure, Madeleine. “The Detective and the Author: *City of Glass*.” Barone, *Beyond the Red Notebook* 71-87.

Srajek, Martin C.: *In the Margins of Deconstruction: Jewish Conceptions of Ethics in E. Lévinas and Jacques Derrida.* Pittsburgh, Pa.: Duquesne UP, 2000.

Taureck, Bernhard H.F. *Emmanuel Lévinas zur Einführung.* Hamburg: Junius,1997.

Troester, Anne. “’Beyond this point, everything turns to prose’: Paul Auster’s Writing Between Poetry and Prose.” *Amerikastudien / American Studies* 47:4 (2002): 525-38.

Vernoff, Charles Elliott. “Hope.” Cohen and Mendes-Flohr 417-21.

Walden, Daniel, ed. *20th Century American-fiction writers.* Detroit: Gale Research Co., 1984.

Washburn, Katharine. “A Book at the End of the World: Paul Auster’s *In the Country of Last Things*.” *The Review of Contemporary Fiction* 14.1(1994 Spring): 62-65.

Wild, John. Introduction. *Totality and Infinity. An Essay on Exteriority.* By Emmanuel Lévinas. Pittsburgh: Duquesne University Press, 2004. 11-20.

Woods, Tim. "'Looking for Signs in the Air': Urban Space and the Postmodern in *In the Country of Last Things*." Barone, *Beyond the Red Notebook* 107-27.